For Johnny.

ROCK CLIMBING IN KENTUCKY'S RED RIVER GORGE

An Oral History of Community, Resources, and Tourism

James N. Maples

West Virginia University Press / Morgantown

First edition published 2021 by West Virginia University Press

Printed in the United States of America

ISBN 978-1-952271-14-4 (cloth) / 978-1-952271-15-1 (paperback) /
978-1-952271-16-8 (ebook)

Library of Congress Cataloging-in-Publication Data

Names: Maples, James N., author.

Title: Rock climbing in Kentucky's Red River Gorge : an oral history of community,
    resources, and tourism / James N. Maples.

Description: Morgantown : West Virginia University Press, 2021. | Includes
    bibliographical references and index.

Identifiers: LCCN 2021009494 | ISBN 9781952271144 (cloth) | ISBN
    9781952271151 (paperback) | ISBN 9781952271168 (ebook)

Subjects: LCSH: Rock climbing—Kentucky—Red River Gorge—History. |
    Tourism—Kentucky—Red River Gorge Region. | Red River Gorge Region
    (Ky.)—History.

Classification: LCC GV199.42.K42 R436 2021 | DDC 796.522/309769—dc23

LC record available at https://lccn.loc.gov/2021009494

Book and cover design by Than Saffel / WVU Press

Cover image: Kris Odub Hampton climbing Swingline 5.13d @ The Dark Side,
Red River Gorge, Kentucky, 2010. Photograph by Elodie Saracco.

Contents

Acknowledgments

This book started innocently enough when I said, "Wouldn't it be great to conduct an oral history on rock climbing in the Red?" at a climbing presentation at Natural Bridge State Park. That turned into a realization that very little had actually been written about climbing history in the Red. As I began to interview climbers, I was impressed by their extraordinary stories and how these events could only have happened in Kentucky's Red River Gorge. Those stories, when examined collectively, also offered a narrative of how outdoor recreation users experienced a unique place while also being shaped by that experience.

This book would be impossible without the support of the Red's rock-climbing community. They have kindly and patiently endured surveys, interviews, and random climbing questions since I arrived at Eastern Kentucky University (EKU), and for this I am thankful. Several climbers require special thanks for creating the foundation of this book. These include Yasmeen Fowler, Rick Bost, Ron Stokley, Dieter Britz, Frank Becker, Shannon Stuart-Smith, Johnny Nowell, Chris Snyder, Hugh Loeffler, Bob Matheny, Brian Clark, Liz Weber, Rick Weber, Tom Souders, Ellen Seibert, Tom Seibert, Tina Bronaugh, Bill Ramsey, Bentley Brackett, Chris Chaney, Kris Hampton, Ray Ellington, Kipp Trummel, Tina Brouwer, Bill Rogers, Kevin Pogue, Otto Mock, Ron Snider, Stephanie Meadows, Bill Strachan, and many more climbers from around the world who kindly did oral history interviews with me in recent years. I am especially indebted to Yasmeen and Rick for answering my numerous and often random questions about climbing. Likewise, it has been a wonderful privilege working with Ron, Dieter, Frank, Otto, and Bill to recover an early Red climbing history that was effectively lost.

This book incorporates material from multiple academic fields, and it would have withered on the vine without help from my colleagues. Mike Bradley, Brian Clark, and Ryan Sharp were a great help in understanding outdoor recreation. On the archaeological side, I am deeply indebted to Wayna Adams, Jon Endonino, Johnny Faulkner, Eric Schlarb, and Kelli Carmean for their support in writing about their extraordinary, important field. I'm thankful to Gary O'Dell, Larry Meadows, Johnny Faulkner, Randy Boedy, and Matthew Davidson for sharing with me their knowledge about niter mines. Likewise, I am appreciative for Charlie Bishop, Catherine Bishop, and Gary O'Dell for their help in understanding the region's caving community.

I would also like to thank several of my colleagues for their support on this book. I am grateful for Jillian Rickly, who read and critiqued the earliest version of the book and offered valuable corrections as both a climber and a professor. I deeply appreciate Holly Ningard's help in editing several chapters and also providing feedback on an early copy of the manuscript. Thanks are due to Neil Kasiak, my colleague at the William Berge Oral History Center, for his support and advice on oral history studies. I am thankful for Rhiannon Leebrick's help in thinking about how place matters in history. Likewise, I am thankful for my EKU colleagues Tom Martin (Center for Economic Development, Entrepreneurship, and Technology), Sara Zeigler (College of Letters, Arts, and Social Sciences), and Paul Paolucci (Department of Anthropology, Sociology, and Social Work) for supporting my research.

I'm appreciative to the editorial team at West Virginia University Press (WVUP) for turning this labor of love into reality. Thanks, Andrew Berzanskis, for originally approaching me about the book. I am grateful for Sarah Munroe's help in getting this manuscript into a publishable form. I deeply appreciate Lee Motteler's revisions to the final manuscript. Thanks also go to Derek Krissoff and everyone at WVUP for walking me through the publishing process.

This story would not be possible without the people who live in the Red and its many in-between county spaces. I interviewed many local residents, officials, and public persons as part of this project. I'm simply grateful for the time I spent with them hanging out in gas stations, town halls, coffee shops, and some of the best restaurants in the region. I am particularly indebted to Joe Bowen, Larry Meadows, the Red River Museum, Dedra Brandenburg, Linda Black, David Terrill, Chris Schimmoeller, Andy Sigmon, and John Ott for their guidance and help in documenting the region's history.

I am grateful for the dedication of the US Forest Service in protecting public lands. One of my singular hopes in writing this book is to see outdoor recreation users and the Forest Service closely work together wherever possible to protect our public lands. I am especially grateful to the staff at the Daniel Boone National Forest here in Eastern Kentucky, who are watching over the Red and fighting to balance access to outdoor recreation areas with protecting irreplaceable natural resources. Public lands matter, and it is critical that they be funded so that future generations can experience them. I am particularly appreciative to Wayna Adams for reading my manuscript and Tim Eling for answering numerous historical questions about the Daniel Boone National Forest's history. Although he passed before I began work on this project, I am also thankful for Robert F. Collins's definitive history on the Daniel Boone National Forest.

I am lucky to have a wife and child who are tolerant of my odd profession. Laura Bost, thanks for tolerating my frazzled brain, crazy schedule, and endless distractions. I don't have the words to express how glad I am that we're together, except to simply say that I love you. Without you, none of this would have happened. And to my dear Josie Maples, you are the singular reason I get up and go to work in the morning. You're a great artist, budding scientist, and world-class *karateka*. You can do anything you set your mind to do.

Thanks go to my parents Ruth and David Maples and my extra parents Barbara and Buddy Burgess for supporting me while I searched for my bearings. Without your support, I wouldn't be writing this today. I am also eternally thankful for my academic mom, mentor, and dissertation chair, Stephanie Bohon. Stephanie, thanks for putting me on my path. I wouldn't be here without your guidance, patience, and support. Thanks for believing in me.

This book is also inspired by climbers and authors who have documented the history of climbing in many climbing areas outside the Red. Authors like Steve Roper, Joseph E. Taylor III, Don Mellor, and Jon Krakauer have inspired me in part to write this book.

This book was indirectly supported by several grants. Those include a grant from the Kentucky Oral History Commission to conduct the oral history of climbers in the Red, grants from the Access Fund and Eastern Kentucky University to conduct economic impact research on climbing in the Red River Gorge and New River Gorge, and the purchase of a scanner by the Red River Gorge Climbers' Coalition to support the scanning of the Cumberland Climbers archive.

I have made every effort to get the historical details correct, but it is inadvertently possible that an error may be made in any oral history. Dates get fuzzy, names fade, and memories revise with time. Moreover, this oral history account is not an exhaustive historical account of the Red's climbing community, meaning that some stories did not make it into the final book. This makes them no less important. I encourage readers to share their Red River Gorge climbing stories and historical revisions with me. I will keep them in mind for any future editions of this book and share revisions/additions on jamesmaples.com.

Abbreviations

BRRP	Bald Rock Recreational Preserve
CCSC	Cumberland Chapter of the Sierra Club
CMG	Rock Climbing Management Guide
COE	United States Army Corps of Engineers
DBNF	Daniel Boone National Forest
EKRPC	Eastern Kentucky Regional Planning Commission
EKU	Eastern Kentucky University
FA	First ascents
FOMV	Friends of Muir Valley
FS	United States Forest Service
KAS	Kentucky Archaeological Survey
LAC	Limits of Acceptable Change
LCO	Local Climbing Organizations
MFRP	Miller Fork Recreational Preserve
MIDI	Musical Instrument Digital Interface
NCO	National Climbing Organization
NEPA	National Environmental Policy Act
OIA	Outdoor Industry Association
PMRP	Pendergrass-Murray Recreational Preserve
RRGCC	Red River Gorge Climbers' Coalition
RRGGA	Red River Gorge Geological Area
T&E	Threatened and endangered
TVA	Tennessee Valley Authority
YDS	Yosemite Decimal System

Introduction

Climbers have been visiting the Red River Gorge for at least a half century now with hopes of ascending its unique, gorgeous sandstone cliff lines. Early generations of climbers called it *the Gorge*, while more recent climbers simply call it *the Red*. Those cliff lines, eroded for eons by droplets of water jostling their way down the hillside, reveal a vibrant, unique, and seemingly endless concentration of overhung sandstone climbing that marks it today among the planet's favorite climbing destinations. In fact, climber Shannon Stuart-Smith feels that "if God created a place to climb, it would be the Red."[1] But understanding the Red's climbing history is more than just the campfire stories of first ascents and climbing feats. This history goes much deeper, weaving in rapid cultural changes in climbing traditions, evolving responsibilities for public land managers, and the long-standing experiences of people living in the Red's wet floodplain.

This is a story that formally begins in 1968 with the earliest climbers in the Red and the founding of the Cumberland Climbers. Their membership included rugged pioneers like Ron Stokley and Dieter Britz who established early routes at *Tower Rock* and *Chimney Rock* in the Daniel Boone National Forest (DBNF). Although most of the routes established in those earliest years are now either closed or lost to history, the Cumberland Climbers fostered an environmentalist-minded clean climbing ethic that has remained in the Red for generations. By the mid-seventies, a new cadre of climbers (including local legends like Martin Hackworth, Larry Day, and Tom Seibert) vastly increased the number of established routes in the DBNF. Their contributions included the famed crag *Military Wall* and a long list of routes (such as "Tower of Power," "Jungle Beat," and "GI") that defined the early Red.[2] In due time, Frank Becker, Ed Benjamin, Ed Pearsall, and Martin Hackworth would all write guidebooks documenting a burgeoning list of new routes in the Red, while Tom Souders and Jeff Koenig pushed the boundaries of traditional climbing in the Red. Still greater growth would come in a new (at the time) approach to climbing called *sport climbing*.

Up to this moment in the Red, climbers had used removable protection wedged into cracks in the rock to protect themselves in the event of a fall, something generally called traditional (or *trad*) climbing. The impact on the rock was minimal, but climbing was limited to natural features like cracks. Sport climbing changed that by installing permanent metal bolts in the rock face, thus creating climbing in otherwise featureless areas inaccessible to trad climbers. And it was Porter Jarrard who would make sport climbing a mainstream offering in the Red's climbing crags, proliferating the number of sport routes across the Red through the use of a rock drill and permanent bolts. His base of operations was an old house at the Rainbow Door, an ice cream shop that would soon begin feeding bread (and eventually pizza) to climbers. They eventually changed their name to Miguel's Pizza. Meanwhile, Chris Snyder found probably the most famed crag in the Red, *The Motherlode*. The Red River Gorge Climbers' Coalition, a new local climbing organization with Shannon Stuart-Smith as executive director, put a collective voice behind climbers' interests. And John Bronaugh wrote a historic guidebook that documented the uptick of new sport routes in the Red, opening the doors to a crush of climbers pounding their way to eastern Kentucky. Unbeknownst, climbers were now in an intercepting orbit with the US Forest Service as a result of climbing's rapid growth and the increasing use of bolts without permission on public lands.

The Forest Service faced an arduous, fluid, and thankless task: finding appropriate balance in maintaining timber sales, keeping public lands open to recreation, documenting cultural resources such as archaeology sites, and protecting a wide list of resources on public lands. In the Red, that included protecting a number of important archaeological areas extensively used by Indigenous peoples and watching over a finicky, endangered plant (the white-haired goldenrod) that liked to live in the drip lines of rockshelters right about where climbers and hikers liked putting their feet. The Forest Service, specifically the Daniel Boone National Forest, had to figure out where and how climbing fit into their pledge to maintain public lands for recreation.

The folks at the DBNF took extraordinary measures to balance climbing use and resource protection, including a number of critical partnerships between the two groups across 50 years of climbing in the Red. Climbers and the DBNF worked together from the start of the Red's climbing community, partnering on many activities. Despite everyone's best intentions (including climbers and the DBNF), this relationship was strained by the rapid growth of sport routes in the late 1980s and early 1990s. Amid strong leaders with firm beliefs on both sides, this entire debate came to a head at a climbing crag (and Indigenous rockshelter) called *Military Wall*.

Everything changed following the conflict at *Military Wall*. It was then that climbers first began whispering a phrase heard even today: "If we own it, they can't close it." Climbers soon began buying tracts of land throughout the region, gradually redirecting the growth of climbing away from Forest Service land and onto climbing preserves. This culminated in two local climbing organizations (LCOs) representing the region: the Red River Gorge Climbers' Coalition (RRGCC) and Muir Valley. These climbing preserves assured that climbing would remain present in the region for future generations without utilizing public land. These areas today even have conservation easements meant to ensure that the land will never be used for any other purpose. While climbing development on public lands (specifically the DBNF) has now slowed to a crawl, new privately or LCO-owned climbing properties appear every few years. As a result, the bulk of climbing routes in the Red are now beyond the borders of the Red River Gorge itself in a continued growth pattern. Yet these new areas (as well as crags at *Pocket Wall*, Torrent Falls, and *Roadside*) all faced the difficulty of balancing climber impacts with the right to climb.

It's an extraordinary history to be sure, but the Red's climbers did not exist in a vacuum. Rather they were subject to the political economy, historic events, and cultural patterns of the region. In a short 50 years, climbers would see the rise and fall of a proposed dam in the Red, a revolution in climbing traditions, sweeping national changes to accessing climbing areas, and a surge in climbing's popularity amid efforts to adhere to Forest Service policy. And then there are the residents of the Red, who watched as more and more strangers came to the region wearing ropes and clinking belts to do the unthinkable: climb the hollers and hills of eastern Kentucky. And so, this book aims to tell a more comprehensive story than might be gleaned solely from the perspective of climbers.

The chapters are built around climbing's historical markers in the Red's climbing history, ranging from evolving traditions (chapter 6's exploration of sport climbing, which radically changed the Red's history), the history of the Red as a place (chapter 3's recounting of the Red River Dam's rise and fall), and even singular historic events, such as chapter 9's fateful archaeological dig at *Military Wall*. Throughout, the story is then put into context by exploring how the Red, imbued with its own extraordinary history, had its own shaping influence on how that story would unfold. The story is told through the words and experiences of many a person who experienced it firsthand. That story continues (and the book concludes) by reflecting on what climbers might have in store for the coming decades, including how their presence and economic activities might be useful to rural regions with climbable natural features.

Methodological Approach

When I started this book, the history of the Red's climbing community was largely minimal and disorganized. There was no central historical account of the community beyond a few standard pages in most climbing guides, a handful of articles in climbing magazines, and a brief description of the Red in Don Mellor's *American Rock*, a book summarizing the history of American climbing communities. Much of the history out there mostly repeats ideas from John Bronaugh's early guides and Ray Ellington's profiles on local heroes. Chris Chaney also organized several climbing stories into his 2019 book on the Red River Gorge. Additionally, the online forums at redriverclimbing.com contained a lot of historical data mixed in among thousands of more mundane topics, such as lost climbing gear and near-constant online ribbing among friends. This small gathering of historical information created a simple outline of the community's history but with a lot of flesh (and even a few major bones) missing from the overall body.

To fill in the many gaps in the literature, I began collecting oral history interviews with Red River Gorge climbers in 2017. By luck, nearly all the pivotal figures in this history were still alive and willing to share their stories. This soon began to add a clearer, personal picture of the community's many historical events ranging from its earliest days right up to recent happenings. This collection also grew to include interviews with local residents (both current and former), regional scholars, business owners, and government employees to provide a more nuanced perspective on the region. This collection is located at the William Berge Oral History Center at Eastern Kentucky University, where it is presently being organized for public release. Throughout the book, I quote extensively from these interviews to give that personal account of climbers' collective history. Quotes that are not attributed to another source come from those oral history interviews; quotes from all other materials are noted in the text or cited in the notes.

One expected issue with oral history interviews (when also overlapping with the lack of a formal, organized history of climbing in the Red) is that the factual contents indubitably disagreed on occasion. In these cases, I made every effort to corroborate stories with a second source, including other interviews, archival materials, or media. In some cases, I simply note unresolved disagreements over basic facts (particularly dating issues or names) for future researchers to consider. In some instances, interviewees were allowed to revise their quotes in the book to correct an omission or error in their interview. Examples include misspeaking a route name, crag, climber name, or ranking. In limited instances, interviewees requested to revise their quotes for clarity and readability, such as removing unneeded prepositional phrases or pauses. In other cases, I have used ellipses or brackets to revise quotes for clarity.

Climber and guidebook author Frank Becker graciously allowed access to the materials of the Cumberland Climbers. These included founding documents, letters, and membership information. These documents are described for the first time in this book. The Cumberland Climbers' records specifically helped depict the early work of climbers in the area. Their newsletters were particularly helpful in recreating some of the early history and activities of this group.

The dozen or so climbing guides written since the 1970s have documented the extraordinary number of climbing opportunities in the Red over time. The guides share changes in how climbers have understood the Red and how they understood themselves. The guides also give some idea of how climbers moved through the Red developing new areas. One important note about route grading in the guides is needed here. Climbing routes are graded by difficulty, but those grades change over time for myriad reasons. When discussing guides (particularly the ones from the 1970s), I list the route's grade as it is listed in the guide. On occasion I will also list the route's current grading as a point of comparison. I am thankful to all the guidebook authors for their work in preserving the history of the Red's climbing community.

The book also benefited from recent economic research on climbing in the region. These include studies in the Red River Gorge, North Carolina's Nantahala and Pisgah National Forests, and West Virginia's New River Gorge. Each of these studies utilize survey data to establish the annual economic impact of climbers within their respective study areas, but they also help establish (for the first time) clear trends in climbers' demographics and spending patterns that relate to the history of the community and how others perceive its members. The data from these studies helped change how we now understand climbers, and these findings are discussed in the final chapter. Those findings are also tempered with the need to better understand climber social and environmental impacts to limit undesired consequences like closures or irreparably changing what it means to be part of the Red River Gorge.

Finally, a number of other media sources help round out this intense story. This includes news articles, video footage, still images, climber internet forums, blogs, and written accounts of climbing experiences in the Red. Each provides background information and a sense of history as it happened. These also helped establish dating for climbing events that were often unexpectedly hard to pin down to specific dates. Occasionally, I also suggest online video media and images found on the internet that help the reader visualize the Red and organize a mental map of the region.

One of the greatest historical resources on the Red's climbing history has, quite sadly, already been lost. That resource would be John (Johnny) Bronaugh. John, a climber, attorney, and unofficial historian for the climbing community, passed in 2004. Ray Ellington, in his first printed guide on the Red, described John as the "King of the Red River Gorge." In my time studying the Red's climbing community, I cannot think of a person more fitting of that title. In my interviews, I so very often heard some form of the phrase, "Man, I wish John were still here, because he could tell the full story about that." We are all fortunate that John documented some of this important history in his two guidebooks. Moreover, he inadvertently documented his own historic accomplishments with the RRGCC via his forum posts to redriverclimbing.com. John's work in the Red lives on in the stories of those who loved him most and in the dedicated work of those he inspired. This book is wholeheartedly dedicated in memory of Johnny Bronaugh, the King of the Red River Gorge.

CHAPTER 1

A Brief Overview of the Red and the Surrounding Region

At mile marker 25 of the Bert T. Combs Mountain Parkway, tourists, climbers, and locals alike drive quickly over an inconspicuous Red River. This specific crossing runs through a cow pasture. A small sign noting the river's presence almost feels like an afterthought. The parkway crosses the river again at mile marker 28, this time sandwiched between a nearby mountain and a floodplain. In both cases, the Red River is small enough that a strategically placed rock and a coordinated skip could suffice to cross it in most spots. First-time visitors to the area might find it inconsequential, unassuming, muted. This is far from the truth.

Now jump ahead farther down the parkway, departing onto Highway 77, driving through Nada Tunnel, joining Highway 715, and cruising through the Daniel Boone National Forest. Nada Tunnel is a 900-foot long, rough-hewn logging tunnel built from 1910 to 1912 that goes right through the mountain. The purpose was to create a shorter route for moving timber out of the area. The tunnel consists of a single lane measuring 12 feet across with a 13-foot ceiling. Today, the tunnel is used as an informal gateway to the Red River Gorge from the Mountain Bypass area. Here, drivers follow along a more brazen and even bumptious Red River that pushes aside boulders during high water and propels the occasional neon-bright kayak or falling fly fisher farther downstream. It furiously etches whatever stone it touches that is unlucky enough to be stuck in the river's charge. It is aggressive and alive.

It is a common misunderstanding that the Red River alone carved a 310-million-year-old valley of sandstone into these rusty-tinged overhangs, cracks, and arêtes found in the Red. That assumption misses a more subtle and easily overlooked force in the Red: the imperturbable power of dripping water. As it moves downhill in a cyclical search for the river, the water erodes features in the stone. These overhangs also create excellent shelters that have kept humans dry for quite some time.[1] This special erosion pattern found in the Red also defines much of the climbing here. Meanwhile, all that water was just trying to make its way back to the Red River.

The Red River is a 97-mile tributary of the Kentucky River. In 1993, the Red River Designation Act declared 19.4 miles of the Red going through eastern Kentucky a federally designated Wild and Scenic River, making it the state's first designation of this kind. This designation means the river will be forever free flowing and cannot be dammed. In 1973, the Commonwealth declared the upper section of the river a Kentucky Wild River from the KY 746 Bridge down to the KY 715 Bridge. This includes a recreational river access point at Highway 715.

The Red River is popular with many kinds of outdoor recreation users. An estimated 70-plus species of fish and 16 mussels are found in the Red River, including smallmouth bass, Kentucky bass, and the occasional rainbow trout, attracting both locals and visitors to the region. When in full force, the river's 10-mile recreational area provides a mixture of Class I (easier) to Class III (harder) rapids to negotiate, along with boulder gardens and catchy landmarks like "Dog Drowning Hole."

Surrounding this unassuming river is the Red River Gorge Geological Area (RRGGA). The RRGGA is situated in Menifee, Wolfe, and Powell Counties and is often treated as the formal definition of what defines the Red. The area consists of approximately 29,000 acres and has been duly designated as a protected area (in 1974) and a National Natural Landmark (in 1976).[2] The star of the geological area would be the 100-plus sandstone arches documented in numerous online guides and printed brochures. These features are created as water and wind erode tunnels through the rock, eventually leaving behind extraordinary sandstone arches. Many of these are popular hiking destinations and the subject of several hiking and arch guides.

The arches found in the Red River Gorge are shockingly vast and gargantuan. For example, the popular Grays Arch is 50 feet tall and 80 feet across.[3] Perhaps the most famous arch in the area is Natural Bridge. At 65 feet high and 78 feet long, this arch attracted tourists to the Red as early as the 1890s. That arch is technically separate from the RRGGA, however. It is celebrated as the centerpiece of the neighboring Natural Bridge State Park. Although the arches here can be visited and often walked upon, a few arches include fenced-off archaeological areas protected from visitors.[4] Additionally, climbing and rappelling is prohibited on all arches in the DBNF and the Natural Bridge State Park.

The RRGGA is overseen by the DBNF. The Daniel Boone National Forest was originally called the Cumberland National Forest, which was created in 1937. The name *Cumberland* comes from the Cumberland Gap, which was, in turn, named for the Duke of Cumberland from Britain (also known as the

Butcher Cumberland for his work against the Scots at Culloden).[5] This did not match well at the time with a marketing campaign being designed for the forest, whereas local hero Daniel Boone was a great (even logical) historical fit. The wheels to rename the forest began turning in earnest in 1958, and by 1965 Kentucky governor Edward Breathitt had placed his support behind the renaming campaign. (The fact that Daniel Boone also had got his eponymous television show the prior year certainly was also convenient.) *Kentucky State Senate Resolution #43* supported the name change as well in 1966, noting that "the life of Daniel Boone was more directly connected with the history of Kentucky and therefore it is fitting and proper to rename the Cumberland National Forest in his honor." Lyndon Johnson signed the proclamation of the name change on April 11, 1966, marking the creation of the Daniel Boone National Forest.[6]

Explaining the purpose of the US Forest Service is somewhat complicated because they play such a pivotal, holistic role in public land management. Tim Eling, a staff officer with the DBNF, explained that "the US Forest Service has a very broad mission as defined by the United States Congress." That mission can include (depending on the national forest) vegetation management, timber sales, special use permits, wildlife habitat management, grazing, mining, recreation, wild and scenic river management, and wilderness management, just to provide a short list of nonetheless critical tasks in managing public lands.

This mission is made further difficult in that each forest can be quite unique. Eling explains that "different national forests across the country sometimes have different parts of that important mission that are more emphasized." For example, Colorado national forests might have different recreational uses than the DBNF, whereas a national forest in Mississippi might be more focused on vegetation management and cutting down timber products for the American people. "We're somewhere in the middle on the Daniel Boone." The Red has heavy recreational use, such as hiking, fishing, and climbing, "but then we also have vegetation management projects around the forest. Just trying to balance all of that and explain to the American public that we're here for a variety of management issues [is a difficult task]." The Red also includes cultural resources, such as numerous archaeological sites, that must be protected.

Today, the DBNF covers a 2.1-million-acre proclamation boundary established by Congress in the 1930s. The Forest Service is allowed to purchase land within this boundary. To make matters somewhat confusing, the boundary area includes private land as well as entire towns, and privately owned areas within this zone have the same rights as privately owned areas outside the zone. This is one important difference between a national forest and a national park.[7] This boundary is fully contained within the state of Kentucky, going all the way to the Tennessee border in the south and just shy of the Ohio border to the north. Over the last 90 years, 708,000 acres have been purchased. Due to its sheer size, the DBNF has four ranger districts: Redbird, Stearns, London, and Cumberland. Cumberland District is the northernmost of the four districts and includes the RRGGA. Overall, the DBNF Cumberland District includes the RRGGA, the upper portion of the aforementioned Red Wild and Scenic River and Red River Gorge Natural Landmark, as well as the Clifty Wilderness and Red River Gorge Archaeological District.

The Clifty Wilderness is a 12,646-acre area meant to provide solitude inside a primitive, largely untouched environment. The 1985 Kentucky Wilderness Act designated the Clifty Wilderness for inclusion in the National Wilderness Preservation System. This wilderness area includes several climbing crags, most importantly *Tower Rock*, which is historically treated as the starting point for climbing in the Red.[8] The wilderness designation prohibits groups larger than 10 or using motorized or mechanized equipment (such as an off-highway vehicle or OHV) to travel across the area. Additionally, no new climbing routes using permanent anchors (such as bolts) can be added here. In comparison, the DBNF Forest Plan (last updated in 2004) does allow for the creation of new routes under specific guidelines and procedures designed to protect flora, fauna, and cultural resources such as archaeological sites. This last point is particularly important given the prevalence of archaeological resources located here.

The Cumberland District includes a 37,000-acre National Archaeological District, created in 2003. This district documents and (where possible) protects potential and known archaeological sites. The DBNF and its surrounding area accounts for over half the Indigenous sites located in the Upper Kentucky/ Licking Management Area 6. Area 6 also had (as of 2008) the most National Register sites in the state, almost all of which are located in the Red. This management area is unique in Kentucky, as it is the only region where the most common site is open habitation without mounds. Moreover, this area includes extensive use of rockshelters by Indigenous peoples.

Rockshelters can be described as very shallow caves. Erosion has removed stone along where the rock wall meets the dirt, leaving an overhanging rock roof. That roof often keeps the area below it quite dry, making it an ideal stopping point for hunting parties or even as long-term shelter. Rockshelters also can run the gamut from being quite small, such as providing modest shelter to a small hunting party, to protecting a small community of residents. The National Archaeological District notably includes the Military Wall Shelter, home to what climbers simply call *Military Wall*. Although not as large as many other shelters found throughout the region, the Military Wall Shelter certainly provided a large, dry workspace for Indigenous peoples in the Red.

Throughout prehistory, most rockshelters in and around the Red saw plenty of use from Indigenous peoples from the Archaic period on, but use varied by season and over time. In our oral history interview, archaeologist Dr. Jon Endonino noted that certain rockshelters may have been used as seasonal residences for harvesting things like hickory nuts, others for wintering in one place, and still others year-round living. In any case, they cemented the Red as a great place to live. Rockshelters were cooler in the summers and, depending on which way they faced, could be a bit warmer in the winter. Water seeps were often nearby, too, offering a source of fresh water.

Indigenous peoples lived in the Red around the start of the Holocene, a geological epoch marking a gradual move towards a warmer climate in the Red. During the Paleoindian period (ranging from 12,000 to 10,000 years ago), humans lived in the eastern Kentucky area. Much of their diet hinged on hunting smaller-bodied animals, although larger animals like bison or now-extinct species including mastodons and mammoth may have also been an option. Smaller animals would have been prevalent in the region, while larger animals like bison would have needed wider expanses of prairie environments in short supply in eastern Kentucky. Very little remains from this era, but archaeologists think that Paleoindian peoples likely used the hides for everything from clothes to containers, and the bones may have served as tools.[9] Archaeologists also think the Paleoindian period marked the first efforts to harness the plant resources available in the Red. Plant resources (both for humans and other animals) would become a central cause of change moving into the Archaic period (ranging from 10,000 to 3,000 years ago), when the Red's forest radically changed.

As the region warmed and transformed from conifer to hardwood forest, Archaic period residents of the Red adapted to a new way of life. During the Archaic period, mast resources (which include fruit and nuts from trees) would have taken on an increased importance as larger animals were going extinct. By this time, the mastodons were gone across North America, possible victims of overhunting, climate change, or a mass death event during the Quaternary extinction. Archaic people instead turned to collecting nuts and hunting smaller animals more familiar to us today. As new nut-bearing species (such as oak, walnut, and hickory) became the norm, deer, elk, raccoons, turkeys, rabbits, opossums, tortoises, and snakes became an important food source for humans, making a life spent in the Red an increasingly attractive option. Perhaps more importantly, however, was the growth of exciting plant innovations.

During the Archaic period and continuing into the Woodland period (ranging from 3,000 to 1,000 years ago), humans harvested weedy plants that thrived in the new Red. Unique plant development occurred in the Ohio River Valley (which includes the Red) around this time, leading to the cultivation of starchy, oily seeds like goosefoot, amaranth, sump weed, and even sunflower. Interestingly, some of the earliest known sunflower seeds in Kentucky were found at the Newt Kash Shelter (which is north of the Red).[10] Gardens became increasingly common finds at shelter sites. The act of gardening occupied more time as well, as humans in the Red became less nomadic and adapted to life in the rockshelters. It also created a form of identifiable cultural remains at shelter sites where cooking fires protected the carbonized plant remains. Some of these early cultigens and their carbonized remains would turn up in the archaeological dig at the Military Wall Shelter thousands of years later.

Kentucky's colonial settlement history farther east of the Red often overshadows Kentucky's Indigenous history today. The Warrior's Path extended from Kentucky into the Carolinas, east Tennessee, and Georgia. It was an important early system of transportation, moving people, technology, and ideas throughout the area. It was also a valuable hunting corridor. Today, this area is often known as the Cumberland Gap. Colonel Andrew Wood (an early financial supporter of exploration in Native American lands in the region) wrote in his journals about the existence of the Gap in the 1670s, along with the so-called plain Indian Road going through the Gap.[11] The Loyal Land Company initiated a 1748 expedition through the area in search for farming land, and expedition member Dr. Thomas Walker was possibly the first nonindigenous settler of note to walk through what is now called the Cumberland Gap in 1750. Walker named it for Prince William Augustus, Duke of Cumberland.

Daniel Boone and five colleagues established Kentucky's second oldest nonindigenous settlement, Fort Boonesborough, after climbing through the Cumberland Gap and hacking out the Wilderness Road. The Wilderness Road created a critical pathway into the region for settlers. Fort Boonesborough remained active from 1775 until 1820, with a few residents lingering into the 1830s.[12] It was briefly planned to be the capital of the upstart Transylvania Colony, which was quashed by the Virginia Colony. Instead, it became the transit point for settling much of Kentucky as the only site for crossing the Kentucky River until the early 1800s. Today it is a state park in Madison County. Within the property one can find pay camping, RV hookups, a boat ramp for river access, a pool, miniature golf, and a gift shop.[13]

The Red's modern history also ties in with this new wave of settlement. The Ohio Company sent Christopher Gist and an unknown enslaved person to explore the Ohio River and its surrounding lands in 1750.[14] After their two-person exploration team felt the risk of attack by Native Americans was too great, Gist traveled down the Kentucky, landing in what is today Powell County, Kentucky. Gist traveled near and may even have ascended Powell County's Pilot Knob, a 730-foot-high outcropping of 280-million-year-old Pennsylvanian sandstone.[15] Daniel Boone and John Finley would later visit the location in 1769, as would other explorers who would marvel at the resources (trees, wildlife, and quarrying) available in this region.[16] The region appeared to have a bright future ahead at the time.

Returning to the present day, the Red is situated in the eastern end of Kentucky, a largely rural area that has faced long-standing issues. The *New York Times* recently described eastern Kentucky as the "land of storybook hills and drawls [that] just might be the hardest place to live in the United States."[17] The great majority of eastern Kentucky is classified by the Appalachian Regional Commission as distressed, which is notably their lowest economic rating. For example, of the counties surrounding the RRGGA, three recently ranked among the top 100 poorest counties (measured as lowest median household income) in the United States. Lee is 11th and Wolfe 39th as of 2016 estimates. In 2015, Lee was 11th, Wolfe 14th, and Estill 96th. As a point of comparison, Harlan County, an infamous coal county much farther east in Kentucky, then ranked 10th poorest. Owsley County, just south of the Red, was third in the nation. Further, 21 (of 120) Kentucky counties made the 2016 top 100 poorest list, with most in eastern Kentucky.[18]

Eastern Kentucky possesses equally disheartening statistics on addiction. Since the 1996 release of the highly profitable drug OxyContin by Purdue Pharma and following through with the spread of heroin and fentanyl throughout the region, Kentucky has suffered two decades of addiction, opioid overprescription, pill mills, and social disruption.[19] This social problem is now even being compared to the 1980s HIV crisis by researchers.[20] There were 1,248 overdose deaths across the state in 2015, up from 1,088 the previous year. In 2016, the trend continued, with 1,404 reported deaths. Four eastern Kentucky counties—Perry, Leslie, Knott, and Breathitt—ranked in the top 10 in the nation for opioid abuse hospitalization rates, with Perry and Leslie Counties coming in as numbers one and two in the nation.[21] In 2010, inpatient and emergency room charges for overdoses hit $78 million across the state. Clay County (in eastern Kentucky) recently gained notoriety for filling 2.2 million doses of hydrocodone and 617,000 doses of oxycodone in a 12-month period in a county with only 21,000 residents.[22]

This era of addiction has resulted in many children now living without their parents in their household. In 2013, Steve Richardson, who works with

Knott County schools, indicated that perhaps half of the school-age children in the district were being raised by someone other than their parents, often due to drugs.[23] This phenomenon resulted in the creation of Grandparents as Parents of Kentucky as a support and advocacy organization. This group, and others, are now pushing the state to support family caregivers in the same way they do licensed foster families.

Indeed, the statewide perspective is not any brighter. Due to shortfalls in state tax revenues, more than $40 billion in underfunded teaching and state worker pension liabilities, and rising costs of maintaining roads amid lowered gas tax collection, the state budget had to remove $1 billion from the 2018–2019 and 2019–2020 budgets.[24] Governor Matt Bevin, in announcing his planned budget, proposed axing nearly 70 programs from the state budget, along with a 6.25 percent reduction at many state agencies.[25] Counties would have still received almost $4,000 per student, but counties must also lower administrative costs to make up for less funding in health insurance premiums. As Bevin stated, "We have far too many people who are not teaching our students who are sucking up the dollars that are being spent." The state is now revisiting critical conversations about its tax structure that will likely make or break the state for the coming decades. Bevin, who lost his reelection campaign in 2019 to present state governor, Andy Beshear, noted in parting from Frankfort that the state could be looking at a $1 billion shortfall in the coming years.

The state's job market is also discouraging. Manufacturing and extraction jobs, both important cornerstones for the state economy, are in short supply. Manufacturing jobs rapidly declined following the Great Recession, with Kentucky losing an estimated 11 percent of its factory jobs between 2009 and 2011.[26] Extraction has also been hard hit, declining from an estimated 13,020 mining jobs in 2010 to 4,043 in 2017, while production has slid by around 50 million short tons in 10 years.[27] Global market changes in coal use have most likely rendered extraction particularly irrelevant. The economy lacks desirable jobs that can support a household. This creates a paradox in which today's young adults must decide if Kentucky can sustain their needs even as older-aged generations make the difficult decision to relocate for better life opportunities.

Yet, even as one door closes on a long history of coal extraction in Kentucky, another window may be looking at a new opportunity in the Red. Eastern Kentucky is awash in outdoor recreation opportunities, ranging from mountain biking to hiking to climbing. In recent years, America's outdoor recreation economy has demonstrated rapid growth. It includes a wide swath of jobs—from retail to lodging to manufacturing—related to fulfilling the economic interests of hikers, hunters, fishers, and, yes, even climbers. In recent years, estimates indicate that the outdoor recreation industry has grown from $646 billion in 2012 (during the Great Recession) to $887 billion in 2017. Kentucky alone can claim an estimated $12.8 billion of that figure, along with 120,000 jobs, $3.6 billion in wages and salaries, and $756 million in state and local tax revenue.[28] The DBNF (with over a million annual visits) is already an important part of this economy, but what about the surrounding area? Rural areas like eastern Kentucky, and especially the Red, are awash in natural features that interest outdoor recreation users, so could those areas support economic revitalization by somehow incorporating outdoor recreation into their economies?

Having that conversation of increasing outdoor recreation use in eastern Kentucky requires a paradigm shift in rethinking natural resources. Kentuckians have often previously envisioned resources (e.g., coal or trees) as something to be removed and sold for profit. That certainly is economically desirable and it decidedly has its place in the national economy, but it is not without problems. The value of that exchange is unsustainable due to finite coal supplies and a changing energy market. Moreover, much of the value in that exchange benefits either corporations or persons living wherever that Kentucky coal is utilized. Kentuckians themselves are most often left in the cold on this value exchange. This long-standing economic relationship has already seen eastern Kentucky become an underdeveloped area as a result.

In comparison, supporting an outdoor recreation economy would require placing value in *preserving* natural features (such as those hills and hollers that define eastern Kentucky) in place and largely untouched except for carefully managed outdoor recreation activities. The value of the resource could be kept local, creating a capacity for Kentucky residents to create businesses built around outdoor recreation user needs ranging from gas and groceries to the more developed manufacturing of locally branded gear. Breaking with extraction traditions, this economic sector need not define the region as a tourism mono-economy. Rather, it could be seen as *one part* of a diverse economy that would need to include more than service-oriented jobs. This approach could also offer some economic growth in the region without sacrificing the region's culture or radically changing the area. Could something like this work for the Red? And what about the surrounding rural region, or even Appalachia in the broader sense? The history of the *The Motherlode* crag offers abundant examples of both the allure and the challenges of establishing climbing as a viable economic option in the Red and in the region, while also providing a starting point for understanding climbing history here in the Red.

CHAPTER 2

The Motherlode

An unmarked Bald Rock Fork Road departs from Lee County's Highway 498 on its way into the eastern Kentucky countryside. The road soon transitions from pavement to gravel, now winding along green rural hilltops as it passes a handful of houses and the weathered Ross Cemetery. To the east, passengers can peer into the valley to see a mixture of pastureland and cattle enjoying the region's cool spring mornings. As Highway 498 fades in the rearview mirror, Bald Rock Fork Road meanders through a gully. Off to the left is a recently constructed campground and cabin rental company owned by a longtime local resident. Off to the right, an oil extraction well explains the scent of petroleum that sometimes permeates the valley. Straight ahead, a sketchy gravel road blindly turns left and rapidly descends into the woods. Only the initiated would know they are now descending into the heart of a world-class climbing area.[1]

The road plummets about three-tenths of a mile down a steep and exposed gravel hill into the valley. That slippery hill is frightening for the uninitiated, and more than a few cars have gotten stuck on the way back up. Like a small stream flowing down the mountain, the county road then splashes and pools into a series of small parking lots scattered at the base of the hill. Here, Bald Rock Fork Road runs alongside its namesake stream, and flooding was a frequent issue for decades. In recent years, the Red River Gorge Climbers' Coalition made several improvements to the area to help minimize erosion and flooding, including having the nearby hill into the valley graded. Each parking lot has its own trails leading to multiple climbing areas on a wide swath of climber-owned land. Climbers disembark here, while the road itself meanders off into the distant wilderness and through the unincorporated rural community of Fixer, Kentucky, located farther down Bald Rock Fork Road. The area was an important oil extraction site in the early history of the Red, and wells are still found there today.[2]

During the climbing season, climbers arrive in these parking lots as early as possible to get first shot at their favorite routes. Renowned routes such as "BOHICA," "Chainsaw Massacre," and "The Madness" will fill up by 9 a.m. on any given spring or fall weekend with decent weather. There is often not enough parking, so climbers carpool to save funds and time. If the lot looks too full, the climbers might go to another crag. It's common to hear folks in the parking lot surveying the crowds by asking who is going climbing where today. In other cases, climbers already worked out first dibs while talking over a campfire at Miguel's Pizza or Land of the Arches, while others conferred in the Shakeout Lounge at Lago Linda.[3] The good news is that there are lots of places to climb in the Red, although the climbing in this region is no longer a secret.

The parking lots form a staging area for the day's activities. Climbers pile out of Subarus and Honda Elements crammed with gear, food bags, Nalgene bottles or water jugs, and the occasional crag dog. Climbers fill the morning with the light clink and rattle of climbing racks loaded with quickdraws and belay devices.[4] They pack their gear into long, rectangular rope bags and overnight hiking packs before setting out for the actual climbing routes. Their noticeably different climbing pants (stretchier than denim) and telltale smooth-soled climbing shoes dangling from their backpacks single them out as climbers rather than hikers. It is common to see climbers here making coffee or scarfing down a quick tortilla-wrapped breakfast before hitting the trail. They are prepping for an entire day spent circuiting between socializing, relaxing, attentively belaying, and then expending every ounce of their being climbing up the Red's unforgiving sandstone walls.

During the spring and summer, the walls will be brutal and hot wherever the sun pours onto the exposed faces. In cooler months, the climbers may seek out these exposed crags to warm up their frozen, aching fingers. Climbers are quick to note that climbing in cooler weather in the Red does allow for better grip and adhesion to the rock.[5] Projects from the spring season are often *sent* (by climbing the route *clean*—i.e., without falling) in the fall months when climbing conditions are at their peak.[6] Climbers often identify projects (selecting a particular route as a challenge to be repeated until it is completed) as a means of self-improving or increasing their abilities. Projects can last for hours, seasons, or even years depending on the route's difficulty, the climber's skill level, the climber's time commitment, and the unpredictable weather.[7] Regardless of the season, climbers may spend the day focused on a single route or return back to their car to visit another crag before retreating to their tents, cabins, vans, RVs, or the long drive home. Several thousand unique climbers find their way to the Red each year and keep coming back again and again during the year. Still others will fly from distant countries to spend a once-in-a-lifetime trip in eastern Kentucky's verdant hills. Of late, still others have decided to uproot their lives and simply live here full time.

Clustered throughout the Red and its surrounding region, climbing crags are gorgeous to behold yet indescribable on first sight. They overwhelm the senses with sheer size and their fantastic multihued stone coloring amid the hardwood trees and nearly impenetrable patches of rhododendron. Swirling iron deposits, compressed and twisted by time, pressure, and erosion pathways, provide almost psychedelic qualities to the rock. Those iron deposits also might offer a nice micro foothold to climbers. Running water creates long stains along some rock faces, whereas others are pocked with indentions, called *pockets*, which climbers often use to ascend to new heights. To first-time visitors, a trip to the crag is a visceral, life-changing event. Yet, perhaps no crag here is so imposing, so awe-inspiring, as *The Motherlode*.[8]

Climbers have collectively agreed that *The Motherlode* (often colloquially referred to as *Motherlode* or simply *The Lode*) is globally famous and a critical part of the Red's climbing community.[9] Yasmeen Fowler added, "The people who know of the Red River Gorge from out of the country [the United States] will know when you say 'The Motherlode.' " Rick Bost described *The Motherlode* as "the most beautiful piece of rock from a rock climber's viewpoint. I mean there's more hard routes and such a big concentration of hard routes in that one area that it is probably the single most well known crag in the United States." Josephine Sterr described *The Motherlode* as the "crown jewel of the Red," in an interview at the 2016 Access Fund conference in Denver. And revered guidebook author Ray Ellington calls it "the hard sport-climbing Mecca of the Red and one of the best sport crags in the world."

The Motherlode is, more accurately, five crags within one huge cove linked together by two approach trails from the west and east. Approaching from the eastern side, *Undertow Wall* feels like a giant wave of 100 feet plus looming above and preparing to crash over everything in its path. Through heavy erosion at its base, *Undertow Wall*'s top end leans far over the trail, providing a fantastic opportunity for steep climbing. This also means that any roped falls while climbing allow the climber to descend through empty space rather than hit the wall. *Undertow Wall* contains a long list of climbs ranked 5.12 (see next paragraph), including classics like "Chainsaw Massacre." The majority of this section was first climbed in the mid-1990s by Jeff Moll and Chris Martin.

Climbing routes have established difficulty levels; take the 5.12a ranking of "Chainsaw Massacre," for example. The Yosemite Decimal System (YDS) is commonly used to rank the difficulty of climbs, with an increase in number meaning a greater difficulty. The YDS ranking has up to three parts. It begins with a five-class ranking system where the first number describes five classes of ascent. Classes 1 through 4 describe increasing difficulty in walking up a particular hill. Classes 1 and 2 are akin to hiking up a trail, and Class 3 would be scrambling up a hill using hands and feet. Class 4 technically begins climbing, although it is more akin to scrambling up an exposed section of the trail, something that could be found while hiking on a few parts of the Appalachian Trail. Technical climbing begins at Class 5. Hence, all climbs will start with a 5 in their ranking. Next, the YDS has a climbing subdivision ranking via a number placed after the decimal (e.g., 5.9) based on the difficulty of the climbing route. As a subtle third category, routes ranked 5.10 and up also have a letter at the end (a–d) indicating slight changes in difficulty (e.g., 5.10d). As of June 2020, the highest-ranked route in the world is "Silence" at *Flatanger*, a 5.15d in Norway climbed by Adam Ondra in 2017. Only a handful of climbers on the planet can climb at this level. In comparison, a 5.8 or 5.9 sport-climbing route would be considered a novice level most any climber could do with practice and time. For the purposes of this book, it is again useful to remember that a higher number means higher difficulty.

Traveling north, *Madness Cave* is named for an eerie cave at the base of the wall. The area was mostly bolted in the late 1990s and early 2000s by local climbing legends like Jeff Moll, Chris Martin, and Bill Ramsey. This area contains "Omaha Beach," and at the crux of this route is a declining sandy area that is difficult to pass, which largely explains its World War II homage name. The *crux* of a climb is often treated as the most difficult part of the climb. Climbers often describe it as the *problem*, hinting they are likely taking a problem-solving approach to completing climbing routes. As such, each route could be considered its own puzzle that is solved by a particular list of specific moves that lead to sending the route. Overcoming that crux might rely on *beta* (information) from other climbers, or the climber may choose to shun that advice. The crag also includes "BOHICA," a 100-foot 5.13 classic with an intense 45-degree overhang near the end of the route.

GMC Wall is the northernmost part of *The Motherlode*, and it contains a very visual cave-like indention around 30 feet above ground. *GMC*'s name comes (per local legend) from a GMC truck that rolled off the cliff above and remains in the valley even today. Chris Snyder bolted four routes here: "8 Ball," "Snooker," "Cutthroat," and "Hot for Teacher." Chris explained that he gave Dave Hume the rights to the first ascent of "8 Ball" in exchange for Dave leaving the rest of Chris's nearby projects alone. Dave was a young climbing prodigy in the Red at the time and was described as a "quiet strongman" by Whitney Boland in *Climbing Magazine*.[10] He was competing against renowned climbers Chris Sharma and Tommy Caldwell in climbing-wall competitions by age 14, and he would later establish many respected first ascents in the Red. This includes *GMC Wall's* famous 5.14 route "Thanatopsis," a fear-inspiring climb with an intimidating blank face and utter lack of holds.

Warm-up Wall is named because of a handful of lower-skill routes (as in one 5.9, one 5.10, and several 5.11s) that climbers could use as warmups for bigger routes around the corner. It also contains a bit of history in the route "Take That, Katie Brown." In the mid-1990s, Katie Brown was a phenomenal young climber from Lexington with a penchant for onsighting routes (finishing a route on the first try without falling). Hugh Loeffler put this route up in 1997 as a "tongue-in-cheek tribute to her kicking everyone's ass—as in 'thank God we finally found a route she can't onsight.' "[11]

Finally, *Buckeye Buttress* is the first area encountered on the western approach trail. It holds several 5.11s and 5.12s on a beautiful feature-filled wall to the right of a long arête. *Warm-up Wall* and *Buckeye Buttress* represent some of the earliest route development at *The Motherlode*. Both have a number of routes put up in 1994, the same year *The Motherlode* first met the Red's climbing community.

Although synonymous with the Red, *The Motherlode* is technically beyond the Red River Gorge itself. In fact, the bulk of climbing in the region now falls into this category. In some small sense, all climber-owned properties in the Red and surrounding region arguably have two common ancestors: *The Motherlode* and *Military Wall*. The issues with sport climbing and Forest Service regulations at the *Military Wall* crag (discussed extensively later in the book) created a strong desire in the community to own their climbing destinations to ensure access, and *The Motherlode* represented an early example of expansion beyond the Red that could be privately owned. Today, Lee County (which is where *The Motherlode* is found) holds a great deal of climbing opportunities, nearly all of which are climber owned. *The Motherlode* also presents an early example of the myriad issues with climbing off public lands.

Chris Snyder recalls the story of finding *The Motherlode*:

> I had the idea to go to the geological survey at University of Kentucky on the campus and buy some geologic maps. I bought several quadrangles . . . and they color code the formations. The sandstone that we all climb on is called Corbin Sandstone and it's got a specific color on the maps, and you could just look at these quadrangle maps and it was apparent that the region that's known as The Big Sinking to the locals had a lot of rock in it, and even though it was August or July and really out of season in Kentucky, a friend and I went hiking down there.

Descending what is now called Bald Rock Fork Road and entering the Big Sinking oil field, Chris looked across the canyon and saw a powerline cut that offered an easier hiking path through the dense forest. "We bee-lined for that [cut] . . . we hiked just straight for that. . . . We looked at the rock kinda to the east of that, and it was okay. There's routes there now, it's called the *Bear's Den* . . . and then we hiked to the west and stumbled upon that drainage that is *The Motherlode*. We were back the very next day."[12]

Chris decided to find the landowner of this natural masterpiece to ask permission to climb there. He scoured through the Lee County tax assessor's records and got a lucky hit. *The Motherlode* was owned by Thomas Hall, then commonwealth attorney for Lee County. Chris visited Thomas's Beattyville office to ask permission to climb there. His response, per Chris: "You wanna do what? You wanna climb on my land?" Chris explained the process of putting up sport routes and establishing user trails there. He explained that this was a fantastic climbing location with the potential for national, even international fame. Chris remembers the conversation like this:

Thomas: "You're not gonna use any spray paint are ya?"
Chris: "No, we don't do that."
Thomas: "You're not gonna grow any pot back there?"
Chris: "No."
Thomas: "You kids do whatever you want."

As it turns out, Kentucky laws are actually quite friendly toward outdoor recreation land use. Kentucky statute 411.190 (*Obligations of owner to persons using land for recreation*) states that "an owner of land owes no duty of care to keep the premises safe for entry or use by others for recreational purposes, or to give any warning of a dangerous condition, use, structure, or activity on the premises to persons entering for such purposes." The noted purpose of the statute was "to encourage owners of land to make land and water areas available to the public for recreational purposes by limiting their liability toward persons entering thereon for such purposes." This wording allows for both "directly or indirectly" inviting persons onto the property for recreation, which creates a loophole for scenarios where the landowner essentially looks the other way or simply doesn't know. In other cases, private landowners can explicitly ban climbers or require a permit (as is today the case with Graining Fork Nature Preserve) or limit climbing access to paid guests staying at cabins on the property (such as Torrent Falls). However, the statute explicitly excludes situations where the landowner charges admittance that would place the risk of liability on the landowner. Instead, landowners can choose to allow for donations or charge for parking.[13]

Having secured permission to climb, Chris still had a big problem: physical access to the site through dense forest. Coincidently, Thomas sold the timber rights to the area soon after his conversation with Chris. Seeing the potential for good fortune, Chris talked repeatedly with the timber crews to ask that particular trees be removed, which helped ease access. Meanwhile, the bulldozers in the valley also helped to clear parking and passages. Before long, a small trickle of climbers could regularly be found in the valley.

Development happened quickly at *The Motherlode*. Chris's first route at *The Motherlode* was "Stain," a 5.12c sport classic. The following year he put up "8 Ball" (5.12d), "Cutthroat" (5.13b), and "Hot for Teacher" (5.12c). In 1994, Chris and other climbers added a total of 15 routes in short order at *The Motherlode*, and the following year climbers added another 31 routes. In two short years, *The Motherlode* had 46 routes, putting it in the same company with locations like *Military Wall* (but with the distinct climber benefit of not being under Forest Service policies). Moreover, nearly every one of those routes at *The Motherlode* was a sport route, taking advantage of the intense overhang available at spots like *Undertow* (one of the subsections within *The Motherlode*). This includes several 5.13s that were among the most difficult routes in the region. The area remains one of the most popular climbing destinations in the Red.

Thomas occasionally visited the area to see the developments occurring there. Chris said that about five years after the area had been developed for climbing, Thomas visited with his entire family. They made a day of it, watching the climbers. Looking at the license plates from around the United States, Thomas realized it was now "world famous." Chris recalled, "It was so fortunate that [Thomas] was the guy who happened to own it, and a lot of the credit for that place can be given to him."

One looming issue overarched the rapid gains at *The Motherlode*: land ownership. In those days, climbers were allowed to access the space due to the good graces of Thomas Hall, with support from Kentucky state laws, but this was contingent on Hall remaining the landowner. And at some point, the property was listed for sale. Climbing continued, but there was always the risk that it could be closed. Ray Ellington noted in his third-edition guide that *The Motherlode* is "privately owned. Although there have been no access problems reported recently, its inclusion in this book does not imply that climbers have the right to climb there."[14]

To put this in perspective, numerous climbing areas have closed in recent decades over concerns about protecting public lands, minimizing environmental impact, or even fulfilling the owner's prerogative to limit access. That sense of risk would stick around the Red. Yasmeen Fowler explained it as such: "If it's not owned by climbers, private property is kind of this loose hopeful verbal agreement between the few climbers that have the landowner's permission and the landowner. . . . That's where the motto comes from: 'If we own it, they can't close it.' "

Making things even more confusing, landownership in Appalachia also includes issues of owning the rights to extract resources. Mineral rights are often released to extraction companies interested in accessing the supply of oil beneath the region. Today, walking around *The Motherlode* area, one can often hear, see, and smell the sounds of well activity. The wells are slow producing but certainly active and must, on occasion, be emptied. In fact, this created a conflict with climbers, as extraction trucks would occasionally arrive to find cars parked in front of wells. The cars would often be towed, creating further conflicts and even fisticuffs. Bill Ramsey explained, "That was always a concern that we had because there was always this uncertainty about Charmane Oil at the time. . . . There was always this kind of sketchy relationship with them where some of the people who were working for Charmane seemed okay with the climbing, where others did not."

Despite the odds, *The Motherlode* is presently secured for climbers. In 2011, the Ventura family (who also own nearby Miguel's Pizza, a globally known climbing hub in Powell County) purchased the property above *The Motherlode*, while in 2017, the RRGCC purchased the property below *The Motherlode*. This effectively keeps the area in the climbing community. The RRGCC area is now known as Bald Rock Recreational Preserve (BRRP). The RRGCC (on September 7, 2017) signed a conservation and recreation easement with Access Fund, a national climbing advocacy and land trust organization. The easement ensures that the BRRP portion of the property cannot be developed in the future.[15]

Reflecting on climbing history in the Red, securing *The Motherlode* was certainly a milestone achievement. Its protection also guarantees that climbers will continue coming to Lee County and the surrounding region for the imaginable future. But this result belies the difficulty of coming to that momentous event. In fact, it took climbers approximately five decades to travel the journey. The path was decidedly uphill and required wading through a long history of politics, generational poverty, and flooding to get to their destination.

The Red River Dam, 1962–1969

Flooding is a part of life for residents of Clay City, Kentucky. The Great Flood of Clay City in 1962 broke flooding records for the previous 102 years.[1] The worst flood on record in Clay City would come on December 9, 1978, when the Red River crested at over 26 feet, resulting in up to three feet of water in local homes and businesses.[2] A June 1, 2004, flood saw the Red River crest at 24 feet. As recently as 2021, historic flooding in the region resulted in Powell County being declared a flood disaster zone.[3]

During regular downpours and deluges, water often submerges roadways here, seeking its escape. Flooded roads happen frequently enough that local residents know the usual areas where the water will rise and plan their lives accordingly.[4] Local residents also know an important rule for crossing flooded roadways—and particularly bridges submerged in water: *never cross at night*. When crossing a flooded area by day, the driver can pick a point of reference on the other side (such as a sign, mailbox, or fence post) and keep aim for that point. Looking just ahead of the vehicle at the water is a bad idea, as the distorted perspective can cause the driver to veer off the road into the flowing water. By night, finding a point of reference is difficult, if not impossible in rain or fog, and this increases the risk of inadvertently driving off the roadway into the flowing water.

Joe Bowen grew up on a hillside farm in Powell County. After leaving the US Air Force in 1967, Joe chose to ride his bicycle from California back home to Powell County, exploring over 14,000 miles on his meandering route across the nation. In 1980 he walked 3,000 miles across the nation on stilts to raise support for muscular dystrophy research, and he holds a Guinness world record for the longest stilt walk as a result. Joe is also a historian and has overseen the creation of two life-sized bronze statues of Bert Combs: one placed at the Prestonburg, Kentucky, courthouse and the other in Stanton a few hundred yards from the Bert T. Combs Mountain Parkway, which brings visitors into the Red. Joe shared that Combs made a fateful decision while driving home to Powell County on the night of December 4, 1991:

He worked late and he was going home and we've got three river cross-
ings, three roads that go through the valley here that floods. Almost all
of us will drive up to those. . . . When the water is getting up above the
highway, we will drive up to it and it's kinda, "Yeah, we can pass, we can
go through it," or we say, "No, it looks too deep." And this was 10 o'clock
at night. He was probably tired, and he pulled up to the high water, and
it had started flooding, and he decided to drive it. And it slid his car off
the road into a deep pool, but he didn't drown. He got his jacket off, and
they found one of his shoes, and about a quarter mile downstream they
found him. He had actually got out of the main river channel and he had
his hand on about a two-inch tree, and it got down to about 10 degrees
[Fahrenheit] that night, and he actually froze to death.

The rushing water of the Red River has previously been part of a short-lived
economic boon for Clay City. Early timber harvesters originally utilized the
swollen river to move cut trees down the valley to be milled. The steam-
powered Red River Lumber Mill (established in 1880) was the biggest mill in
the state at the time and was reputed to be one of the largest in the nation by
1889. Rails were needed to get the timber to cities. This mill was supported by
the Kentucky Union Railway Company, which established rails to help move
timber from the mill to cities. Kentucky Union was chartered March 10, 1854,
originally to create several lines linking eastern Kentucky's coal and timber
resources to areas like Lexington and Cincinnati.[5] However, this plan was dis-
rupted by the Civil War. Scaling down their project, they constructed a railway
linking Clay City to a junction near Winchester on June 6, 1885. From there,
the timber could be sent to Lexington.[6]

High demand for seemingly endless timber stands and the new rail connection created ongoing economic support for the town, and the timber kept
moving down the river. Unfortunately, that sawmill operation burned down in
1906. By December 1910, the Dana Lumber Company was working on Nada
Tunnel (near Slade), which would provide even better rail access to the Red's
timber supplies. The tunnel was finished by 1912, but the economic bloom at
Clay City had fallen from the vine.

Clay City's story is not dissimilar to many mountain towns throughout
Appalachia, where boom and bust cycles built around finite resources made
for a way of life. Eastern Kentucky's long history of timber (such as that in the
Red) and coal (which is found farther east of the Red) is built on the premise
of removing natural wealth that cannot be replenished in our lifetimes. Good

jobs are developed as extraction occurs, but they are, at best, temporary good jobs. Those jobs will eventually be relocated or lost as operations move from site to site, and little is left behind for those living in and around the exhausted extraction site.[7]

A good example of this process in action is the high concentration of coal operations in West Virginia's New River Gorge.[8] In a matter of 70 years, coal extractors and workers established numerous new camps and towns singularly focused on mining. It took that long for the bulk of the coal to be removed, leaving numerous towns that depopulated as miners and their families moved elsewhere for mine work. Amid those now abandoned towns were banks, grocers, schools, churches, and company stores, which, once extraction at a particular shaft became unprofitable, also closed their doors. This coal town boom and bust cycle is largely normalized and rarely subject to questions outside of geography, sociology, and perhaps critical history. Rather, it is now just an accepted way of life affixed to Appalachian culture.

Extraction offers unequal returns based on where one falls in the exchange process: the company that removes the resource receives more benefit than the location where the coal is extracted.[9] In other words, the creation of wealth in extraction is effectively one sided: profits are largely made on the ownership end of the process, not as much at the site where the resource is removed. But as part of this extraction process (whether dealing with coal or timber or other extraction industries), the environmental costs remain at the site of extraction. The idea goes that these areas, often described as *sacrifice zones*, are effectively set aside for deforestation, pollution, and environmental loss in pursuit of economic value.[10]

Sacrifice zones begin with unequal exchange between a provider and receiver.[11] One side provides a resource (or a service) to the other, who may then use that resource for another purpose (even selling it again in another form). The value of that exchange, however, falls mostly on the receiving end. The resource costs but a fraction of the value it serves removed from the dirt, and little is deposited in the community it comes from.[12] For example, Clay City's timber and milling industry provided timber for use outside of Powell County. Lexington, an urban area, would have little timber, whereas the Red has lots, so Lexington businesses (and perhaps even the city managers) would have had interest in obtaining timber for construction and resale. As the supply of timber was quite plentiful, Clay City's saw mills could sell it for relatively little. An interesting side effect is that there's often little reason to develop the economy further at the site of extraction beyond the infrastructure needed to continue extraction.

Sacrifice zones also differently experience the costs and long-term effects of conducting business. This is particularly the case for negative environmental impacts. For example, the costs of timbering in the Red risked deforestation in Powell County, not in Lexington.[13] Deforestation creates issues with erosion and timber trail development, and these effects would be felt in areas like Clay City and Slade, not Lexington. Over time, these relationships inherently created unevenly developed linkages where one location grew further through using the resources of another location. There was little cause to further develop businesses at the extraction site. As a result, Clay City really had on hand only what was needed to continue the timber extraction economy and developed little else in the economy. Lexington, however, could benefit from the value added of manufacturing products from timber, creating jobs far from the extraction site. This results in an unstable relationship where, once the resource being extracted is gone, there is little left in terms of economic development.

There are also cases where the resulting impacts of this relationship are acutely felt by the community living around the extraction cite. A tragic example of this is the Martin County coal slurry pond spill. Martin County, located along Kentucky's eastern border with West Virginia, is located in a coal-rich region of the state. Massey Energy owned a mine for which they created a pond to hold coal slurry, which is a by-product of coal preparation. Water used in cleaning coal includes fine particulates that render the water black and effectively untreatable, necessitating the use of storage ponds. These ponds can include toxic metals and elements inadvertently mined while extracting coal, such as cyanide and mercury. On October 11, 2000, the impoundment broke, flooding an abandoned mine below and sending coal slurry out of the mine's openings. An estimated 306 million gallons of slurry dumped into the Tug Fork River, polluting over 200 miles of the Big Sandy River, contaminating water supplies for the 27,000-plus residents in the area, and killing all aquatic life in Coldwater Fork and Wolf Creek.[14]

Today, sacrifice zones can take multiple forms beyond extraction and are often treated as important economic sources for local economies. These include public works such as landfills, prisons, and waterworks. One local example is the Estill County landfill. This landfill was recently illegally tainted with radioactive waste. The state has now elected to encase the radioactive waste rather than relocate it. Notably, the landfill is located right across the street from the county high school.[15] Another example is the US penitentiary, Big Sandy, located in Martin County. Although having a high-security prison does create needed jobs amid the decline of coal in the region, it also means increased noise and light pollution. Landfills and prisons aren't ideal neighbors to have in any community, so they are often pushed out to rural areas. In academics and community development, these have been nicknamed NIMBYs, an acronym for *not in my backyard*. The idea goes that existing residential and commercial areas would not want a landfill near their community, so they would fight against it, whereas a rural community or less economically privileged area might choose to take on this undesirable activity as a necessary source of revenues and jobs. The end result is that these developments are pressed out into rural areas with extensive land and an interest in jobs.

Public works such as dams and reservoirs represent an intriguing version of sacrifice zones. Dams can certainly provide flood relief (something needed throughout the Red) and an influx of jobs relating to constructing, operating, and maintaining the dam. They can also create a source of drinking water, a source for water recreation, and even a source for tourism growth in the area. Recall that the Tennessee Valley Authority (TVA) built a series of hydroelectric dams on the Tennessee River under the rationale of providing electricity to rural residents, including Appalachian residents. Later, TVA would provide power for the Second World War effort. In 1942, there were 12 hydroelectric dams running, and they employed around 28,000 workers. As of 1959, TVA was a self-sustaining force in the region even as the demand for coal (and coal-fired energy) increased, and they continued the series of locks and dams on the Tennessee River. Farther west, dams were also a hot topic. There, western states were looking for ways to turn arid land into farms, and the Colorado River provided one of few opportunities.[16] Lake Powell (an artificial lake on the border of Utah and Arizona) would be filling with water during Bert Combs's time as governor.

Clay City native Bert Combs was elected Kentucky's governor in 1960. This was a true accomplishment for a local Appalachian kid from the hollers of eastern Kentucky. Although Combs's family was not wealthy, they did have one handy resource: Combs's mother was a teacher who ensured that the family valued education.[17] Her love of learning would help see Combs graduate high school at age 15 as valedictorian before heading to Cumberland College, where he reportedly lit the furnaces and cleaned campus buildings to support his tuition.[18] He then worked as a state department clerk, saving funds that later afforded him a bachelor of laws degree at the University of Kentucky in 1937. He graduated second in his class. He soon passed his bar admission and returned to Clay County to practice law before later taking a firm job in Prestonsburg. World War II would soon put those legal skills to work in unexpected ways.

In 1943, Combs enlisted in the army. He completed Officer Candidate School. Given that he was a lawyer, he joined the Judge Advocate General's Corps, where he conducted war tribunals for Japanese war criminals. After the war, he returned to Prestonsburg. In 1950 he was elected city attorney and soon filled in as the Commonwealth's counsel in the 31st Judicial District. He then ran for and won a seat on the Kentucky Court of Appeals. This set the table for Combs's first attempt at running for governor, a race he decidedly lost. He would have his chance again four years later when the current governor and previous victor, Happy Chandler, was term limited out of office. This time, Combs was victorious, and he would serve as governor from 1959 until 1963.

As the new state governor, Combs inherited a region that, Ronald Eller argues, was "devastated by economic stagnation, out-migration, and environmental depredation in the postwar years."[19] The state was effectively behind the curve in multiple areas. High school dropout rates often exceeded 50 percent, with few graduates going to college. Roads were in bad shape, often inadequate for heavy travel, hindering industrial development in the region. The state park system was woefully underfunded and in dire need of repairs. The flooding in 1957 had damaged the state economy, particularly in eastern Kentucky, yet relief funds were simply not available in the budget.

Improving education would be a central tenet of his administration and earn Combs the historical reputation as Kentucky's "Education Governor."[20] In a presentation to the Frankfort Rotary Club on September 11, 1963, Combs explained his administration's focus on education and echoed some of what he had learned from his mother all those years ago: "We gave our attention first to education, because every survey of public opinion indicated that education of children held first place in the hearts of Kentuckians. I think most Kentuckians feel that if there is a single key which can unlock the door to a brighter future that key is education."[21]

Combs increased funding to both primary schools and the state community college system by raising the state sales tax by 3 percent. Teacher salaries increased during the Combs administration by nearly double. The school system was also restructured, eliminating 500 one-room schools, building 30 new high schools and 102 new elementary schools, and expanding 87 existing high schools and 181 elementary schools.[22] Over four years, Combs increased support for higher education by 115 percent, established the state's Community College System, and started the Kentucky Educational Television (KET).[23]

Combs second priority was infrastructure, particularly transportation and supporting tourism.[24] He issued $100 million in bonds to support highway growth, including the mountain parkway that would eventually bear his name. He secured $20 million, half in bonds, to begin renovations in the 26 state parks existing at that time.[25] He also established a state park system that would go on to be the model for others states.[26] In sum, Combs's work resulted in a doubling of out-of-state tourism to the region and an unexpected glut of persons seeking lodging and campsite reservations across the state, including Natural Bridge in the Red.

One of Combs's early efforts was working with the Eastern Kentucky Regional Planning Commission (EKRPC). The intent of EKRPC was to provide state and local policy makers with innovative recommendations on strategies to deal with localized flooding following the disastrous 1957 deluge. They were also to recommend a pathway to improved emergency relief and transportation/infrastructure improvements. B. F. Reed, a coal operator, chaired the committee, and its membership included representatives from the gas and timber industries, real estate, religion, news media, education, and medicine, each representing interests in the region. EKRPC soon nominated John D. Whisman as its executive director.

Whisman envisioned eastern Kentucky's problems from an underdevelopment perspective, believing the region provided potential that had to be unlocked. He stated that the region's transportation, utilities, education, and water control facilities (among others) had not adequately been developed to serve the people who lived there. (That part about water control facilities would prove important for the Red in the following years.) Ronald Eller argues that Whisman saw the problems as essentially a lack of resources, both human and physical, that resulted from isolation. Arguably, the correct application of resources would then unlock its potential and, so to speak, bring it up to speed with the rest of the nation.[27]

EKRPC crafted *Program 60* as a plan to integrate development strategies ranging from education changes to economic diversification. Their plan covered extensive parts of the region's political economy. They proposed revisiting existing zoning and planning policies to promote growth, invigorating the job market through job training and increasing job diversity, and improved transportation throughout the state. Moreover, they included a plan to support flood control. As someone who knew about flooding from his days in Powell County, Bert Combs was an important proponent of Program 60's ideas on flood control as the new state governor.[28]

Official conversations about a dam in the Red River Gorge were already underway when Program 60 released their historic report outlining their plans for the region. As early as 1954, talk of creating a flood-prevention dam along the Red appeared in US Corps of Engineers (COE) reports, and the 1957 flooding in Appalachia furthered this cause. The *Kentucky River Report* (a result of a COE study of the Kentucky River Basin) included suggestions for a Red River reservoir.[29] The report was shared in Senate and House hearings without any signs of dissent but with little further action. It was only a matter of time before another flood would come.

Joe Bowen was there for the 1962 flood: "In 1962, I remember delivering groceries to people on my horse from the grocery store 'cause the water just stayed up and stayed up . . . February '62 . . . and I remember I took groceries to Eugene and Shirley Reed and they've got that little driveway . . . and I'm on my horse, okay? And all the sudden the horse goes under. I'd missed the driveway [laughs] but my horse was getting out of there, baby! I knew just stay on!"

Efforts to address flooding along the Red River gained renewed support among Congress soon after the waters receded. By the end of the year, the Red River Reservoir had been authorized by Congress as part of the Flood Control Act of 1962. Options in this act included a levy, a diversion channel, a flood wall, or building a dam and reservoir. The dam and reservoir won out. Under the name of the Red River Lake Project, the COE held a 1963 public meeting in Stanton to discuss the plans and the extent of the dam proposal, again with no recorded dissent.[30] The planned location would be on the North Fork of the Red. It would flood approximately 1,400 privately held acres and another 2,000 acres of national forest land. Surrounding developments (which included management facilities and public use facilities) would cover another 8,000 acres of the national forest and 2,000 more acres of private land.

From the COE perspective, there were relatively few issues with the proposed dam.[31] It would mean the loss of vegetation and wildlife habitat, but it would create a fish hatchery habitat in its place. One arch in the Red (Moonshiner's Arch) might experience water lapping at its base on high water days. KY-715 would be lost to the dam and KY-77 would need to be redirected via a bridge across the dam. There were also other perhaps less transparent motivations for creating the dam.[32] First, the reservoir behind the dam would guarantee water access for cities like Lexington. Curiously, Lexington reportedly sold their two existing water reservoirs at a profit of over $2 million when the dam was initially funded by Congress. The Commonwealth of Kentucky then offered to pay for the dam to be built higher, thus impounding more water. Second, the COE envisioned that having a reservoir would create new opportunities for accessing the Red as a recreational space, not unlike lake development such as Lakes Powell and Mead on the Colorado River. The COE plan assumed that the DBNF (which endorsed the plan insofar as they, like the COE, served as a government agency) would establish best practices to protect existing resources as new recreational development occurred as a result of the dam.

Throughout this process, local and state support for the dam remained quite strong. Few political figures dared oppose the dam, as it was popular among their constituents. Representative Gene Snyder from Kentucky's 4th district in Oldham County was a rare exception, noting the "peculiar coincidence" that Lexington had sold their water reservoirs as the dam moved forward.[33] Journalist Edwin Shrake's article on the dam also noted that the original proposed dam would limit flooding only on the North Fork, and only in the case of major floods, which would be lowered by two inches based on COE figures. Thus the dam might not be as useful as local residents hoped.[34] Local residents founded the Red River Dam Association, which voiced support for the dam. This group also largely suppressed local dissidence, which pressured a clear minority to keep their views on the dam quiet.[35]

In 1967, the COE held a meeting in Stanton to discuss how land would be purchased for the project. The Cumberland Chapter of the Sierra Club (CCSC) registered formal opposition to the project at the COE hearing. The CCSC was very new, having been organized in February 1966 by Carroll Tichenor, Dorris Tichenor, Bill Holstein, Jim Kowalski, and others whose names are presently lost to history. They collectively argued that this project, if completed, would destroy the scenic quality of the Red and its intrinsic and instrumental values as a natural area. Although difficult to prove, as the area had been largely cleared for farmland or forested in recent decades, the CCSC argued that the dam would also irreparably damage the unique habitats found in the Red. Notably, the Sierra Club *did* support a dam project five miles downstream that would avoid flooding 80 percent of the Red River Gorge at the increased cost of around $3 million.[36] The CCSC's stance was not a popular one in places like Clay City. Local residents who had long supported the dam were none too happy about *outsiders* shaping how local space would be used.

The CCSC initiated a *Stop the Dam* protest in 1967. Members began a letter-writing campaign that targeted national-level political figures. The CCSC gained support of the National Audubon Society (something that would prove very important later on), but similar efforts to garner support from the League of Kentucky Sportsmen, National Wildlife Federation, and Kentucky Conservation Council were all rebuffed.[37] Regionally, favorable coverage from the *Louisville Courier-Journal* newspaper likely helped the CCSC's cause. Meanwhile, the CCSC worked to bring in national-level political figures to see and experience the Red. One such case was Supreme Court justice William O. Douglass. Today his visit is considered a watershed moment in the overall fight against the dam.

In an interview with Kentucky Afield Radio, CCSC cofounder (and Cumberland Climbers member, an organization discussed in the next chapter) Carroll Tichenor recounts encouraging CCSC president and Union College professor Jim Kowalski to contact Justice Douglass.[38] Justice Douglass had recently marched at a similar pro-environment event, and Carroll suggested Jim write him on Union College letterhead to give the group more legitimacy. Instead, Kowalski sent a postcard. Regardless, it worked. Douglass agreed to come visit the Red for a short hike through the area on the premise that the CCSC would reimburse his expenses. Dorris Tichenor prepared 15 or so lunches for the CCSC and their guests. Justice Douglass and his wife arrived around 1:00 in the afternoon, ate lunch, and went for a scheduled walk to Moonshiner's Arch. Approximately 800 to 1,000 protesters against the dam joined in on the hike, as well as a few hundred antiprotesters. That short walk to Moonshiner's Arch would become an event known today as the 1967 Protest Hike, which got the attention of the state, particularly as it was amid an election year for the state governorship.

By the time the 1967 Protest Hike was happening, Bert Combs had completed his term as governor and had already returned to his private law practice.[39] On April 5, 1967, Combs accepted a judge appointment to the US Court of Appeals Sixth Circuit, where he would remain until 1970. Combs's former campaign worker, Ned Breathitt, had replaced Combs in 1963 as state governor. Louie B. Nunn lost against Breathitt in 1963 but won the governorship in 1967. He proposed a license fee increase (from $5.00 to $12.50) on motor vehicles and a sales tax increase from Combs's 3 percent to a proposed 5 percent to cover a projected $24 million shortfall in the state budget. Meanwhile, fierce debate over the dam had moved from the Protest Hike into the State Senate. Republican senator John S. Cooper, who originally supported the dam, now opposed it. This change was quizzical, given his support for public works along the Big Sandy River and reconstruction of locks and dams on the Ohio River and in the Green River Valley. In July of 1968, Cooper suggested an alternate location for the dam on the Middle Fork of the River. The site was farther downstream and would have had a lower height, thus reducing the lake's height in the Red.

In 1969, new state governor Louie B. Nunn also publicly announced that he no longer supported the proposed dam. His announcement came after meeting with Elvis Stahr, president of the National Audubon Society, whose organization had been an early supporter of the CCSC's work in the Red.[40] Soon thereafter, Senator Cooper approached President Richard Nixon in a bid to stop the dam. Nixon finally nixed the dam. On April 10, 1969, the New York Times ran a story entitled "Victory at Red River," signaling what most thought was the end of the Red River Dam project. The proposed dam site was scrapped, at least for the moment.

The dam fight had long-term ramifications. The issues raised by the project supported the creation of several important environmental laws, including the Endangered Species Act and the National Environmental Policy Act (NEPA).[41] Author Wendell Berry would write The Unforeseen Wilderness, a Muir-worthy environmental text focused solely on the preservation of the Red River Gorge. Red climbers would take on a noted environmental tone in several of their early guidebooks from the 1970s (discussed in chapters 4 and 5), thinking the Red might still be lost. The DBNF would conduct many archaeological site examinations, some of which would relate to select climbing closures decades later. And two decades later, Bert Combs would make the disastrous decision of crossing a flooded bridge at night.

Collins's history of the Forest Service cites an article in *American Forest Magazine* published just a few years after the dam struggle (1972) in which Glen Rutherford gave readers a word of warning: "By the late 1960s, people swarmed over the Gorge, from the top of Chimney Rock to the depths of hollows crowded with giant hemlock, tulip poplars, sycamores, beeches, hickories and oaks. They came with packs on their backs and in $15,000 camping vehicles. They came to see the place the Army was going to destroy with water—and in doing so, they succeeded in destroying much of it themselves." [42]

Likewise, Edwin Shrake's article on the Red and the proposed dam assumed it was now a foregone conclusion that the Red's geological features would be lost despite outsiders (such as the CCSC) attempting to sway local perceptions about the scientific value of the Red. [43] The Red had been put on the national stage. Now, people wanted to see what was so great out there in eastern Kentucky.

Just one year after that brutal 1962 flood in Powell County, Howard Becker published a seminal text called *Outsiders*. [44] This text provides useful insight on additional long-term impacts of the proposed dam. Becker's work examined how groups might include or exclude others based on perceptions of keeping or breaking norms defined by that group. Norms, or rules for social behavior, can be formal or informal. Formalized norms are easier to learn because they are written into laws and policies and are generally well established. For example, visitors to the region know they cannot steal from stores, as theft is a codified law. However, informal norms can be particularly hard to follow for those entering a new area. Informal expectations for how people should behave are not written and are often based in long-standing traditions in one place that do not apply in others. For example, one may be expected to dress a certain way even though there is no clear dress code or be expected to participate in specific activities that have long-standing cultural ties. Their uncodified nature makes the rules difficult to know and interpret, but the penalties for violating them (e.g., being labeled as a deviant or an outsider) are no less real. Consequences of violating informal norms can be relatively minor, like getting bad service at a restaurant frequented by locals, or it can be quite extreme, such as being the target of violence.

Appalachian culture prevalent in the Red involves long-standing traditions that acknowledge hunting, gathering forest products, hiking, or swimming as perfectly normal behaviors. Likewise, gathering archaeological items, moonshining, or even growing marijuana (each having their own histories in the region) might be considered in the range of acceptability even while violating formal rules prohibiting these behaviors. In contrast, vocally expressing interests in birding, climbing, or even environmentalism might raise eyebrows among other Appalachians. This was especially true around the time of the dam.

In the 1960s, Ella Carroll ran a small motel and general store on Highway 15 near Nada. In a 1972 magazine article chronicling the history of the dam, Ella was quoted as saying, "Everything was fine down here for a long time—we were going to get our dam and flood control and everything. Then some danged outsiders had to pipe up." Ella was frustrated in how nonlocal activities shaped local issues. She continued, "It beats me how some attorney or something up in Lexington or Louisville can suddenly become an expert on what ought to be done down here. . . . [Local residents] know what needs to be done, and if some of those people who began raising all the fuss over the dam had seen Clay City washing away down the Red River, they'd never said a word." [45]

Ella's perceptions about outsiders were also shared by other local residents. Kentucky native Lionel Johnson was quoted in the same article as feeling that the growing rush of people now coming to the area as a result of national attention would destroy the Red: "The single most adverse impact on the area as a result of the new dam and reservoir won't be the water, but the additional people they will bring to the Gorge." Lionel felt the increase in visitors needed to be curtailed: "We've just got to begin limiting, in some way or another, the amount of people visiting the Gorge. If we don't, the whole thing will be gone in a few years." [46]

By the time Ella and Lionel's words were printed in 1972, climbers had already been in the Red for a couple years, and that history begins in the next chapter. Could the dam have created a moment in which one generation of local residents defined climbers as outsiders? There are some ancillary issues that make this likely. The late 1960s marked an epoch for the hippie movement in the United States. (Recall that Woodstock was happening right around the time climbers would first appear in the Red.) The Sierra Club, an external organization based out West, brought in individuals to protest the dam at a time when the hippie movement was socially visible for protesting. The Sierra Club held ideals that did not entirely mesh with how the Red's residents understood reality. From a local perspective, fixing the flooding was a logical idea because it was devastating the region. But externally, the value of this fix was overshadowed by risks to natural areas and environmental conservation.

There's another dynamic afoot that labels climbers as outsiders: they played in a forbidden zone (the Red) where locals were taught to do otherwise.

Territorialization is the process of establishing norms dictating who can be found in a particular area, when that can happen, and under what conditions. In conducting interviews with local residents, the Red was often described by their parents and other kin as being off limits for children. Effectively, children were either forbidden or discouraged from going too deep into the Red. Certain areas were open to cultural uses such as hunting and fishing. These often included family land or familiar areas where her older family members felt comfortable. Here, cultural norms treat the Red as an off-limits space except under certain conditions. It points to the power of cultural norms in guiding our behaviors without much thought about questioning those behaviors.

This also created a scenario where older generations could shape how children understood outsiders, such as those against the dam. Much of what children in the Red knew, both then and now, about visitors in the Red was largely handed down across generations and subject to a healthy injection of myth. In fact, it was common for older generations of residents (particularly those who had lived through the Red River Dam's tumultuous history) to take a fairly negative view of outsiders and remain wary of visitors. Taking a distrustful view of those who used the Red for recreation was arguably a cultural norm for the people of the Red, and it was something passed down long after the dam was lost.

Local author and climber Chis Chaney provided perspective on this relationship between climbers and the outsider status in his book recounting his years in the Red.[47] Chris grew up in Stanton, a stone's throw from Clay City. There his family ran a local business for many years. He experienced what climbers who aren't from here could not quite understand. And it goes back to that dam. Chris explained, "You had two groups when the dam was going in: you had the group that lived in that North Fork area that were going to be directly impacted, they were against [the dam] . . . and then the rest of the community, the entire rest of the county, everybody else that lived in the area wanted the dam." Much of the activism, Chris felt, was tied into that small number of folks who were local and against the dam, and that these persons helped mobilize protests and lawsuits that eventually got the national attention of the Sierra Club, and history tells the rest of the story. "All those people from outside came in and told us what we were going to do, what we could do and what we couldn't do." Over time, locals began to apply that same logic to most anyone found in the Red. "When I grew up, it was 'those dirty hippies in the Gorge,' you know? And that's what you heard all the time, and that's the perception I had until I started climbing."

CHAPTER 4

Cumberland Climbers, 1968–1975

Departing on foot from KY-715 and walking up Forest Service Trail #229, the hike to *Tower Rock* winds through the beautiful flora of the Red. Hemlock and oak dominate the hillside, while rhododendron bushes block the view of the nearby Red River. At the top of the hill, *Tower Rock* is a huge fingerlike rock extension that rises 90 feet amid a field of gargantuan boulders. From a distance, it feels like a strong-willed Brobdingnag giant has jammed its fists up through the dirt ceiling and extended its pointer finger to the sky. Nearby, tree roots twist around rock, making the area feel almost mythical. On a research trip there in 2016, my colleague Brian Clark (a recreation and park administration professor at EKU) aptly described it as "something out of Lord of the Rings, like a hobbit might come walking by at any moment." The terrain certainly fits the description. The Red truly is a magical place, and *Tower Rock* provided an extraordinary location for climbing to begin in the Red.

This wooded path leads a full circle around the tower, passing alongside a number of classic routes. There's "Africa," a 5.9 route aptly named after an African continent–shaped indention in the rock at the route. Nearby is "Tower of Power," Larry Day's favorite 5.10c that went around 25 years without being repeated. "Delta Blow," a 5.10b route, nearly killed its creator.[1] *Tower Rock* also holds one of the most historically significant routes in the Red: "Caver's Route." This route is located along the eastern end of the tower. Climber lore here records this route as the first climbing route in the Red.

By today's standards, "Caver's Route" is relatively easy (5.3 on the Yosemite Decimal System), but climbers have described it nonetheless as a fun route and a rite of passage for all climbers. Several climbers insisted in interviews that it could be done free solo (without a rope or other protection from falling) since there are really few opportunities to place reliable protection. The route leads first up an unprotected face climb to the left of a large crack and then up this crack between two rock pillars (what climbers call a *chimney*), giving the experience a spelunking feel, which might explain the route's name. At one point, the climber actually shimmies up through the roof and onto the top of the tower.

Once at the top, climbers enjoy the view of the valley before rappelling down the outside of the chimney.

By the time Red climbers began documenting routes on *Tower Rock* in the late 1960s, climbing was already enjoying a revered era out West. Royal Robbins had been in Yosemite for a decade and had put up an envied list of first ascents there (including the coveted Northwest Face of Half Dome), along with climbing greats like Tom Frost, Chuck Pratt, and Yvon Chouinard.[2] Royal, a standoffish climbing aesthete, resisted using permanent protection (e.g., drilled and hammered-in bolts) or any other assistance beyond the rock's natural features while climbing and discouraged others from using them. Royal's foil (but still friend), Warren Harding, a hard-living and harder-nosed climber, had an equally enthralling list of first ascents—perhaps most importantly a first ascent on "The Nose" on El Capitan—but was best known for aggressively using permanent protection.[3] This included now legendary cases of hammering in a long line of pitons or drilling holes for expansion bolts right up a section of rock otherwise deemed unclimbable. Perhaps the difference came down to the purpose of climbing: where Warren placed importance on getting to the top as the purpose of climbing, Royal valued the journey getting there. Thus, Royal and Warren came to represent two sides of the same climbing coin.

Royal's ethic sought balance between pure climbing and safe climbing. He argued that the climber should avoid using any artificial aid as part of the climbing process as a means of moving up the rock.[4] This still allows for safety functions (such as putting a removable piece of protection into a crack, discussed later in this chapter) that would catch the climber in the event of a fall. However, the climber should not attach a rope ladder and ascend from there, use jumars (clamps) to ascend a route, hang their weight on protection to rest, or pull themselves up by using the protection as an anchor. These would each be considered an aid that detracted from the climbing experience. That said, there are times where Royal himself used permanent protection on some routes, so these principles served as an ideal for climbers of the era across the nation rather than an absolute. This overall approach was quite common among the earliest climbers in the Red.

Three climbers stand out in the guidebooks as the earliest documented climbers: Ron Stokley, Dieter Britz, and Robert (Bob) Stokes. They are credited with the earliest recorded first ascents (FAs) in the Red at *Tower Rock*, *Courthouse Rock*, *Natural Bridge*, and *Half Moon*. Oddly, that's about all one will find about them in the scores of Red River Gorge climbing guidebooks published over five decades. Although climbers have an amazing oral tradition of memorizing routes and their details and communicating this information to other climbers (something deserving more research), the community knew little else about this founding generation. Ron, Dieter, and Bob represent important foundational members in the Red's climbing history. Their lived experiences in the Red helped connect the dots between Kentucky's speleology and climbing communities, as well as the origins of "Caver's Route" and the linkages between climbers and several regional and national organizations—Cumberland Climbers, BlueGrass Grotto, the University of Kentucky, and at least two Explorer Posts—which collectively shaped the story of climbing in the Red.

Today, Ron Stokley is a familiar face in Boulder, Colorado.[5] Born in Lexington, Ron moved from the Red to Colorado in 1976 with his job at IBM. He did some climbing there: "I tried. It was so different. . . . [The Red] is a really unique area, and out here [in Colorado] it is granite and a lot of cracks. You can drive a piton in and expect them to hold . . . totally different kind of climbing." After retiring from IBM he spent 12 years at REI and currently works at Neptune Mountaineering. Recently, he founded the Boulder Lightpackers, a group dedicated to ultralight hiking. He's also hiking segments of the 486-mile Colorado Trail. Ron took to serious backpacking after a car accident ended his cycling career. That cycling career began in Kentucky, where he founded the Bluegrass Wheelmen (renamed the Bluegrass Cycling Club in 1994) in either 1966 or 1970, no one is quite sure which.[6] But before all that, a young Ron Stokley got his start on ropes early in the caves of central Kentucky.

Ron is an experienced caver. His interest in caving originated while in Explorer Post 97 in his hometown of Lexington.[7] As a youth, Ron had a lucky opportunity to explore Mammoth Cave and link up with the caving community at the University of Kentucky: "My dad was in construction and he did some ceramic tile work in the Snowball Dining Room [at Mammoth Cave], and as a youngster I was able to go down there while he was doing some of the work and I did a lot of cave exploring with some people from the university [of Kentucky]. . . . We used to practice rappelling, ascending, jumaring up the cliff faces."[8]

Ron also had another lucky opportunity to explore an old commercial cave at Cumberland Lake. The US Army Corps of Engineers lowered Cumberland Lake, located south of the Red, for repairs to the (since halted) Wolf Creek Dam. The lower water level exposed the cave that quickly became the target of the spelunking community. Ron recounts that this lowering created the opportunity for cavers to gather and share techniques, as well as information about new caving areas. It would also be the catalyst for creating an organized cavers community that would eventually become the BlueGrass Grotto, a speleological club that exists still today.[9] Several climbers from the 1970s would eventually become members, including Ron, Martin Hackworth, and Frank Becker.

Ron's involvement in caving and association with cavers at the University of Kentucky via Mammoth Cave introduced him to Dieter Britz: "We used to practice for deep caves on Chimney Rock in the Natural Bridge State Park and that sort of got me involved in a little bit of rock climbing, but later on, Dieter Britz was at the university. He's a fellow from Australia who was attending the University and he contacted me, oh, I can't remember how far back, but he contacted me about wanting to do some rock climbing because he had done a lot in Australia, and I took him to the place where we practiced and he and I, after several times, did a first ascent on Chimney Rock."

Dr. Dieter Britz now lives in Denmark, eight time zones away from Ron in Colorado (and six from the Red).[10] He is professor emeritus since 2010 at the Aarhus University. Dieter completed his PhD in electrochemistry in 1967 at the University of Sydney and was in the Red for only two years (1968–1970) while completing a postdoc at the University of Kentucky. Interestingly, his time in the Red almost didn't happen. In an email message, Dieter shared the story of his arrival in the Red: "I then applied to a postdoc in Colorado where there was a bloke doing my kind of work and using a minicomputer, and got offered the position one day after I had accepted another one, in Lexington, Kentucky, where my PhD supervisor now was. I had a great time there for about two years." In our first email interactions, Dieter was quick to tell me, "By the way I still climb but these days, indoors, twice a week here in Aarhus, and also am an instructor." He sent a video of him moving gracefully and confidently across the holds at an indoor gym and doing overhand pull-ups in his 70s.

Ron shared the story of his first climb together with Dieter at *Chimney Rock*: "The first time [we] climbed *Chimney Rock* we hiked in. Later we would rappel down from the top. We asked a landowner if we could cross her garden property to get to it. The base of it was loaded with copperhead snakes!!! Everywhere we stepped they were there; in the bushes, on ledges, at our feet. We flicked them out of the way with a stick." Dieter seconds memories of all those snakes: "There were copperhead snakes galore at the bottom of the climb." Dieter referred to this route as "Tourist Horror" (which would later be listed as "Tourists' Horror") because tourists who visited the arch across the valley from this spot could make out climbers on "what looked like a blank wall, hence the horror."

Ron described Dieter's climbing rack as having some cutting-edge technology for the time: "Chouinard chocks, big bongs, lots of runners and nuts." To the nonclimber, these are kinds of removable protection that, until then, were technologically absent in the Red. Dieter also possessed earlier climbing experience in Australia where he abseiled (rappelled) with hemp ropes because they limit the amount of bounce (or stretch) when stopping. Still, some of the techniques Dieter and he used would make climbers today cringe. These included self-tied swami belts and belays around the waist using gloves for friction ("quite a useless belay," Dieter noted). They also worked with a Lexington parachute manufacturer to make leftover seatbelt material into climbing harnesses. Ron recalled, "It was a discontinued color and they sewed up the material for us." Dieter, who now teaches climbing safety, winced at recalling the gear and techniques of the era: "I teach this stuff now and am amused at our methods back then, and I horrify people telling them about it."[11]

It isn't clear exactly when Robert Stokes linked into the climbing community. Most likely it happened while he was a professor at the University of Kentucky, which fits into Ron's explanation of how university members got involved in caving, rappelling, and climbing. A physicist by training (earning a PhD from Princeton in 1968), Stokes returned back to Kentucky where he had received his undergraduate training and began a new career as a professor. He was promoted to associate professor while there and has since left the university to become an entrepreneur.

Together, Ron, Dieter, and Bob put down several notable FAs in fall 1969. At *Chimney Top Rock*, they established "Tunnel Route" (Britz and Stokley, September 7, 1969); "Chimney's Chimney," aka "Stokes-Ledford Chimney" (Britz and Stokes, 2nd pitch on June 8, 1969, and full route on August 31, 1969); and "Chimney Direct," aka "Bob's Mummery" (Stokes, Britz, and Hubart, September 1969).[12] Across the valley from Natural Bridge, Dieter and Bob established "Tourists' Horror" (October 12, 1969). At *Half Moon Rock*, they also put up "Ron's Garden" (Stokley, Britz, and Stokes, September 1969).

At first there was no effort to formally document these new routes. Guides (or guidebooks) are often used to formalize existing routes and record who first climbed them and when. They offer a useful system for introducing new climbers to the area and giving them the locations of existing climbs. In this case, the community was still very small, so everyone simply knew who had climbed the routes. As Ron explained, "We did a lot of first ascents, but a lot of them were not publicized because there wasn't really a need for anybody to follow things that were going on back then." Quite interestingly, the community was slightly larger than even Ron may have known. At the time, there was also a group of four or so firefighters practicing their skills in the Red, but they were generally keeping to themselves. One of those climbers, Otto Mock, put up "Bolt Route," a reportedly dangerous route at *Courthouse Rock*, most likely in 1969, making it one of the earlier routes in the Red. Otto noted that this group largely wanted to keep to themselves as going to the Red was an escape from people in general. Hence, the two groups apparently never encountered each other, and if they did, it went undocumented.

Probably the first instance of fully documenting a route in the Red would be Dieter and Ron's report on *Chimney Top Rock* focusing on the "Ledford Route."[13] The report was likely published in a Sierra Club newsletter.[14] It notes that Dieter and Ron first found the route by looking at *Chimney Top Rock* via a telescope on Route 715. The duo parked their car at the property of Floyd Ledford (a rare local who opposed the Red River Dam), and with his permission they bushwhacked across his land to *Chimney Top*.[15] The route was completed in two pitches (or stages), and the duo rated the climb as a 5.1 or 5.2 using the Yosemite Decimal System. The report notes that Dieter and Ron placed a plain 7/16th-inch bolt near the top, allowing one 120-foot rappel to reach the base of the climb. Given the difficulty of the hike to the base, Dieter and Ron suggest that rappelling down and then climbing up may actually be the better way to approach the route. They also note a fair number of copperheads at the bottom: "We found six of them curled around one small bush alone!"

Dieter and Ron's article represents an important link between the early climbers in the Red and the Sierra Club. Recall that the Sierra Club had been a leading opponent of the Red River Dam. As part of establishing its Cumberland Chapter in the Red, a subchapter called the Cumberland Climbers had also formed.[16] The Sierra Club was a natural pairing for this new climbing organization. In fact, the Sierra Club's first president was a climber: none other than John Muir. The Sierra Club's climbing clubs offered a social arrangement of mentoring new climbers while protecting natural areas. They promoted safety, too, through training and mentorship. A good example is the work of Richard (Dick) Leonard, an important American climber in the 1930s and president of the Sierra Club, who invented a way of testing and certifying climbers to ensure they could safely handle themselves and others at the crag.[17] Dick had formed the Cragmont Climbers in California, which, after being absorbed by the San Francisco Sierra Club chapter, would morph into the Sierra Club's Rock Climbing Section. The Cumberland Climbers fell under this section.

The Cumberland Climbers (officially founded in 1969) were the first known local climbing organization in the Red and would be an integral part of the climbing community's history for the coming years. Membership in the Cumberland Climbers was initially $1.00 per year and was limited to Sierra Club members. The first entries on the Cumberland Climbers' mailing list are dated September 8, 1969. They included the following names on that date: Ronald Stokley (misspelled as Stokely), Roger C. Westman, Bill Andrews, Grace M. Donnelly (who was a professor at the University of Kentucky at the time), William (Bill) L. Rodgers, Clifford Bond, Dave Kelly, Jim Kelly, Duane Kelly, Dean Jaros, Sonia Jaros, Robert A. Stokes, and Dieter Britz.[18] Additional names were added in the coming days and weeks: Mary Francis Reed (September 9), Wini Mastin (September 18), Robert C. Funk (October 23), David Irving (November 1), R. Brooks Howard, MD (November 3), John Potts (November 3), Alfred Mattox, MD (November 3), Victoria Mattox (November 3), and Rush E. Cassady (November 3). Later pages include important names like Carroll Tichenor (an early organizer of the Cumberland Chapter of the Sierra Club), Frank Becker (the 1974 guide author), and Ellen and Tom Seibert. The list of early members in the Cumberland Climbers includes several interlocking pivotal names who shaped the history of climbing in the Red.[19]

Dr. Clifford Bond, now professor emeritus at Montana State University, represents an early linkage of the Cumberland Climbers into the next generation of climbers. Clifford (often simply called Cliff in the community) was a graduate student at University of Kentucky during the Cumberland Climber era.[20] He was working on a PhD in microbiology. Tom Seibert was Cliff's roommate for a time in graduate school. Tom shared that Cliff had already climbed in the Bugaboos and Cascades: "So he was really a mountaineer, but he liked the Red. It was the best he could find nearby to get out of the lab and go and do something on the weekends." Cliff did not create any new routes in the Red (at least none that were recorded), opting instead to go to familiar places like *Chimney Top, Tower Rock*, and *Half Moon*. Tom shared that "Cliff probably had the first set of nuts in Kentucky. Chouinard had started making hexagonal nuts to protect the climbs. Cliff ordered all the sizes." When they came, he stacked them on the table and Tom and Ellen remembered taking a picture of them.

Cliff taught both Tom and Ellen Seibert how to climb. Tom remembers that "with Cliff, we pretty much climbed climbs that had already been done," rather than establishing new routes. "He taught us all the safe ways, belaying, and all that other stuff," early evidence of the strong mentorship that continues today among experienced and neophyte climbers. Tom was in Kentucky "because I was interested in caves and caving" and to attend graduate school at the University of Kentucky in cave biology. Tom and Ellen met while caving. Ellen, too, was in college at the University of Kentucky.

William (Bill) Andrews is another particularly interesting name in the early Cumberland Climbers days because anecdotal evidence points at him as a possible starting point for "Caver's Route." [21] As previously mentioned, "Caver's Route" has long been accepted as the first climbing route in the Red. Guidebook author John Bronaugh (who plays a pivotal role in the Red's climbing history and is discussed at length later in this book) described "Caver's Route" in his first-edition guidebook as being the Red's first route, as being from the 1950s, and as probably being created by cavers. Ron Stokley also adds important context to John's history of "Caver's Route": "There were two twin brothers, last name was Andrews, and one of the Andrews brothers was extremely interested in caving and I believe did a lot of caving for the insect environment that was in the caves. . . . He's pretty prominent for beetles and things like that that were in the caves. As far as I understand it, he and his brother or he and the caving community at the time were the first ones to put up or at least climb that."

Bill and his twin brother, Doug, were both part of the caving community and would have certainly practiced caving in the Red, as was normal for the spelunking community at the time. Bill was certainly a member of the BlueGrass Grotto. The Red does not offer much in terms of caves, even though the rest of the state of Kentucky is flush with them. However, the Red did offer an ideal spot for practicing caving techniques above ground. True to its name, "Caver's Route" would be ideal as it includes several techniques that could be practiced above ground. Given the facts, it seems highly plausible (although not certain) that Bill established "Caver's Route."

The Cumberland Climbers' files reveal a quite active group with at least 133 members in just four years, the bulk of which were in the first two years. Despite those numbers, only a small group was focused on climbing. Cumberland Climbers Bill Rogers and Ron Stokley both felt that there was essentially a smaller number of experienced climbers (which includes several of the names listed thus far) and a much larger list of novice climbers looking for mentors and training. Still greater may have been persons mostly interested in the Red as environmentalists rather than climbers, for reasons that become clear in the next chapter. Despite that imbalance, Bill remembers it fondly: "It was our playground. We could park anyplace we wanted to in the trail pulloffs to go hiking or climbing . . . we could climb anywhere." Tom Seibert similarly remembers the Red: "It was a lot different [from today]. We would go there and there would hardly be anybody else in the Gorge, and there weren't too many trails to any of these climbs."

The organization's major source of communication was a club newsletter that shared the ideas of the organization as a whole. The newsletter published information from the Sierra Club and Sierra Club's Rock Climbing Section for the Cumberland Climber membership, as well as safety tips, climbing advice, and many personable climbing sketches and humor that brought levity to the newsletter.[22] It also fulfilled a social role in the community long before the days of social media, announcing meetings and scheduling talks, instructional sessions, and slideshows. It appeared to be somewhat irregular (a membership recruitment notice from perhaps 1974 indicates that the newsletter's "publication was often irregular. However, the letter will be published monthly, with the exception of the summer months, beginning in October, 1974."), but it was certainly important in keeping this organization connected.[23]

Tom Seibert recalls that the Cumberland Climbers served clear purposes: "It was a lot for camaraderie, but it was a lot for safety, training, making sure everybody had the communication between their belayer and the climber down pat, and to make sure they could catch somebody if they fell." Evidence shows the Cumberland Climbers were quite focused on safety and training. For example, Tom recounts Cumberland Climbers' use of a weighted dummy for practicing safe belaying: "They had this 130-pound cement chunk of rock with a hook on the end of it, and they had a tripwire [which would release the rock] and it would fall like 30 feet or so . . . and that tripwire was how we learned to belay. . . . We didn't have figure eights or any of those mechanical devices then, so we were just belaying around the back and with hip belay." With a laugh, Tom recalled, "Back then the leader wasn't supposed to fall, but it happened." Training also included working with pitons, carabiners, and break bars.

Safety was an important component for Sierra Club climbing chapters of the era. Members were required to be trained and pass evaluations before leading climbs, for example. One entry in their newsletter notes that the Cumberland Climbers received a $10 sum from the Sierra Club to subscribe to the *Mountain Safety Research Newsletter*, which they in turn shared through seminars, technique sessions, and climbing days. They also had clear rules, such as specific terminology to be used while climbing, practical (and lifesaving) advice like making sure to double-check knots, and reminders about not walking on ropes. They also encouraged wearing hard hats while climbing to protect from falling rocks and debris.

Mentorship was also a very important component of this organization. This was an important safety function, as a mentor could teach a neophyte climber the correct way to do techniques, which in turn minimized risk and promoted safety. This mentorship relationship was present in other Sierra Club climbing groups, but it was also common in the Red's caving community. In caving, mentorships have those same safety functions, but they also include the sharing of information about where certain caving areas can be found. While some caves are certainly publicly mapped and listed, many more are kept fairly secret. Mentorship served as a means of sharing this knowledge and expectations with the next generation, establishing behavior norms (e.g., safe climbing and minimum-impact behaviors) along the way.

As is often the case, there were more interested mentees than available mentors. Ron Stokley, then serving as activities chairman of the Cumberland Climbers, in a letter to the members dated January 4, 1971, noted that the group had grown from a handful of skilled climbers to a great number of novices—in just a year and a few months! These few skilled climbers were spending a lot of their time teaching others the basics of climbing (a good thing), but this also probably limited how often they could climb new routes and explore the Red in general. Ron felt the need to nurture these climbers for myriad reasons, the most prevalent being safety. Thus, he proposed leadership seminars in the winter months (out of climbing season). The seminars were "designed to produce leaders familiar with the best climbs in this area."[24]

Another important leader was present in the Red during the earliest days of climbers: a respected Daniel Boone National Forest employee named Don Fig. Don grew up in Virginia and joined the Forest Service in 1960. He was assigned to the Red and never left: "The arches, the great cathedrals of rock, they all made an impression on my young mind." Don Fig served in the DBNF for 47 years and is a central part of the DBNF's modern history. One particularly important area of service for him has been search and rescue; Don himself took part in 1,660 rescues in the Red during his career. He is often remembered for his friendliness with climbers. Perhaps it was because Don somehow related to climbers' desire to be in the Red. In an interview with *Kentucky Living*, he recalled, "When I was a young man, I wanted to climb every rock in the Gorge, and I've climbed all the important ones." But Don also knew the allure and risk of those same rocks: "Just stay away from that edge. People are fascinated by the edge and want to get close to it. They'll grab a tree and lean as far over it as they can. Lots of times that tree will give way or a branch will break." Don would go on to write several books and articles about the Red River Gorge.[25]

The Cumberland Climbers (if only briefly) were also part of Don's early rescue work. Tom Seibert shared that Don "gave us some training with rescue. A lot of us with the Cumberland Climbers—Cliff [Bond], Ellen and [Tom], Martin Hackworth, probably Larry Day and Frank Becker—all went to at least one training session on the Stokes litter and if somebody was on a ledge, we practiced hauling them up in a Stokes litter, and we had some practice with the Forest Service." Tom recalls that climbers participating in safety training were asked to place a red dot in the back window of their vehicles. In the event the DBNF needed help on a rescue, they could enlist trained climbers who happened to be in the Red to assist. Although it was a great idea, finding vehicles with red dots during an emergency proved unwieldly. Instead, the Forest Service soon organized with local residents who could be safety trained and developed a rescue squad approach with them. This tradition continues today. That said, this still shows the value of a close working relationship between climbers and public land managers.

Frank Becker's transition into leadership around 1974 shows increased interest in developing policy in close partnerships with organizations like the DBNF. There are multiple correspondences between the Cumberland Climbers and the Forest Service, Sierra Club, and local organizations. One particularly interesting correspondence was in 1974, when Frank corresponded with Ranger John Moore (with the DBNF) regarding the two groups working together to create a marked trail to *Tower Rock*. Moore had purportedly asked climbers (in an earlier letter not found in the archive) to help build the trail, but Frank declined, noting that safety precautions for nonclimbers (e.g., tourists) visiting the site reduced safety and seclusion for climbers (again due to tourists) and increased damage to the rock. Frank did offer, however, to help in search and rescue missions as volunteers. Frank's reply letter to John also included another big worry: "We are very concerned about the damage that could possibly be created by irresponsible or unenlightened rock-climbers who hammer pitons into the soft and fragile sandstone. We would therefore desire to work with you on formulating a policy statement on the use of such damaging equipment." [26]

Minimizing impact was clearly on the minds of many Cumberland Climbers. Tom Seibert recalls that, when he met Cliff Bond, Cliff was still using pitons, which were hammered into rock crevices. This risked leaving scars in the rock and changing the natural experience. As Tom recalls, "Since the Sierra Club stressed leave just footprints and take just pictures, we didn't like the idea of using pitons that left scars." New gear such as chocks, bongs, and nuts were gradually entering into the community, partly due to experienced mountaineers like Britz. This offered opportunities to limit impacts. Tom continued, "We didn't want to leave a trace we were there. We didn't put in bolts or use chalk or anything like that. . . . We didn't consider it a real climb if we top-roped it, although we did top-rope some things that looked interesting. But to be a real climb we thought the leader had to protect it."

The development of policies regarding recreational use in the region, however, could also work against the climbers. The Cumberland Climbers experienced the earliest announced climbing closures in the Red. First, it was decided by Ranger John Moore to close *Chimney Top*. The Forest Service reportedly was not concerned about the safety of climbers but the threat they posed to tourists at the site. Per Frank Becker's notice in the newsletter, Ranger Moore believed that "the presence of climbers on Chimney Top enticed tourists visiting the rock to put themselves in danger while trying to get a good view. Tourists climb over the guardrails and stand close to the edge of the cliff to see the activities of the climbers below them." This first closure would be only a partial closure, as climbers could use the area during the tourist off-season from December to April. A second closure was tentatively announced in the May 1976 edition of the newsletter, this time at *Sky Bridge Arch*. Again, tourists were listed as the cause. Although these were the earliest known climbing closures in the Red, they certainly would not be the last.

This early era of climbing in the Red stormed in and briskly went, lasting really just a matter of years. Dieter Britz had already left Lexington at the end of his postdoc in 1970. Ron Stokley stuck around until 1976 before leaving for Colorado with his job at IBM. Cliff Bond would finish his PhD in 1973, leaving for California for a postdoctorate at UC San Diego.

The Cumberland Climbers remained until around 1976 before dissolving as an organization. Still, they left behind a clear and strong presence going into the next generation. Moreover, the next generation of climbers in the Red remained concerned over ideals such as clean climbing and outdoor ethics, which, when paired with the Cumberland Climbers' dedication to safety, mentorship, and policy, set precedent for a strong, conservation-minded community going into the future.

CHAPTER 5

Trad Climbing Growth and Climbing Guides, 1974–1986

Military Wall is located in the DBNF's Martin's Fork area. Take the Slade exit off the Bert T. Combs Mountain Highway and keep left onto Kentucky Highway 11. In about two miles, keep right onto Kentucky Highway 77 (also called Nada Tunnel Road). Along the way, travelers pass a handful of local residents offering a last chance to purchase camping permits, firewood, groceries, and assorted sundries before entering the DBNF. Up ahead, Highway 77 sneaks through the 900-foot-long hand-hewn Nada Tunnel. Over a century ago, locomotives used to bring timber to the sawmill in Clay City. Now, this tunnel brings visitors to the Red. Coming out of Nada, the Red makes a strong first impression, showing off a mix of its intense greens and craggy outcrops. The road itself feels precariously placed, heightening the experience. About a mile ahead near the bottom of the valley is Martin's Fork trailhead, a parking lot, and bathrooms. Most any morning during the climbing season, this lot will be completely full with a mix of climbers and day hikers. The occasional celebratory (or perhaps falling) yell of a climber echoes through the valley.

Visitors departing their cars and entering the lush forest are immediately greeted by a very sturdy bridge over a friendly stream. This bridge actually has quite a bit of climbing history attached to it. Working in tandem with the RRGCC, the Access Fund tapped Jim Angel, a founding Access Fund member and respected trail developer, to come to Martin's Fork and construct this bridge. The bridge was made from locally sourced Powell County lumber. And again working with the DBNF, climbers also turned an unmarked user trail leading to *Military Wall* into an official DBNF-mapped trail. User trails are a major problem on public lands. Once a few people go off the official trails, the sight of trampled vegetation can result in more people taking that trail or even getting lost off the mapped trails. Over time, erosion takes hold as vegetation declines. For example, the loss of rhododendrons to user trails increases sunlight on the forest floor, which kills out plant life that requires shade and begins to change the entire ecology of the area. The original user trail to *Military Wall* ran the risk of causing such a change to the area and was not designed to be a sustainable trail. Working together to make Military Wall Trail (#230) sustainable was quite a big deal.

Lasting only a quarter mile, the trail leads west up to the valley ridge to its namesake. After winding among trees and a few boulders, much of the northern end of *Military Wall* sits in plain view along the right of the trail. From the trail, climbers are readily evident on the wall as they seek out miniscule fingerholds and smear their rubber soles along nearly invisible rock features. Below, their belayers tend to the ropes that, in the event of a fall, should keep the climber safe. Quietly standing along this trail allows nonclimbers an opportunity to watch and learn a great deal about the climbing community.

From a nonclimber perspective, climbing may seem unnatural and risky. In reality, there is quite a bit of safety and risk mitigation in play. It starts with the belay loop on a climber's harness. The climbing rope follows through two hard points: one on the waist part of the harness and one through the leg part of the harness. These securely connect the rope to the harness. This system uses a figure-eight knot, a knot that retains the strength of the rope while tightening itself when weighted.[1] The figure-eight knot offers the advantage that one's climbing partner can see if it has been tied correctly. As they ascend, climbers will clip their rope into protection placed in the rock.

At *Military Wall*, climbers have many routes using permanent bolts placed in the rocks or classic routes that allow them to place their own removable protection, using quickdraws for sport routes and traditional gear for trad routes. Below, the climbing rope is threaded through a belay device that is clipped into the belayer's harness belay loop. This device can altogether stop a rope from moving through the device. Thus, should a climber fall, belayers can stop the rope at the last place the climber clipped in, plus any amount of rope above that point, and rope stretch over those lengths. If everything works as designed, the climber's fall is arrested, at which point they can get back on the wall and begin climbing again or be lowered to the ground. Taking a step back in time to the 1970s and 1980s, climbers instead would have been using removable protection placed in cracks to complete this same safety function. While many a climber has taken extraordinary falls on removable pro (even using the gear from the 1970s and 1980s), a common climbing mantra of the era was plain and purposeful: *don't fall.*

Walking a bit farther to the end of the Military Wall Trail also reveals an important part of both natural history and climbing history. The trail effectively ends at the centerpiece of *Military Wall*: a medium-sized rockshelter.

Indigenous peoples used these shelters in the same ways that humans use homes today: to keep out of the elements and to keep safe from unknown threats. This particular shelter at *Military Wall* is quite dry. The soil here rarely gets exposed to the rain and even snow. Looking directly above the shelter, lines of bolts extruding from the rock face trace out six sport routes from the 1990s, while a dihedral and crack mark three trad routes (using removable protection) from the 1980s. And extending to both sides of the shelter are another 50-plus routes established from the 1970s to present. It was an exciting time of rapid growth in the Red's climbing community, but it was also a time overshadowed by ongoing concerns about a *second* proposed Red River Dam site. That's right. The proposed dam was only *paused* in 1969. Now, the US Army Corps of Engineers (COE) redoubled efforts to place the dam at a second location.

Recall that the original proposed site for the Red River Dam was abandoned by the COE following protests and declining support. Later that year (1969), they announced plans to examine their second proposed site, which had previously been considered more costly. That site was 5.3 miles downstream from the original site. Public meetings began in 1973. By the following year, Save Our Red River (a group that reportedly included both local residents and conservation groups) filed for an injunction against the corps. A second reprieve was found in 1975 when Governor Julian Carroll ended state support for the dam and the plan lost steam. Conversations about placing a dam on the Red River continued until George H. W. Bush's presidency, when he recommended the Red River be given Wild and Scenic River designation. Bill Clinton later signed this into existence, making the dam an impossibility. But in the 1970s and even early 1980s, the dam still seemed like a legitimate threat to climbers.[2]

The second proposed Red River Dam clearly had a major impact on climbers, and it is prominently noted in one of the important climbing events of the mid-1970s: the publication of Frank Becker's *Red River Gorge Climber's Guide*.[3] Recall that Frank, who would take over as secretary and de facto leader of the Cumberland Climbers from Ron Stokley, had been in the Red only a few years at the time. Still, he had the foresight to see the need to document the Red as it stood then. And given that he was working on his law degree around then, he may also have privately understood how sincere a risk the Red faced at the time. The guide's early pages have a bleak tone, noting the Red was "doomed to impoundment. Though it is likely that the lake will directly affect the climbing routes, it will certainly deteriorate the aesthetic experience of climbing." Becker decidedly saw his climbing guide on the Red almost as a documentation of history before it could be lost. He even notes in the preface that this book serves to "record as much as possible concerning the Red River Gorge in its 'natural' state." It also bears a theme that carries forward in future guides, that of environmental awareness and preservation that, ostensibly, was shaped by the presence of the Sierra Club chapter: "This guide does have potential for causing damage, and therefore I would urge all users of this guide to make all attempts to minimize their impact on the climbing environment."[4]

In all, the guide includes 34 routes across ten crags on DBNF land. The guide lists several developments at previously climbed (per the records of the Cumberland Climbers) crags *Natural Bridge*, *Half Moon Rock*, *Chimney Rock*, and *Tower Rock*. *Natural Bridge* has five routes listed, none with difficulties over 5.4: "Lookout Crack," "Lookout Crack South," "All Face," "Face Escape," and "Tourists' Horror." Incidentally, this is where "Tourists' Horror" inadvertently becomes an early example of a lost route. Despite Dieter and Ron's notes on the route, Becker's guide notes that they were unable to identify the route. Climbers today think the route may have been renamed something else, but as the area would eventually be closed to climbing, this route was quickly lost to history.

Half Moon included six routes. "Ron's Garden" was an early Cumberland Climber route, while "Bob's Moon," "Full Moon," and "Ellen's Descent" were new 1973 or 1974 routes. "Rockhouse" and an unnamed route (that per the description sounded more like a rock scramble) may or may not have been Cumberland Climber routes given the lack of dates. *Chimney Rock* contained eight routes, four with ties to the Cumberland Climbers. The other four included "Tunnel Overhang" (which was FA'd by Frank Becker, Ellen Seibert, and Tom Seibert in August 1974), "Chimney Direct" (Becker, Seibert, Seibert, April 1974), "Connection Ledge," and "Zig-Zag Bond."[5] The last two had no FA listed, and "Zig-Zag Bond" was specifically noted as not having been climbed as of the guide's printing.[6]

Tower Rock now officially included four low-skill (5.3 or less) routes: "Caver's Route," "Mighty Eidson," "Tower Backside," and "Tower Corner."[7] However, one higher-skill route (at least for the time) stood out, and that was Tom Seibert and Larry Day's "Arachnid." This route is particularly notable in that Becker reported, "in the 1960s, a bolt was placed under the ceiling" for layback practice. Note that Tom Seibert shared that this bolt had been used by the Cumberland Climbers to practice working through layback cracks. Charlie and Catherine Bishop (cavers with the BlueGrass Grotto) similarly reported this bolt was used by cavers to practice layback techniques.[8] Tom Seibert agreed that the bolt had probably been set by cavers as a practice area, which would place this route as one of the earliest climbing routes in the Red alongside "Caver's Route." Bill Rogers, a Cumberland Climbers member, noted that climbers and cavers were certainly overlapping at the time, and that both practiced techniques at locations like *Natural Bridge* and *Chimney Rock*, too. Bill recalled that the Greater Cincinnati Grotto (another speleological club) was visiting the area at the time, as well. Thus "Arachnid" likely also holds an interesting claim to being one of the earliest climbing routes in the Red as a result of its caving ties.

The guide also offered a listing of several new crags that were likely or certainly visited by Cumberland Climbers. First, Tunnel Ridge Road along the Double Arches Trail (which is near Nada Tunnel) had an early Martin Hackworth route called "Tunnel Ridge Crack," which he ascended with Frank Becker and Tom Seibert in spring 1973. A second route, "Rainy Days," has no first ascent listed. *Princess Arch* held only "Beginner's Nightmare" (climbed by Cliff Bond, Tom Seibert, and Ellen Seibert in 1973), while *Jewel Pinnacle* had three routes: "Diamond in the Crack," "Jewel Corner," and an unnamed (and uncommon) top out route leading to the summit. *Good Tang* (a crag that would eventually be renamed *Lower Small Wall*) included the eponymous "Good Tang," an unusually long (106-foot) route for the Red climbed by Larry Day and Frank Becker in February 1974. Additionally, the guide lists *Courthouse Rock*, which had only one route listing, "Bolt Route." Although not listed in the guide at the time, this route was FA'd by Otto Mock most likely in 1969. That route included, per the Becker guide, "the remains of a chain that was once bolted to the side of the rock." [9] Potentially cavers had, again, established this route years earlier, but this also may have been a leftover from Otto Mock and other firefighters climbing in the Red at the time. Therefore "Bolt Route" should also be counted likely among the earliest climbing routes in the Red with "Caver's Route" and "Arachnid."

The guide includes a few historical tidbits of interest. The guide includes an addendum listing the "Frenchburg Overhangs" without a specific crag. Today, "Frenchburg Overhangs" is located at *Dunkan Rock*. The addendum updates the first ascent information for "Diamond in the Crack" (Larry Day, Tom Seibert, Bob Hill, and Eric Bostrum, November 3, 1974). [10] It closes describing the upstream Red River area as having potential but no serious attempts to document a climb.

The guide also lists *Raven Rock*, "the most obvious sandstone structure seen while crossing Red River on KY 77," but notes it has "seen little climbing activity as it is privately owned and is 'off limits' to rock climbers." [11] Raven Rock had been a private development back in the 1960s and 1970s. A private road was established taking visitors to the top overlook, but a fee was charged to access that road. The land below had been subdivided into lots called the Daniel Boone Estates. The estates proved unsuccessful over time, with lots remaining unpurchased and few houses built. Since then, the DBNF has obtained most but not all of *Raven Rock*. Today, climbing still occurs there on seven routes, with a local resident offering parking for a donation.

The Becker guide also sets precedent for future guides by noting a brief geology of the Red, a summary of the types of climbing available, a summary of equipment needed, a (very brief) history, information on the Red's unpredictable (and often rainy) weather, and camping opportunities. It may be of historical interest that the guide lists only two camping options: Koomer's Ridge (DBNF land) and Natural Bridge State Park. Even this early in the Red's history, he notes on page seven that "both campgrounds may be full to capacity on summer weekends."

This exciting level of growth continued through the remainder of the 1970s, quickly leading to the need for another new guide. Ed Benjamin and Ed Pearsall published *Rawk!: A Climbers Guide to the Red River Gorge* in 1978. *Rawk* in the title is likely a play on the local dialect, which also would have been used by many climbers from the Lexington area. The Red now contained 54 listed routes, up from 33 routes in the Becker guide. Page six of this guide shares a few remarks about the Red's recent climbing history, including the fact that much of the early history of climbing here was lost: "Most Gorge climbing before the publication of Frank Becker's Guide Book [*sic*] is lost in the mists of time. Almost all our pioneer climbers moved away. . . . We occasionally hear rumors of climbing in the Red River Gorge in the 1950s and early 1960s." This note may have formalized the belief that climbing had extended back into the 1950s, when climbing more formally began here in the late 1960s, while spelunkers had been practicing here before then.

Benjamin and Pearsall's guide showed a mix of development at new and old areas. For example, one old location, *Tower Rock*, had grown to 10 routes. *Princess Arch* also had three new routes: "Golden Fleece" (a 5.6 route), "Face Farce" (5.8), and "Rip-Off" (5.4). But it was the newer areas—*Daniel Boone Hut Trail, Haystack Rock, Small Wall, Hole in the Wall,* and *Fortress Wall*—that really saw the most growth. Among those, *Fortress Wall* would particularly stand out for the coming decades.

Fortress Wall was probably the most important contribution of the new guide. It included 10 new routes, mostly developed by Bob Molzon and Dick Schori in November and December 1977.[12] Benjamin and Pearsall note that the crag was "a large wall with many potential routes on it."[13] New routes included "Horny Bitch," "Snake," "Cussin' Crack," "Calypso," "American Crack," "American Wall," and four unnamed routes. At "American Wall" the authors noted that the rock face has features resembling the North American map. Even today, *Fortress Wall* is a valuable trad climbing crag. This crag holds the only FAs reported by Bob and Dick in the entire Red. Tom Seibert knew both Bob and Dick and recalled with a chuckle that the two climbers had treated *Fortress Wall* as their secret crag and didn't share word of the area until they had finished all the strong routes. That said, many more great routes would be developed at *Fortress Wall* in later years.

There were certainly even more routes out there (including some really historic route development happening in the region; more on that later in the chapter) than those listed in this guide. Benjamin and Pearsall noted that they did not know the routes at *Rough Trail* beyond the fact that Larry Day, John Lamb, and Rick Ratliff had set routes out there. As an indication of how small this community was at the time, Benjamin and Pearsall added in their guide that anyone who knew of additional routes could simply write them.

As previously noted in Cumberland Climber newsletters, closures were now a formalized part of climbing in the Red, and it was this guide that would be the first Red guide to discuss closures in the area. The guide included two notes of interest at *Chimney Top*. First, "When climbing on *Chimney Top* beware of tourists throwing things."[14] This was a very different take on Ranger John Moore's perception that tourists were leaning over the edges to see climbers, placing the tourists in danger. Second, the guide also mentioned a closure at *Chimney Top* from the Thursday before Memorial Day to November 1. This closure was first announced in the Cumberland Climber's newsletter years earlier, although at the time it was closed from April to December. Today, *Chimney Top* experiences occasional fatalities when tourists cross the barriers to jump across onto the chimney. The jump across is possible because the chimney sits slightly lower than the viewing platform. However, jumping from the chimney back to the viewing platform is difficult because the jumper now needs to jump across while also jumping up. The end result has been over 20 deaths at this site, despite extensive Forest Service signage, warnings, and barriers.[15]

While new routes popped up in the Red, Sage Outfitters, a small shop specializing in climbing and outdoor recreation gear in Lexington, acted as an off-site centerpiece for the Red's growing climbing community. Many of the climbing greats of the 1970s worked there at some point. For example, Larry Day and Frank Becker worked there together. This would also introduce Ed Pearsall into the climbing community. Larry Day explained that "[Ed's] introduction to rock climbing was through a class that Frank and I taught. But then years later, after I moved West and would come home [to Kentucky], Pearsall was now climbing very hard and he and I teamed up for a bunch of routes. . . . He did 'Tower of Power' with me."

Ed Benjamin was a manager at Sage Outfitters. Ed Pearsall, from an email interview, remembers purchasing "my first climbing rack off him for $60 . . . stoppers, hexes, and tube chocks." Pearsall would later work there, too, as would Kevin Pogue, who knew Ed Pearsall from Explorer Post 360 (for which Ron Stokley had served as a leader). Ed and Kevin would also establish a guide service (Sky Bridge Guides) in the Red, probably one of the first of its kind there, which would eventually bring in Ron Snider as a student. Ron would go on to begin development at *Roadside*, an important new climbing area in the Red, in the 1980s, and would climb with John Bronaugh, who was a central part of understanding climbing in the Red in the following two decades.

Ed Pearsall addressed all the new routes being established in the region by creating a third guide, *Climber's Guide to the Red River Gorge*, in 1980, just two years after the Benjamin and Pearsall guide. It turns out that this guide would be one for the history books for multiple reasons. First, it quietly documents a changing of the guard in the Red. By this time, nearly all of the Cumberland Climbers had moved on except for the Seiberts and Frank Becker. Tom and Ellen continued to climb but stopped doing first ascents around 1980, as they were then in Owensboro, Kentucky. Frank Becker received his law degree from the University of Kentucky in 1979 (first in his class) and was admitted to the bar that same year. However, all three play important linkages in the climbing community: the Seiberts through their connection to Martin Hackworth and Frank through his connection to Larry Day. Both Martin and Larry would go on to play important roles in the Red's history. Moreover, Larry and Frank's connection to Ed Pearsall would also lead the transition of climbers (like Kevin Pogue and Ron Snider) going into the 1980s.

Second, the guide also technically looks back in time to document several missed developments. The guide now identified 30 distinct and accessible crags in the Red, meaning the Red now held, in just six years' time, nearly as many *crags* as the number of *routes* listed in the Becker guide. The Red now had 133 routes on the books, more than doubling what was listed in 1978. Moreover, among those routes there were some major inclusions in this guide well known even today among trad climbers in the Red: "The Quest," "Insanity Ceiling," "Tower of Power," the three "Calypso" routes, and "Jungle Beat." The guide effectively caught up with route development happening in the Red up to 1980, going back in time to document route development happening as early as 1974 that was missed in the previous guides. Of these missed developments, *Military Wall* stands most prominent.[16]

The first route at *Military Wall* was called "German-Irish," or "GI" for short. The route was established in 1974 by Tom Seibert and Martin Hackworth.[17] Tom and Martin met as part of the BlueGrass Grotto and their mutual interest in caving, but the route name linked back to the climbers' ethnic backgrounds: German for Seibert and Irish for Hackworth. Tom shared the story and its long-lasting impact: "That's what Martin [wanted to call it]. . . . His heritage was Irish . . . and my name is German. . . . We did that climb and Martin wanted to name it the 'German Irish' route, which got shortened to 'GI,' and we laugh about that because that turned into the whole *Military Wall* thing." In fact, later guides (and generally most climbers today) simply refer to the route as "GI," giving the crag a military theme that was later repeated in a handful of other routes (and potentially at the nearby *Left Flank* crag).

Military Wall is interesting in that it's not exactly clear who may have discovered it or when climbing began there beyond Tom and Martin's first route there. The crag is generally within sight of the Rough Trail, which bisects DBNF, and depending on the season, it might even have been visible from Nada Tunnel Road. Yet none of the early climbers were sure of its finder. Tom, when reflecting on his first climb there on "German-Irish," declared, "I don't know why we found that rock or anything. . . . It was mainly it was just, when you come around the corner, that was the first crack we saw that looked halfway decent. So that's why we took that and climbed up that route there." At some point, the trail approach to *Military Wall* changed. The original trail (since removed) led to the far northeastern end of the crag. Today, a Forest Service trail leads to the center of the crag, right in front of the rockshelter. At the time, the climber's original user trail to the crag incidentally led almost right to "German-Irish," so it truly would have been one of the first things seen there.

Alongside Martin and Tom, Larry Day and Frank Becker would have been climbing at *Military Wall* in the early and mid-1970s. Like Tom and Martin, Larry and Frank both were interested in caving.[18] Martin would play a part in seeing Frank and Larry into the climbing community. As Frank recalls, "I think Martin was actually too young to drive at the time. I think he was 15, you know, might even have been younger." Frank described Martin as "just full of personality . . . very precocious, very ambitious, very lively person. A great personality." Frank remembers that Martin told him and Larry, "If you want to be a great caver, you gotta learn to climb." The trio headed most likely to *Tower Rock* to do "Caver's Route" per Frank.

In the Pearsall guide, *Military Wall* has only seven routes listed. "Jungle Beat" (a four-pitch 5.9 by Larry Day and Tom Seibert, November 4, 1979) and "Pink Feat" (which has a tricky first ascension story, discussed later in this chapter) both stand out today. "Jungle Beat" is today treated as a classic trad route.[19] It represented an accessible but challenging long route (long for the Red, at 175-plus feet). Tom Seibert recalled that he led the first pitch of "Jungle Beat" and that Larry led the second pitch. He noted that Larry was a very determined leader and was good at placing protection. "Pink Feat" was described as a boulder problem in the Pearsall guide. Larry Day is listed as the first ascent in Pearsall's 1980 guide with no date, and the climb was listed as a 5.9. Other routes at *Military Wall* in this guide were "Things That Go Bump in the Night" (FA'd by Larry, Tom, and Ellen), "Armed Forces" (Jim Sharp and Ed Pearsall, FA'd November 15, 1979), and two single-pitch routes by Larry Day ("Green Gully" and "Decay's Way").

Small Wall showed dramatic growth since the previous guide. Recall that in the Benjamin and Pearsall guide, this location held routes with nothing more than their route names. In the Pearsall guide, *Small Wall* was now two locations (*Lower Small Wall* with eleven routes and *Upper Small Wall* with seven routes). As a point of comparison, recall that in the Becker guide this area had been called the *Good Tang* crag, named for the singular route found there in 1974. Now, *Upper Small Wall* had "The Quest," treated as one of the longest routes in the Red. The original route was a three-pitch 175-foot route with a very early 5.10 rating. The route was first ascended by Larry Day and Ed Pearsall on October 20, 1979, but they relied on aid climbing to complete the final pitch. In 1984, Tom Souders (a very respected, hard trad climber discussed later in this chapter) and Bob Hayes would free-climb all 220 feet of the route.

Larry Day and his climbing partners made two more big contributions in this guide at *Tower Rock*: "Insanity Ceiling" and "Tower of Power." *Tower Rock* itself had now hit 20 routes, doubling its listings from the previous guide and adding the two new aforementioned 5.10 routes.[20] "Insanity Ceiling," a 5.10 by Larry Day, Tom Seibert, and Ed Pearsall (featured on the back cover of the guide) utilized a large roof at *Tower Rock*, which puts climbers in the position of either choosing to keep their back horizontal with the ground while working across the roof or letting their feet dangle as their hands lead the way. Either is a highly physical feat. On redriverclimbing.com's notes about the route, Larry Day described it at the time as "the hardest thing I'd ever onsighted, definitely on the ragged edge of my ability at the time." It has since been upgraded to a 5.11a. "Tower of Power" utilizes another ceiling at *Tower Rock* to great effect. There's a famous picture of Larry climbing this route in 1984, leaving the horizontal rock face and pulling himself up on a ledge. Aside from being climbed a few times in the early 1980s, "Tower of Power" went over two decades without being repeated.[21]

Fortress Wall continued to see strong trad route development by Dick Shori and Bob Molzon. In the Pearsall guide, it now contained 15 routes. Three routes named "Calypso" are still climbed today and represented three important train-ing routes. All three were lower-difficulty (5.5) single pitches with good stances for placing gear. This offered a great opportunity, then, for socializing in new trad climbers at a crag still known for trad routes today.

This guide also includes a few valuable historical notes. First, it notes that the Forest Service was in the process of trying to buy *Raven Rock*, which had previously held climbing routes but was no longer accessible to climbing, being prohibited by the current landowner. Second, it lists Heartwood Far Dept. (the spelling utilizes a linguistic play on the eastern Kentucky pronunciation of *fire*) as offering food and drinks for sale, as well as climbing gear. Finally, it talks about the toll roads in this region. One thing climbers today may not realize is that the Red once included toll roads. Kentucky law allowed for roads to include tolls to help pay for them but required ending the toll once the cost was recovered. The Pearsall guide clearly describes those tolls: "The Red River Gorge lies within the Daniel Boone National Forest in eastern Kentucky. It is best reached via the Mountain Parkway, a toll road, which starts from I-64, 2 miles east of Winchester. The first toll is 30¢, the next toll is at Slade and it is 25¢ to get off." The commonwealth removed the tolls on July 1, 1985, when the Parkway had paid for itself.[22]

In 1981, the Red's climbing community received some of its first national coverage. Frank Becker authored an article in the September-October edition of *Climbing*. The two-page article, simply titled "Red River Gorge," highlights the increasing difficulty of recent (at the time) route development by Larry Day, Ed Pearsall, Kevin Pogue, and Doug Hemken. Frank notes that Chouinard's tubular chocks as well as the valuable creation of Ray Jardine's Friends made protection much safer in the Red's "soft, shallow, and usually flaring" cracks.[23] The article also talks about Larry Day's historic climb at "Tower of Power."

Around 1983, two new names stood out as additional representatives for complicated, demanding climbs: Tom Souders and Jeff Koenig. In a few short years the duo established 17 routes, including several very difficult 5.11 routes that proved challenging for up-and-coming climbers. Interestingly, Tom, who arrived in 1983, had not seen the Red as a climbing destination. "[I] really just came down there hiking . . . didn't really think that, even though there was some climbing down there in the past, we really didn't think that soft sandstone was even possible to climb." After visiting Chattanooga, Tennessee's climbing community, and the work being done by Rob Robinson and others on *Tennessee Wall*, Tom reconsidered the Red's possibilities and returned with a new perspective on first ascents.

In 1983, Jeff and Tom got to work on their technically challenging Beene series of routes, which would continue through 1986. The name originates from Jeff's stature: "Jeff was just kinda long and lanky, so we just called him Jeff Beene. Or we just started calling him the Beeneling or the Beene." The theme continued onto "Beene Material" and "Beenestalker," both 5.10s at *Military Wall*. When Jeff returned from time in Colorado, they continued at *Sky Bridge* with a 5.10d, "The Return of Geoff Beene" (using a different spelling of Jeff's name). Tom noted that John Bronaugh and Ron Snider originally worked "The Return of Geoff Beene" and called it "Western Crack," but they had not completed the first ascent. When Tom and Jeff completed the route, John and Ron supported the name change. Hence, it became a Beene route. Beene routes also appeared through 1986 (with all but one a 5.10c or higher), culminating in "That's Enough of this Beene Shit" at *Lower Small Wall*.

Up until the early 1980s, climbing technology in the Red had hit the pause button. By the late 1970s, most of the protectable cracks had been done or at least attempted, resulting in over 200 routes in the Red. Trad climbing remained a very physical pursuit: climbers focused on features like the huge cracks down a rock face that allowed the climber to jam in fists and feet to ascend. But the real problem was the ability to place protection. The right gear could open up many more climbing lines in the Red.

Removable protection had already seen great advances in just a few decades. Pitons (which are hammered into cracks) had appeared by the 1930s in alpine climbing but were now eschewed for aesthetic purposes. Jeff Achey's article on the history of nuts documented British climbers carrying "pebbles in the pockets of their knickers, slotting these stones into wide spots in cracks and tying them off—with scary-looking hemp cord—for pro." [24] Taking advantage of technology in the area, Welsh climbers at *Clogwyn Du'R Arddu* began using metal nuts from the nearby railroad as a more reliable form of protection. The center hole would be tied to a cord that could hold a carabiner (metal ring), and the nut was wedged into various cracks to create protection. With work, other industrial nuts could be made to match various sized cracks. John Brailsford produced early commercial nuts starting in 1961, with others making their own designs throughout Wales and England in the 1960s. [25]

In 1966, Yosemite climber Royal Robbins would visit the UK to climb, and he soon began using nuts rather than pitons in the United States. This would form the basis for his clean climbing ethic in Yosemite, particularly in the removal of nuts after use. At the time, the use of pitons (a metal blade of varying thicknesses hammered into a crack) was prevalent because they offered a convenient and safe (if used properly) approach to climbing into otherwise inaccessible areas. However, removing these (again, as was the ethic of the time) was scarring the rocks. Robbins argued that nuts offered a better solution, and his clean (nuts only) ascent (with Galen Rowell and Dennis Hennek) of *Half Dome*'s "Regular Northwest Face" in 1973 gave the device the credence and exposure needed to promote its use.[26]

Yosemite's mechanically minded climbers had a field day developing new nuts and pitons. In 1945, John Salathe began making pitons (called Lost Arrows, after his ascent of the *Lost Arrow Spire*) from high-carbon chrome-vanadium steel, as existing pitons were too soft for Yosemite's hard stone. By 1959, Tom Frost and Yvon Chouinard had created the RURP (realized ultimate reality piton), which greatly aided climbing in the region. With Royal bringing in nuts, Chouinard was soon back in the workshop, creating his Hexentrics sets in 1972. This device was a versatile tool that could be wedged into three different-sized cracks. Tom and Yvon teamed up again in 1975 to create Tube Chocks, which fit into off-width cracks (cracks too big for a fist to hold but too small for using chimney techniques). These were effectively lengths of pipe with a length of cable tied through holes drilled in the pipe. It was simple but highly effective for its time. That year, they also created the Crack-n-Up, which was designed for very thin cracks. All this technology gradually crept into the Red, making riskier climbs an option. Yet it was a device made by a Yosemite climber, Ray Jardine (who also happened to be an aerospace engineer), that opened up a new round of route development following a lull in growth: the Friend.[27]

Jardine's (aptly titled) Friends' removable protection would support a new level of climbing in Kentucky and around the world. Friends worked by a trigger mechanism that relaxed two gear-like points on the end. The device could then be stuck into a crack and the trigger released. This effectively allowed a smaller item to be put into a crack and then expanded to create a much better grip in the crack. Ray and Chris Walker tested several generations of the device in the 1970s before releasing the idea to entrepreneur Mark Vallance, who manufactured the devices and sold them through the company Wild Country.

Tom Souders remembers how big a change Friends were at the time: "There was kind of a big break (in first ascents in the Red). . . . That's when the Friends came out. . . . A lot of those cracks and overhangs that were really hard to protect for [climbers in the 1970s], we could all the sudden protect them. That was great for us [laughs]!" This new level of protection now allowed physical climbers to push beyond their earlier limits.[28] In 1983 alone, over 30 routes would be added to the Red. This included multiple routes now rated as 5.11s, a high-skill ranking for the time and still considered a difficult route by today's technology standards.

One of those routes was Tom and Jeff's new work on "Pink Feat" at *Military Wall*. Recall that "Pink Feat" had previously appeared as a Larry Day route in the Ed Pearsall guide. Larry and Ed had aid climbed the final pitch of the route, leaving the option open for future climbers to free-climb the pitch. Tom Souders remembers that an early version of the route was a boulder problem built around mantling up a ledge. In 1983, using that ledge as a starting point, Tom and Jeff "decided to make a route out of it, so I think you could get a couple of those little Cam-a-lots [which are very similar to Friends] . . . put them in a little hold, and then we ended up putting like a bolt or two. . . . from there it was just that blank wall that we needed to put a couple bolts. . . . It's a really well-protected route." This change resulted in the route being attached to Tom and Jeff in later guides.

In 1984, Martin Hackworth would put out a pivotal guide for the Red's history. He had diligently worked his way through the Red, attaching his name to over 60 routes, and now he added to that potentially the most comprehensive, detailed guide to the Red yet. The guide opens with a hint of irony in noting that the proposed Red River Dam had, in many ways, created the Red we know today. Although the dam, had it continued, would have irreversibly changed the Red, Martin felt the extensive media coverage had also opened the Red to an entirely new audience. In the first edition of his guide, *Stones of Years*, Martin explores the source: "In the wake of extensive coverage by the media, Red River Gorge was 'discovered' by hundreds of new visitors yearly. Along with the hikers, campers and tourists came climbers; few at first, then in greater numbers with each passing year." [29]

Stones of Years recorded a massive amount of new growth in the Red. In just four years since the last guide, the Red now contained over 230 routes. The Hackworth guide listed 31 crags in the Red, too, including *Roadside Park* (more on that in a moment), *Muscle Beach*, *The Dome*, *Buzzard's Roost*, and added the recent Forest Service acquisition, *Raven Rock*. But that growth had come with caveats: the climbing community was changing, too. The guide almost wistfully denotes the moment the Red's small community had expanded: "Fourteen years ago, nearly everyone climbing in the Gorge was from a close-knit group, mainly from Lexington. The possibilities for new routes seemed endless and climbing was then a leisurely pastime. Today, many climbers who regularly visit the Gorge are from widespread, distant areas. Competition for the best new lines is becoming more intense." [30] And looking through the guide, a growing list of new names is found alongside the dozen or so featured over the last decade. Quite a few of those newer names were respected trad climbers, including folks like Tom Souders, Greg Smith, Ron Snider, Grant Stephens, and John Bronaugh.

One of the important contributions of the Hackworth guide was the addition of *Roadside Park* (later referred to simply as *Roadside*). *Roadside* was so named because climbers could park on the side of the road and walk right up to the climbing. This crag saw early development by Greg Smith, Ron Snider, Martin Hackworth, and others in 1984. Ron remembered that *Roadside* "was a cool place. I couldn't believe it that nobody had climbed there before. Greg found it, and he says, 'Come here and check this out,' and he drove me up there past it and turned around and came down, and he's like, 'Look at that crack!' " The two went on to put up the eponymous route "Roadside Attraction" (a 5.7 from 1984), which is visible from the road and was probably the first route at the crag. In the spring of 1984, Greg Smith completed "Synchronicity" (a 5.10+ that later guides listed as a 1987 FA with Tom Souders). That summer, Ron Snider teamed up with John Bronaugh on "Andromeda Strain," a 5.9 route, while Greg Smith crafted "Psycho Killer."[31] In August, Greg Smith completed 5.11- "Harder Than Your Husband" (today a 5.11b).[32] Tod Anderson, Martin Hackworth, and Grant Stephens completed "Five Finger Discount," a 50-foot 5.8 in November 1984.[33] Grant's route "Motha" was also preemptively listed in the guide, most likely while he was finishing up the first ascent. Looking forward, Grant would also be listed as author on the third edition of the Hackworth guide in 1994.

Muscle Beach was another valuable contribution from the Hackworth guide, and it can essentially be treated as a crag of which Hackworth was the main developer. The guide included 15 routes there. Martin's work at the crag started in 1981 by climbing the "Minas Tirith" route up a pinnacle (an isolated, generally tall section of rock) at the eponymous crag. On March 26–27, 1982, Ron Snider and Martin completed multiple routes: "Casual Corner," "Carnivorous," "Muscle Shoals," and "Cruising for a Bruising."[34] On June 20, 1982, Martin and Ed Pearsall would finish "When Gravity Fails" and, later that year, Martin and George Robinson would ascend "Mama Told Me Not to Come" (October 10) and "Surfin' with Grizz" (October 17). In April of 1982, Martin would ascend "Minas Ithil," another pinnacle located at this crag. In January 2, 1983, Martin and Joe Pulliam completed "Close Encounters with a Wench." That November, Martin rope soloed on "Woman Trouble" and "Last Wave." On September 25, 1983, Martin and Grant Stephens completed "Rocket Man." In all, Martin's name was on every route at *Muscle Beach* in this guide except for one: "Rock Rash," first ascended by Ron Snider and Bill Rieker in spring 1983.

There is an overlooked piece of interesting history at *Muscle Beach*. Hackworth notes that one of the pinnacles (which holds the route "Minas Tirith") in this area was first climbed by Joe Hayden in 1968 with aid. Bob Compton climbed the route "Minas Tirith" without aid in the 1970s, although it was not listed in the guides at the time. The route listed in the guide was a variant of this route and was FA'd by Martin in 1981. This historical tidbit notes yet another area where climbers were probably active earlier than has previously been considered. It also puts "Minas Tirith" among the early routes in the Red.

The Hackworth guide also included *Cloud Splitter*, a crag with only one route: "Hobnoblin," a 5.7 trad route. This route was located near one of the Red's many overlooks, which was also a very popular hiker destination. The route was first ascended by George Robinson on December 30, 1982. In later years, "Sebaceous Crack" (a 5.8) would be added by Anders Lindgren, Bryan Scott, and Phil Schneider in November 1997. This crag was still listed in the 1990s guides but would fade away in the 2000-era guidebooks. In his 1997 guide, John Bronaugh notes that the crux (most difficult part of the climb) at *Cloud Splitter* was the hiking crowds.

The Hackworth guide was the first instance of a Red climbing guide sorting routes by interests. Along with the usual index of routes based on skill rankings, Hackworth offers sublistings of routes by six categories: face climbs, finger/hand cracks, off-width/chimneys, layback/underclings, dihedrals/stemming, and overhangs. The guide also included an index (by order of route descriptions in the guide) listing the skill rankings for each route. This gave some idea of the clear diversity of routes then available in the Red, both in terms of type and skill. Later guides (such as the Bronaugh guides coming up in the 1990s) would include a listing by difficulty, although Hackworth's guide stands alone on listing routes by type.

This guide also offered a new sense of urgency regarding environmental impacts from climbing and the need for the community to self-enforce efforts to minimize their impacts. Conversations about climbing ethics to date were not new—every guide to date had included some element of this—but Hackworth's guide went somewhat deeper than previous guides. Hackworth noted, "Climbing is a sport without formalized rules. Whatever code of ethics that you chose to adhere to or ignore is strictly your business, up to a point: If your principles allow you to trash a route or it's [sic] surroundings by destructive or thoughtless actions, then it becomes everybody's business. The vast majority of climbers who now visit the Gorge regularly are very responsible people who adhere to local standards and use common sense in environmental matters. It is a minority then, who are responsible for the litter, wanton destruction of native plants and vandalism that is increasing in some of the more popular climbing areas." [35]

And Martin wasn't alone in his concerns. Larry Day reflects on ethics from this era: "The one thing that I'd like to communicate is that preserving the particular and unique beauty of the Red River climbing experiences was foremost in the minds of even those of us who were most desirous of bagging the best lines. We were so determined not to spoil the place we loved that we refused even the temptation of chalk. If we couldn't do a route without chalk, then it would just have to stand until we could. We were not absolutely against bolting, but we would never have committed the grid bolting horrors that happened later." [36]

Even when removed from the risk of dams and permanent flooding, climbers in the Red were still mindful of impact and long-term access. In this case, Hackworth's environmental ideas were well ahead of national programs like Access Fund's Climber's Pact, which is discussed later in the book, and well in line with the climbing ethic of Yosemite climbers like Royal Robbins.

One element present in both comments is the idea that impact is a *community problem* rather than exclusively a fault of the individual, and only a few persons in the community are to blame. In his guide, Martin Hackworth specifically notes concerns over climber-related trash (cigarette butts, climber tape, and snack wrappers on belay ledges) and damage to trees at *Tower Rock* (most likely from using them as an anchor). He particularly calls out two issues: don't start campfires close to rock walls and limit (or altogether eschew) chalk use. Hackworth also gives cause to grandfather in existing fixed pieces in the Red, such as the gear at "Arachnid" (which again was probably installed by cavers) and that existing gear should be replaced when it is damaged rather than putting in more permanent gear. In addition to preservation, Hackworth notes a secondary aesthetic reason for avoiding chalk use: it is a form of aid to other climbers that may spoil the complexity of the route. Chalk is used to improve gripping at first and to remove sweat from the hands (much like gymnasts), but over time, chalk outlines remain where most climbers (at least in popular climbing areas) are putting their hands. Thus, this gives additional (and often unwanted) information on solving the climbing problem.

There's a long-standing joke (or perhaps it was a eulogy, depending on one's perspective) in the Red that, around 1989, one could hear the sound of a hand drill or hammer echoing through the Gorge. Out on the West Coast, a new approach to climbing—sport climbing—had made its first appearance to a mixture of laud and lambasting. It borrowed ideas from earlier generations about using permanent anchors for protection but involved using far, far more of them to access areas of rock generally otherwise deemed unclimbable. A new era was afoot, and this one would prove to be a bit more complicated than before, one that diverted several climbers away from a clean climbing ethic. Gradually, a portion of Red climbers began to embrace sport climbing, which involved drilling holes in the rock to insert more permanent protection. This opened up a wide array of previously unclimbable areas lacking features, while also opening an entire Pandora's box of new ethical and environmental concerns.

As the 1980s waned, the appearance of the Red's climbing community changed. Much as Martin Hackworth had predicted, new climbers began appearing on the scene to see the Red firsthand. Unlike climbers in the 1970s and 1980s who largely went unnoticed by locals and essentially knew the entire community, this next generation would be more visible. They dressed in neon Lycra leggings and shorts, took up semipermanent residence in the Red, and their sole focus was climbing as much as possible. Their tight community had its own unique vibe going that was just a notch different than how most locals lived at the time.

CHAPTER 6

Sport Climbing Begins in the Red, 1987–1995

Bob Matheny first came to the Red in 1987. "I came back to Lexington to do a residency at the university [of Kentucky], and we would just get away. I had an old rope, so we'd come and rappel and occasionally set up top ropes, and one of the people I was doing a residency with liked to climb, as well, and we came out to do some trad lines." When his residency ended, Bob took a job in Washington State, but his stay was brief. He soon returned to an emergency room physician position. "Sure, I'll come back and do that for a year or two. And that's turned into 26 years."

Bob's climbing trip frequency slowed for much of the 1990s, turning his interests instead to backpacking and coping with 12-hour shifts in the emergency room. He kept his gear, however, and did occasionally shake off the dust to go rappelling. "It was one of those things that just faded until Lee said, 'Would you like to get back into it?' " His colleague Lee Irwin, also a climber on pause, suggested they return to the crags.

Around 1998, Bob and Lee visited California's Owens River Gorge, spending two weeks climbing with guide Bruce Hawkins to get reacquainted with new advances in climbing. There Bruce would introduce them to the very new field of *sport climbing*:

> After the first day when he was going over building anchors, equalizing trad anchors, things of that sort, he said, "What do you guys think about sport climbing?" We really had no idea what it was. "Well, bolts are already in the rock. It allows you to climb without having to put in gear as much." The buy-in for sport climbing is so much less because realistically you don't have to learn how to place gear . . . so we spent the rest of the time we'd hired him sport climbing in the Owens River Gorge. And we constantly heard when we'd speak to people, "Why are you out here? There's this place called the Red River Gorge where there's [sport] climbs

all over the place, is what we hear. It's the Mecca!" And when we came back . . . the first place we went was to *Roadside*.

The Red's *Roadside* was indeed on fire with new sport routes by the mid-1990s. Over a decade of work at *Roadside* already led to nine trad routes by 1994, mostly routes created in the 1980s. However, sport climbers would soon surpass that with 23 sport routes in just six years of development.

The earliest sport routes at *Roadside* go back to 1987 and come from some important names in the trad community. That year, Greg Smith and Tom Souders climbed "Pulling Pockets" (a 5.10d), and Roger Pearson and John Bronaugh completed "Valor Over Discretion" (a 5.8). But it was a calculated and quiet newcomer to the Red, Porter Jarrard, who would soon make his mark at *Roadside*, attaching his name to *ten* routes (solo or with a partner) in the next few years. Moreover, Porter's routes would continue Souders's recent pattern of creating difficult climbs in the Red. Thus, *Roadside* became a symbolic interaction point between the long-standing trad community members and the new sport climbers finding their way to the Red. Sport climbers soon found a ragtag home at an ice cream stand turned pizzeria about four miles down the road.

Miguel and Susan Ventura have been living in the Red since 1983. Miguel's friend, Neville Pohl, had recently purchased farmland in Slade as part of creating a holistic healing center. He invited Miguel and family to buy into the land (at a cost of $4,000 in savings) and join their community. The property contained unused houses and buildings, a few of which would later play into the Red's climbing history. One in particular stood out in setting the Ventura family's roots into the Red: a shuttered storefront called The Old Jottem Down Store. This name itself has history going back to the 1930s and 1940s, when the Lum n' Abner radio show played during the golden era of radio. Lum and Abner, a stereotypical country/Appalachian take on Amos and Andy, ran a fictional store called the Old Jot'em Down Store in Pine Ridge, Arkansas.[1] The store name referenced the practice of letting customers buy goods on credit. Lum and Abner (played by Chester Lauck and Norris Goff) would go on to release over 5,000 episodes and several movies built around the store and their characters.

Miguel and Susan soon renovated this vacant building to make an ice cream shop called The Rainbow Door. Out front, Miguel (who is an astounding artist) hung a door bearing probably one of the best-known faces of climbing today: Susan Ventura. Miguel explained, "I was looking out the tent's screen at the moon when we were camping. And the moon created all these arrays of light around her," so together they carved and painted her on [what would eventually become] the door of their restaurant.[2] Miguel and Susan soon fed their three kids (Dario, Sarah, and Mark) on a mixture of income from the store and eking out a subsistence farming lifestyle from the Red's sandy soil.

Monumental changes were happening, starting around 1985, for both climbers and the Venturas. First, Martin Hackworth opened up a climbing shop on the property. Called Search for Adventure, Hackworth's little store sold climbing gear for the new flock of climbers coming to the area. It was quite well placed, right there on Highway 11 just across from Natural Bridge.[3] Next, climbers began asking about camping in the floodplain behind The Rainbow Door, which the Venturas allowed. Miguel then began making bread for the climbers. Miguel is originally from Maçores, Portugal, where his family worked at a flour mill and the community used a communal oven to bake bread. In the coming years, Miguel's bread offerings for the climbers would transition into pizza with a few ingredients from the family garden. In 1986, Miguel's Pizza would officially open its doors, with Susan's face still on the front door.

Over time, Miguel's became a central hub for the climbing community of the era.[4] As Chris Chaney remembered, "You'd climb all day, you'd go sit [in Miguel's], you'd get a pizza, you'd eat the pizza, and you'd hang around and people would just tell stories, and you'd just be like mesmerized by what was going on, you know?" It was also the place for climbers without partners to come find a climbing buddy for the day, get beta (or information) on new climbing locations, talk about new gear, and learn (often from hearing others' stories) about safety in climbing. Climbers also set up an entire tent community in the woods and grass behind the restaurant, which had a reputation for parties and unconventional living. The abandoned houses would also become famed destinations in and of themselves. And saying one spent an entire climbing season at Miguel's (particularly if it happened in the 1990s) is still today a great credential in the climbing community. In all, Miguel's created a location for the climbing community to dramatically expand the amount of climbing in the region without having to actually leave the area to go home. In doing so, it also replicated a long-standing tradition of dirtbag lifestyle climbing found farther west in California's Yosemite National Park.

Lifestyle climbing is an important part of the climbing identity and ethic. Although the idea of lifestyle climbing has different names (most frequently called dirtbags and more recently called lifers or vanners), the overarching idea is that the climber gives up common comforts to focus first and foremost on climbing.[5] This could mean living in vans near climbing areas to climb more often. It could be living (and sometimes working) at Miguel's to take advantage of its proximity to climbing within a thriving climbing community. Poverty is a given in exchange for more time and resources being dedicated to climbing.

Lifestyle climbing ideals were prevalent in Yosemite's climbers, particularly those who lived in Camp 4.[6] The Park Service eventually banned them from living in Camp 4 (which really had already been a rule for some time). Still, it changed American climbing forever. These persons clearly lived to climb, eschewing most everything else misconstrued as being important by the predominant American culture to be at the crag. Today, *dirtbag* is typically a term of endearment and respect among climbers. The use of the term between climbers is a commentary on dedication to the art of climbing. For the Red, lifestyle climbing was readily evident around 1990 with the arrival of Porter Jarrard.

Porter got his start climbing in North Carolina. His first introduction to climbing happened as a junior in high school when he and his classmates visited *Moore's Wall* in Hanging Rock State Park.[7] As a college student at the University of North Carolina at Greensboro (UNCG), he again went climbing in fall 1986 with Ken McPherson, Porter's longtime friend and experienced climber. In an interview with Bodie McDowell, Porter explained, "I went climbing with Ken . . . and I just became thoroughly engrossed with the sport." Porter learned a great deal from Ken's mentorship and applied what he learned in the world of competitive climbing, winning the Southeastern Regional competition in Atlanta. He would also broaden his climbing experience across the United States before eventually getting into bolting his own routes.

Porter's early work is a good example of the cyclical nature of climbing lifestyles. As the weather changes, climbers often change where they are climbing. In his 2010 interview with *Dead Point Magazine*, Porter explained his annual climbing movements and how he counterbalanced his own life with his climbing:

> Late fall and early winter always sent me scrambling, usually south, looking for warmer temps and hoping for sun in Alabama's northeast corner. Lookout Mountain, Little River Canyon, Sandrock, Jamestown, Steele. We would camp near the first overlook at LRC under the roof of an abandoned gas store with our bags on a concrete pad floor. It was ideal. Just off of that rough slag canyon rim road back in the briars. Nobody ever bothered us there. We drank a lot of bad coffee from an aluminum espresso maker, but that store roof made it bearable during the drizzly rains and we could comfortably leave wet clothes and bed rolls there. We drove into Fort Payne every night to Golden Corral to charge the Hilti and while

away the hours. We'd do, maybe, one of these trips before Christmas then a much longer stay through New Years and into early January until I had to head back to a semester of Tuesday-Thursday classes at UNCG. When I was based out of Greensboro, I'd do four day trips up to the New [New River Gorge] each week, with Wednesday reserved for climbing at Moore's Wall only an hour from home. When the weather was bad, I still drove to the New to endure it and eke-out a few more routes which was an outright massacre of time.[8]

Porter here also gives some examples of the dirtbag lifestyle and how it relates to organizing living around climbing. One detail that might escape nonclimbers was Porter's use of the Hilti, a well-known rock drill used for placing bolts in routes.

Porter made a name for himself establishing new climbing opportunities in West Virginia's New River Gorge. His work in the New is among the first of the sport routes developed there, and his work is today well respected. Ray Ellington notes that as the weather turned cold in West Virginia, Porter worked his way south to the Red. There, Porter famously left a note in Miguel's visitor log with his name and number and the legendary message, "I'm interested in bolting routes." Per his own writing, he arrived in the Red in the summer of 1990, making a detour on the way home from a climbing trip out West. He had previously heard of the Red from two sources: a Martin Hackworth article on the Red in *Climbing Magazine* and a PBS documentary about climbers at *Tower Rock*. Following his first visit and having "got a good look at the rock," he returned in the fall of 1990, meeting Rob Turan, Mark Williams, Matt Flasch, and Tom Fyffe in the parking lot at *Roadside*.[9]

Chris Snyder, originally from Indianapolis, moved out West to climb in his early adult years. There he met Porter, who brought with him a slideshow of climbs in West Virginia, North Carolina, and Kentucky. "That's what everybody did back in the day. You'd have your slides and you'd get together at night, have a few beers and show each other your slides," explained Chris. Chris had been to the Red as child, and Porter's slides spurred a return trip. The following Thanksgiving while visiting his parents, Chris related, "I borrowed my dad's car and drove down to the Red, and the first thing I walked up on was *Military Wall*, and I was hooked." Chris would later go on to discover *The Motherlode*, arguably the most important concentration of climbing in the region. But back in the 1990s, Chris, Porter, and others were solely focused on expanding sport-climbing opportunities in the DBNF while solving the conundrum of living hours away.

The dedication and time required to be a lifestyle climber is immense, but climbers are truly problem solvers. The problem in those early days was that it was hard to climb and live outside the Red. Miguel Ventura provided a solution for this. Chris explains the importance of the Love Shack:

> The climbing season in Kentucky is winter. Spring and fall are nice, but they can often be too hot, especially for hiking around. [In the Winter] it can be horrible to camp as we do get occasional snowfall. Miguel was kind enough to offer the shelter of the Love Shack to Porter and myself for that first winter. . . . Commuting back and forth to Lexington became too much. It became nice to hole up in that thing, dilapidated as it was. He had given us a kerosene heater, we had that in there, and some old couches, eastern Kentucky Style. People would show up on the weekends. Even then rock climbing was becoming more and more popular. So there were lots of different people from Cincinnati and Indianapolis who would come down on the weekends. But for us, it was like full time. I structured my life back then to make it possible to take extended periods of time to concentrate on route development and rock climbing, as silly as it is, I mean, that's how it is when you're a kid. That's the kind of energy youth has, where you can go in and have no visible means of support, sort of a Don Quixote style crusade to make something out of nothing. Miguel was so nice to us.

Porter and Chris used the Love Shack as their base of operations for what would be a momentous era in the Red. In a few years, Porter (alone or with a partner) tied his name to almost 100 sport routes. Remember here that the 1980 Pearsall guide had fewer routes than this, and those routes took over a decade for a few dozen climbers to assemble. Porter systematically began bolting routes where previous climbers had seen only featureless rock. His routes took advantage of the overhung climbing that today often defines climbing in the Red. By placing bolts at specific locations, climbers could now ascend where no climbers had gone before.

Military Wall arguably saw some of the best early sport-route development in the Red in 1990, and Porter was at the heart of this growth. "Fuzzy Undercling" (a 5.11b) was put up by Porter Jarrard, Phil Olenick, Rob Turan, and Mark Williams in the winter of 1990, as was "Tissue Tiger" (5.12b, again Porter, Phil, and Rob). Alongside Mark Williams, Porter developed "Gung Ho" (5.12a), "Reliquary" (5.12b), "Thirsting Skull" (5.12d), "Jac Mac" (5.11d), "Rad Boy Go" (5.12b), "Bozo's Bogus Booty Biner" (5.11c with Matt Flach and Mark

Williams), and "Special Impetus" (5.12b, also with Matt and Mark). There is also "Forearm Follies" (a 5.12b with Tim Toula), and earlier that year, Porter and company had developed "Mule" (5.12c with Doug Reed). That's 11 well-known routes at one crag in one year.

Growth at *Military Wall* would continue for the next few years. Porter and Steve Cater (in 1991) established an early 5.13a called "Revival," which was long treated as a proving route for climbers who wanted to earn street cred. Porter and Steve also added two very popular 5.9s: "Sunshine" and "Moonbeam." On weekends, it is normal for three or four climbers to be in line to climb these lower-skill routes. That same year, Porter and Doug Reed also bolted "Another Doug Reed Route" (5.11c) in the same alcove where early greats like Larry Day had charted famous trad routes like "Jungle Beat" in the 1970s.[10] Doug and Porter teamed with Steve Cater to put up "Nicorette" (a 5.12a). Nearby, Chris Snyder would add the respected route "Nicoderm" (5.12b), which shares a start with "Nicorette." Chris Snyder and Brian McCray also teamed up on 5.11c route "Minimum Creep." Additional new routes included "Hurricane Amy" (5.11c, Porter, Mark Williams, Tom Fyffe, and Matt Flach); "Government Cheese" (5.11d, Porter Jarrad, Mark Williams, and Matt Flach); "Left Turret" (5.11c), "Right Turret" (5.12a), and "Nothing For Now" (5.12a, Porter, Shannon Langley, and Frank Waters); "Etrier" (5.12b with Tim Powers); "Daisychain" (5.12c, Porter and Jamie Baker); and "Super Slab," a 5.12c route by Porter alone. In a matter of years, Porter's work accounted for the majority of routes developed there on the Forest Service's land. Today, his collaborative work still represents a lion share of sport routes in the Red.[11]

Porter's collaboration with Chris Snyder was particularly special and celebrated. The pair created two routes included in a recent list of the top 100 American sport climbs.[12] The first, the 5.10a "To Defy the Laws of Tradition," is located just across the hollow from *Military Wall* at *Left Flank*. This route was FA'd in 1992. It is now a Red classic that has seen extensive traffic over the years. Second is "Mercy, the Huff," a 5.12b route from 1991. Mark Anderson described the route as "one of the best sport routes on the continent," while Ray Ellington suggested that climbers "take your time, breathe, relax, focus and don't fall at the top!"[13]

Around the same time, Porter and Chris Snyder put out a climbing guide in 1992, *Selected Climbs at Red River Gorge, Kentucky*, listing many innovative and nuanced routes from the era. The guide is particularly noted for its detailed geographic maps (which happened to be one of Porter's many strengths) as well as humor throughout. Porter has a lasting reputation as a funny guy, if occasionally dark or crude. His route names range from odd to socially relevant to hilarious: "Stunning the Hog" (1991), "Sex Farm" (1991), "Too Many Puppies" (1992 with Chris Snyder), "King Me" (1990 with Tim Toula), "Super Dario" (a reference to Miguel's son, Dario Ventura; 1991, Doug Reed and Porter Jarrard), or "Bozo's Bogus Booty Biner" (aka BBBB, 1990 with Matt Flash), just to name a few. Bob Matheny gave a classic example of Porter's humor while talking about how Porter put up some of his early routes: "The stories I've heard are that he would go in and scope lines and essentially drop a rope and basically fire bolts in wherever he stopped. Then, they'd pull the rope and he'd send it. And the rumor is that he would, after firing a bolt, he would always say, 'Yeah, you need to watch this one. Don't fall on this bolt.'"

Porter also hinted here at the decidedly sketchy homemade climbing gear often being used as protection. Over in Yosemite, innovative climbers used cast-iron stove legs and other homemade gear to climb cracks. Like the innovators at Yosemite, Porter used some odd items to create these new routes, largely to address a lack of gear at the time blended with a dirtbag vow of ingenious poverty. One of his famous innovations was his bedframe hangers. Terry Kindred (whom you'll meet again later in the book) and Bob Matheny collected several of Porter's bedframe hangers while rebolting those routes for obvious safety reasons. Bob explained the rationale behind those unique devices: "[Porter] would cut [bedframes] into a section about say three inches long, drill one hole here [which bolted into the wall], one hole here [which held a carabiner], [and] bolt it in as a hanger." This innovation, albeit scary by modern safety standards in bolts, is part of the ingenuity often seen in climbing. Bob continues from our interview, "You can buy hangers and at the time they probably cost $3–4 apiece, or you can cut up an old bedframe, which you can find on the side of the road, but it's not appropriately tested steel, a lot of them are fractured, they're really scary when you pull them off, but . . . they were putting in all sorts of weird bolts." Today, those unique handmade devices (now simply called Porter Hangers) are valued collector's items among Red climbers.

This was certainly not Porter's first go at creating gear. His 2010 *Dead Point Magazine* article describes an early version of the Porter Hanger: "Sometime in the late 1980s Porter Jarrard, strapped for cash and with an insatiable desire for new routing, crafted 200 of these in his dad's shop out of 1/8th inch angle iron. Years ago all 200 could be found scattered about the Cumberland Plateau, from Kentucky and West Virginia all the way to Alabama but most have rusted beyond usefulness and been replaced with modern hardware. A few of these historical Easter eggs are still out there though."[14]

Climber Hugh Loeffler (who in just a few short years would become a central figure in the Red climbing community) spent time with Porter and Chris at the Love Shack. He provides a good perspective on the time before and after Porter in the Red:

> We didn't know [about] overhanging climbing. I don't know, we just didn't have a vision. We did not have a vision, and because the New [River Gorge], we'd been to the New and they were climbing vert sport routes. Smith Rocks . . . the paradigm [there] was vertical sport routes. So it took Porter coming over . . . he came over and exploded, you know? Showed us the way. And the rest is history. So we were ready for it. We were ready for the message. There was such a vacuum, and we were waiting for the message, and then he came and delivered the message.

Although many accepted the message, there were detractors. As it would turn out, not everyone in the climbing community was excited about the growth. There was a general pushback from trad climbers. While trad climbing is something requiring years of mentorship on protective gear placement, sport climbing opened climbing areas to most anyone with a rope and the right gear. This mentorship period for trad climbing also allowed climbers to learn the cultural norms of the crag, whereas sport climbers skipped that learning period and could go straight up the route. These tensions occasionally overflowed into arguments, and there are rumors that the differences occasionally led to physical altercations in Miguel's parking lot.

That conflict lingered for several years within the climbing community. Although its exact origins and first use are unknown, the comical phrase "Sport Climbing Is Neither" essentially captures the essence of this conflict. The wordplay here is subtle to nonclimbers; it means that sport climbing (using bolts) is neither a *sport* nor is it *climbing*. Kris Hampton has a great perspective on this conflict as someone who began as a trad climber and transitioned to sport climbing:

> When I first began trad climbing, it seemed like this bastion of better ethics, and that there was more history, it was steeped in this incredible history and sport climbing was still something that was relatively new, and I took those ethics and ran with them. . . . At the time I believed so strongly that putting bolts in the wall was destroying this history that traditional climbing had built that I was angry at sport climbing and definitely waged this war against sport climbers, and that's what that phrase meant, that sport climbing is neither. When you put the bolts in the wall,

you take the adventure out of it, it's no longer a sport and it's no longer climbing, you've bastardized it into this other thing.

Tensions between trad and sport climbers are less of an issue now, particularly as the Red developed a greater renown for being a sport-climbing destination. Kris feels that the "next generations of climbers have gotten a little smarter in a way that it doesn't exist anymore." From Kris's perception, the "Red River Gorge is some of the best sport climbing in the world, and if bolts weren't accepted, we wouldn't even know that." In a matter of years, the Red had transformed from a small-time trad climber paradise to a sport mecca. Today, the difference between trad and sport climbers in the Red is no longer palpable.

Porter left town in 1993, headed toward the next big challenge. Hugh Loeffler put it this way:

Porter was young. Porter certainly didn't know [the historical importance of] what he was doing. He knew he was bolting great routes. He didn't know the historical impact he was making. And to this day, Porter still, he was an accidental icon. He didn't know what he was going to do was going to make him reverential 25 years later or whatever. He had no idea that was going to happen, and I suspect that if he'd known, he never would have done it. He hasn't dealt well with the hero worship. He doesn't like it, but hero worship he gets, you know?

From his interview with *Dead Point Magazine*, Porter recounts that "I made a decision to finish my [graduate] studies before I turned thirty so I moved to Lexington, KY and [re]enrolled in UK, quit climbing." He went on to explain further: "My sudden disappearance from the scene fueled rumors, scandals, and outright lies about my mental status and whereabouts. I helped start this Red River Gorge sport climbing explosion thing then poof vanished. All those young climbers that enjoy climbing on my routes somehow have created a wormhole in the time-space continuum and I have slipped through it." [15] Porter eventually returned to the Red after a hiatus from climbing, explaining that a so-called 9 to 5 life had not been fulfilling. He remains one of the legends of the Red today. His climbing ethic, reminiscent of Yosemite's Camp 4 days, lived on at Miguel's.

While Porter was leaving the Red, John Nowell showed up when lifestyle climbing at Miguel's was probably at its early height. John vividly remembered his time living there:

To some extent, if you were living at Miguel's full time, you really didn't need a guidebook. You were hanging out with a crew that pretty much knew, and there was no Internet, there was no Wi-Fi, and there were no cell phones, so at night it was wax about rock climbs and prowl through climbing magazines [like] *Rock and Ice* and memorize guidebooks and all that stuff. I'm not one of them, but there were a lot of guys who could flip through that and memorize an entire crag, and we'd go up to the crag.

Although dirtbagging was about giving up comforts to redirect resources to climbing, "we tried to be as comfortable as possible." John reminisced:

The dirtbagging thing was more of people living on as little as they possibly could to spend as much time there as they possibly could. Even today you get absorbed into that community, and there's a strong bond, and obviously there [is] somewhat of an addictive quality to climbing, especially the climbing in the Red. . . . There was one season I was sitting there counting my change and my crumpled up one dollar bills trying to figure out, "Okay, if I'm going to pay them $2.00 a night to camp and I can't just keep living on Ramen noodles and how long am I actually going to be able to stay up here before I have to go back and work?"

The tents they lived in (often fairly cheap) may have been filled with goodies like air mattresses that made living in a tent a bit more hospitable. There was also a sense of competition as climbers improvised their living quarters, such as having *two* air mattresses stacked for arguably more comfort. But it was still a Spartan lifestyle. Although Miguel's provided a high calorie source of nutrition, climbers were mostly living off the symbolic foods of poverty: Ramen, Pop Tarts, and canned meats. John remembered his preference for barbecued Vienna sausages over the classic variety: "I always loved the barbecue ones because you could eat those and the barbecue sauce would cover up the taste of [climbing] chalk on your hands. Chalk and regular Vienna sausages were just not a good mix."

Lifestyle climbing at Miguel's went deeper than climbing, though. The experiences of this lifestyle created a makeshift family structure for climbers:

Once I actually started living at Miguel's, I think the big thing was just how tight-knit it was . . . and just the general silliness of it. Now, there was this very serious air when we were out climbing and everybody's trying their hardest and everybody's cheering for each other and all of that good stuff, but when you're back at Miguel's and bored or trying to figure out what to do, it was definitely a sense of family. And it was different from your biological family in that you're of the same age and you've got these common bonds and have this incredible trust with one another.

As a result, being a resident climber at Miguel's meant a rapid expansion in one's social capital in the climbing community. Climbers there met folks from around the world, including some of the Red's greats. It provided immense street credentials, too, as other climbers respected the dedication to climbing. There is also the obvious effect of climbing and training daily, which translated into becoming a better climber. The end result—for those who could swing spending a year (or more) at Miguel's—was a transformative experience.[16] The scene evolved each year, and Miguel's evolved alongside it. John reflected on this: "You know, each season with our little crew, it kinda changed year to year, but there was probably a dozen of us, we would kind of strategically place our camp around Miguel's. One year [Miguel] came out and actually screamed at us because we had, that was actually the first season we had built our little Ewok Village of tents."

Others followed, John explained: "Tarp City was the first one, and underneath those giant pine trees that are all now gone and are actually where the basketball court is, there were some giant pine trees there and we strung ropes up everywhere and had this massive, tattered, unsightly collection of tarps to keep the rain off our tents. And that was Tarp City, and that was actually Miguel who would point at that and say, 'Oh, he's back at Tarp City.'" South Forty, Survivor Island (based on the television show), and other makeshift temporary communities followed. Over time, the number of tents gradually grew. An outdoor shower was added, though it had a reputation for being only semiprivate—if a Miguel's patron caught the right angle through the restaurant windows, they could see inside it. The outhouse was also replaced with more modern toilet facilities. Later years would see a pavilion and short basketball court appear alongside a pay shower facility.

Entertainment was always at hand, even among the self-imposed poverty of dirtbag life. As John mentioned, the lack of cell phones and internet combined with the prevalence of unscheduled time and the poverty of lifestyle climbing led to intense, close social ties. There is also the life and death nature of climbing that ups the ante a notch. There was always beta (information) to be shared about new climbing areas or new routes. And then there were the wax bombs, explained here by John Nowell:

So the wax bombs were basically, again with no Wi-Fi, no internet, we had to entertain ourselves, but Ghetto Chris [Chris Karash] would take a massive cooking pot or a #10 can and stick a couple of those giant 10-inch diameter three-wick candles in there, put it over a Coleman stove and heat it up to the point that the liquid wax would actually catch on fire. And then, from a distance with a long pole or stick clip, another #10 can wired and duct-taped to it [and] full of cold water, he would dump [the cold water] in the boiling, flaming wax, which would then vaporize and ignite and create most often a 40-foot-tall mushroom cloud of fire. Even if you knew it, it would wake you up if you were sleeping with this [makes a loud wooshing sound]. And always a crowd pleaser, and lots of fun, and covered the parking lot and any surrounding vehicles with wax.

The wax bombs still occasionally happen at Miguel's even in recent years, footage of which can be found on YouTube.

Around 1993 or 1994 (no one seems quite sure of the date, or as Dario Ventura put it, "lots of memories over the last 33 years . . . just hard to remember it all"), the Love Shack burned down. Or, "My understanding," John Nowell thought, "it was intentional. It was in pretty bad shape, disrepair. When you walked inside you were wondering if you were the one it was going to land on." Perhaps the only fitting end for the Love Shack would be a Viking pyre, which it got. It had taken a beating. Hugh Loeffler and Chris Snyder both shared that some of the boards from the walls and even the furniture had been used as firewood along the way by climbers trying to keep warm, and it had gradually become unsustainable.

One of the unintended elements of sport climbing and lifestyle climbing from this era in the Red may be that the climbing community became increasingly visible to local residents. Miguel's convenient placement along the highway was great for climbers, but it also made their presence known to local residents driving through the community. Thinking back to issues of local residents and the proposed dams, climbers were ostensibly already labeled as outsiders via their affiliation with the timing of their arrival in the Red and their links to the Sierra Club. Miguel's (through no fault of their own) now provided a chance for locals to confirm their labeling of climbers as outsiders in witnessing lifestyle climbing from the road and parking lot.

The style of the era compounded this issue further: climbers of the day wore form-fitting neon Lycra prints, which aided in sorting them from local residents. And tourists also perhaps played a role here, as life at Miguel's became its own source of entertainment for outsiders. Overall, this may have created issues for climbing, as more and more came into the area to live the life even while it gave it a strong foundation for growth. Today, Miguel's continues to allow climbers to camp in the backyard for a few dollars a night and four-minute showers for $1. The restaurant recently underwent a major expansion, offering more space and pizza ovens, even while keeping the original restaurant space intact. Susan's face is still on the door.

Looking forward in time, climbers would find additional places where they could interact with (rather than simply be seen by) local residents. The first was the Beer Trailer. More formally known as C&S Carryout, the Beer Trailer is an important climber stop in a mostly dry area. In those earlier years, they carried around 12 domestic beers, and John Nowell recalled that the line "If we ain't got it, it ain't worth drinkin" was a common reply from the counter. Wolfe County voted to go wet in 1991, while Powell County (where Miguel's is located) stayed dry until May 2018. This funneled everyone looking for alcohol to a few select spots. Due to its location, the Beer Trailer became very popular for both residents and climbers. Several climbable spots behind the business were also developed over the years and still see traffic today. And there was another reason to visit the Beer Trailer: cats. Crag dogs (dogs that climbers bring to—you guessed it—the crag) are fairly common sights in climbing areas, but not cats. John explained this further: "You can get your cat fix at the Beer Trailer. The Beer Trailer cats host personalities for every type of cat aficionado. Rowdy and aggressive cats, check. Friendly and lovable cats, check. Lap cats, check. . . . There were even cats for those that don't like cats, herds of feral ones that loved a game of chase." [17]

In the coming decade, climbers would also begin developing routes farther south of the Red, leading climbers to eschew the Bert T. Combs Mountain Parkway for county roads leading through Lee County. Local gas station and restaurant, Koops, became a common stop for climbers. Interestingly, Koops was also an important part of the region's OHV/ATV community, which counts many local residents among its members. Climbers now use it as a safe place to park cars, get storage lockers, buy gas, and fill up on calories in the form of chips and homemade sandwiches. Meanwhile, ATVs and side-by-sides are being worked on in the parking lot, and the occasional ATV rider may simply ride up into the parking lot from the nearby Hollerwood Offroad Park. This gradual increase in interaction with local residents may also become a source of a gradual change in how climbers are understood in the region in subsequent years.

CHAPTER 7

Climbing Guides, Climbing Bans, and Climbers Organizing, 1993–1997

Christina Bronaugh and Jennifer Rannels added the 5.7 sport route "C# or B♭" to the guidebooks in 1993. Climbers aren't likely to struggle on the route itself, but the name is more troubling for nonmusicians in the Twitter hashtag era. "Let's name it a music name," Christina recalled saying to Jennifer, who was also Christina's music student. "And now, people don't know what to say with it, C hashtag B what? What? What is this? It was a sharp way before it was a hashtag." Music was also a binding tie between Christina and her husband, John. "John and I were both musicians. John was a fabulous guitarist. We played in bands together for years." Beyond music, they would also put up several routes together. These include "Put Me in the Zoo" (5.9+), "Make a Wish" (a 5.10b), and "Armadillo" (5.10d). Why Armadillo? "Because it's *The Zoo*, and it looked like it had plates" like an armadillo's back, Christina recalled.

Ron Snider, an important part of route development at *Roadside* in the early 1980s, climbed in the Red with John Bronaugh, Christina's husband. "He was just a real passionate rock climber. He loved it. He loved exploring, finding new places." Ron described John as a person who "wasn't afraid to put on a big heavy pack" and go exploring for new routes: "He put the time in looking through the topo maps. He'd get the Forest Service topo maps and look for what looks like it might be a cliff and then he'd go hike in in the wintertime and see what it was. He found a lot of these obscure places [in the Red]." Ron and John also put up several first ascents together, such as "The Battlement," a 5.10 trad route at *Fortress Wall*, and "Whiteout," a classic 5.8 trad at *Emerald City*. John and Ron also found and put up early routes at *Jailhouse Rock*, which is a trad area on Forest Service land. Over the years, John would attach his name to over 100 routes in the Red, which puts him among the great route developers of the Red.[1]

After their early climbing days together, John and Ron went their separate ways. Ron headed to New York to climb in the Shawangunks. John headed to college, earning his bachelor's degree in wildlife biology at Colorado State. Ron recalled that John then began "working at Phillip Gall's [a climbing and outdoor equipment store in Lexington, Kentucky] and learned to play guitar, decided he really liked music." John soon departed for California to attend the Musician's Institute in Hollywood, where he studied guitar. John returned to Kentucky with a new skillset: MIDI.

Musical Instrument Digital Interface (MIDI) allows a musician to control an array of digital instruments, as well as most any characteristic of those instruments, through a single controller. That controller can be a computer, a keyboard, or even a guitar, as was the case in John's work. Through MIDI, Christina and John could work as a duo but with the sound of a full band behind them. "It was in the 80s . . . so we were like a Top 40 band, but only with two of us, so we got paid like a band [because of MIDI], but there was just the two of us." Christina and John enjoyed a long tenure in Lexington as the first and only duo band doing this kind of music in town, and Lexington residents and visitors from the era may still remember the band Special Effects, a cover band singing the hits of the period.

Ron recalled that John went all out with his performance. "He would get up on stage in these Lycra tights and play AC/DC or whatever, which was totally out of character for John. John was more of the outdoorsy hiker kind of guy . . . and next thing you know he's a lawyer." Law school was no accident, though, and was likely in John's mind the whole time. Christina felt that "he always, in the back of his mind, thought that he would end up being an attorney. He was I think the seventh generation [in a] direct line of attorneys [in his family]." Early in their work as a band, John told Christina, "I'm not a musician like you." Christina continued: "He said, 'You're probably going to be a musician for the rest of your life,' and I was like, 'Well, yeah! Of course. What else am I going to do?' " But John had another route in mind: "I'll probably end up in law school."

Christina also shared a poignant story about John that helps explain more about his perspective on access to climbing in the Red in the coming years:

We were playing a gig downtown and we were dressed in our gig clothes, we dressed kind of stupid 80s hip. We were waiting in line to get a table. We had our name in . . . and these other people came in like dressed in suits and things and they got seated right away and they didn't have reservations. And then these next people dressed in suits and things, they got seated right away, and there were like five [groups] that passed us up, okay? John went up to [the host] and he was like, "Why did you seat them and not us?" And [the host] goes, "Have you looked at yourself?"

John was understandably furious: "We're not eating here. You don't deserve our money." They left. But John wasn't finished just yet. Christina shared that John later came back to the restaurant, now dressed in a suit as an attorney. He spoke to the same host, "and told him how awful he treated him just because of the way he was dressed, and now he has a lot of money to spend there, but he won't be spending and neither will any of his friends, and he walked out."

John had a strong reputation as someone who was fully engaged with his interests, whether that was doing an 80-day canoe trip with his brother, Whit, down the Back River to the Arctic Ocean, climbing "The Nose" on El Capitan in Yosemite with Stacy Temple, building a music studio in his basement, or keeping up with playing music even after becoming a lawyer. Christina also emphasized this important characteristic about John: "If he's going to do something, he's going to do it well, like he throws himself into whatever he's going to do."

Likewise, John carried a clear, dedicated perspective on climbing: that he was singularly responsible for his own safety. Amid a 2013 bolting debate on redriverclimbing.com, Shannon Stuart-Smith shared John's perspective on climbing and risk management approach: "I personally subscribe to what I call the John Bronaugh rule (from whom I borrowed the following) . . . 100 percent personal responsibility for all of my climbing decisions, actions and risks, rely on no one for anything, be able to extricate myself in all situations as if I climbed alone." [2] Climbers also respected his ferocity in the face of a challenge. He wouldn't back down if he felt that his cause was in the right. In an informal discussion on redriverclimbing.com (a local website that acted as a de facto source of community information), John is listed several times as one of the four most important climbers in the Red's history, often for his contribution in routes, history, and documentation. Elsewhere, he is described as a "true selfless pioneer of the Gorge." [3]

So it is fitting that, in 1993, John Bronaugh published his *Red River Gorge Climbs* guide, the most comprehensive Red climbing guide to date. The Bronaugh guide (a spiral-bound guide featuring Stacy Temple at *Roadside* on the front cover and Porter Jarrard at *Phantasia* on the back cover) included 76 crags (81 if including subcrags at two locations), up from 31 in the Hackworth guide a decade earlier. The guide included over 680 routes, more than doubling the routes listed in the 1990 edition of the Hackworth guide. Among these is a touching route at *Global Village* in the Natural Bridge Region called "Father and Son." The 5.7 route's first ascent included two pairs of fathers: John Bronaugh and Miguel Ventura and their sons Alex Yeakley and Dario Ventura.

One interesting innovation in the Bronaugh guide is the clearer use of regions. As crags were exceeding routes from the earliest guides at this stage, it became possible to reclassify them into groupings. For example, the Gray's Branch Region now included the Nada Tunnel Area, *Military Wall* and *Left Flank* about a mile down the road, and *Raven Rock*. Many of the classic climbing areas from the 1970s (*Half Moon, Chimney Top*) now fell into the Eastern Gorge Region, while others like *Tower Rock, Hen's Nest*, and the recent growth at the *Small Walls* was included as the Middle Gorge. The guide featured regional maps locating crags alongside major landmarks such as roads, bridges, streams, and even cemeteries. This designation of regions continues even today.

Bronaugh also utilized a map system and numbered routes to provide specific route locations at crags. One major issue with early guides was that finding routes at a particular crag relied upon text description. In many cases, the route would be obvious, such as finding a particular crack or feature to use as a reference point. In other cases, the routes could be quite hard to find and in some cases even lost (such as "Tourists' Horror" from the earliest climbing days in the Red). These crag maps provided a best-case scenario for climbers to find the exact routes they wanted. The overview maps identified approach trails and landmarks and used numbers to identify each route's precise location. Along with grouping routes and crags by regions, these map formats are still used today.

The higher-skill levels of routes found in the Red really started to show up in this guide. These included "Phantasia" (at 5.12d/13a in the guide and located at the eponymous crag), "Revival" (5.13a at *Military Wall*), and "Table of Colors" (5.13a at *Left Flank*).[4] Rankings of 5.12d (four in all) included another *Military Wall* route, "Thirsting Skull." In all, 67 routes were rated at 5.12a or higher.

Along with the higher-skilled routes (including a few now famous routes), the guide also added the *Phantasia* crag to the list of known climbing areas. *Phantasia* actually began life in the climbing world as part of *Dunkan Rock* (which itself was previously referred to as *Frenchburg* and *Dunkan Branch* in earlier guides). The crags were separated by a road (Route 77), so Bronaugh divided them in his guide, with *Phantasia* getting three trad routes from the 1970s ("Bobsledding," "St. Alphonso's," and "Tomfoolery") amid 10 new sport routes. First established was the eponymous route "Phantasia." Porter Jarrard and Tim Toula completed the route in winter 1990. Porter would later work with Chris Snyder on "Twinkie" (spring 1992) (now one of the popular 5.12s in the Red) and with Snyder and Jeff Moll on "Creep Show" (a 5.10d). Porter also worked on two more routes that summer ("Luck's Up" with Scott Lazar and "Count Floyd Show" with Mark Strevels).

Kevin Pogue, a trad climber who had started in the Red in 1980s, also made new sport contributions at *Phantasia*. These included "Pogue Ethics" (with Doug Hemken and Elisa Weinman Pogue in December 1991), "Lord of the Flies" (with Elisa in July 1992), and the first pitch of "Creature Feature" (also with Elisa in July 1991). "Creature Feature" is an example of a less common mixed route where both trad and sport climbing overlap. The first pitch of this route is bolted as a sport route and is generally where most stop. In 1992, Chuck Keller, Steve Faulkner, and Tim Schlachter pioneered a trad route second pitch above the first route.

Two additional dynamics are present in the Bronaugh guide. First is the clear (and quite rapid) expansion of sport routes throughout traditional Red climbing areas. For example, *Military Wall* now had 46 routes, over half of which were established since 1990. *Long Wall* is another example. *Long Wall* first appeared in the Ed Pearsall guide back in 1980 and saw a lot of growth by folks like Martin Hackworth, Grant Stephens, Ron Snider, John Bronaugh, Tom Souders, Jeff Koenig, and Tom Seibert, to name a few, in the early and mid-1980s. However, a blitz of route development in 1992 added 14 of the 37 routes listed in the Bronaugh guide. Next is the number of smaller, new crags where a handful of climbers developed numerous routes in just a few years. A good example of this is *Wall of Denial* in the Upper Gorge Region. There, 20 routes appeared in just two years. The crag saw its first development in March 1990. Climbers such as Hugh Loeffler and Neal Strickland developed the bulk of the routes at this remote crag.

Bronaugh included a conversation about environmental concerns in the guide. One concern involves first ascensionists developing new routes and crags. Bronaugh discouraged cutting down trees or rhododendrons as part of making an area more climbable and bunching routes together. Bronaugh noted that the norm (at the time) was to camouflage hangers and rappelling stations using paint or through buying gear that was precamouflaged by the manufacturer. This would limit the visibility of the gear at the crag, minimizing the visual impact. He concludes with a warning that access to climbing is a nationwide problem, noting "solutions must be started before the problems begin."[5]

The guide already included ongoing closures for climbing in the DBNF: Natural Bridge and the entire state park remained closed year-round, while *Sky Bridge*, *Chimney Top*, *Grays Arch*, and *Nada Tunnel* all had seasonal closures in place from April 1 to November 1. In the description about *Tower Rock*, Bronaugh explained that visitors (who included cavers and hikers then) had cut down most of the trees at the top of the crag for firewood in recent years. The DBNF had subsequently banned camping in that area. Another camper's campfire at the base of the crag had burned down many other trees, leaving the area scarred. Although DBNF did not specifically attribute the damage at

Tower Rock to climbers, it did reflect badly upon climbers regardless. Moreover, it represented some of the growing concerns about the rapid rate of unauthorized sport-route growth in the DBNF in recent years.

In fall 1994, the DBNF issued a blanket ban on putting up new sport routes in the Red.[6] The DBNF needed time to understand this use of the land and how it would be maintained while protecting public lands. They also needed to figure out exactly what sport climbing was. Recall that climbers had long used removable pro up to that point in the Red, and sport climbing was still quite new. Moreover, the DBNF rightly was concerned about impacts to the area, including trampling species like the white-haired goldenrod and damage to archaeological areas. Trampling can gradually change the area's ecology by disrupting what living things can survive there. This moment presented a potential sea change for how climbers used the area with long-lasting implications. That ban was a valid pause button for the Red's public land sport development, which, unfortunately for climbers, made up the bulk of sport-route development at the time.

As part of the ban, DBNF notified the climbing community that rangers would be cataloguing in a logbook all of the existing climbs on Forest Service property. This was, no doubt, made easier by the existence of the recently published Bronaugh guide, which was as comprehensive a climbing guide as existed for the Red. Cataloguing routes would also allow the DBNF to identify routes in high-risk areas, such as rockshelters, that might hold important cultural resources. It provided a perfect opportunity for the DBNF and climbers to work together in finding areas that were problematic, such as climbing routes that started over an unsigned archaeological area. This also could clear routes in areas that did not hold protected resources.

Existing climbs would be grandfathered in to any existing climbing access plans so long as it could be demonstrated that they presented no threats to "plants, animals, rock structures, or archaeological artifacts."[7] However, new routes would need to be approved by the DBNF via a yet unannounced system. This point presented a mixed bag. Climbers, especially route developers, were probably unhappy to hear that bolting routes could not continue as it had in recent years. The extraordinary news for climbers here was that the DBNF was not going to go remove all those sport routes altogether, which they certainly could have done.

As a whole, the Forest Service was already discussing how to address bolted climbing routes. For example, by 1988 there was a bolting ban in place in the Tonto National Forest in Arizona. The ban restricted all bolting, framing it as a violation of existing rules about leaving behind property in the national forests. Tonto National Forest appealed to the Forest Service for advice, leading to a national task force to study this new use of public lands.[8] They proposed guidelines for monitoring anchor use (with density and visibility of anchors being key measures) using limits of acceptable change as a guideline to prevent damage and overuse.

Ideas from the Tonto National Forest ban, in part, would eventually be put into play in the Red, and this may have made the Red into a proving ground for those policies. Louisville, Kentucky's *Courier-Journal* newspaper ran an article on the closure titled "Rock Climbing in Gorge to Be Regulated" by Linda Stahl. The article argued that land managers' collective eyes were on the DBNF to possibly become the national standard for addressing climbing routes on Forest Service land. Stahl felt a total ban on climbing was not off the table: "Others predict the new rules will be unenforceable because the Forest Service's staff is too small to patrol all the cliffs. Eventually, these people think, climbing will be banned because it cannot be controlled."[9] In turn, the Red quietly served as a proving ground for subsequent Forest Service decisions on climbing. These include later policies in Idaho's Sawtooth Wilderness and Granite Mountain in Arizona, bans at Cave Rock in Nevada, and temporary bans for religious reasons at Devils Tower in Wyoming.[10] Moreover, other public land managers were certainly watching, such as the National Park Service, which noted that "the increased impacts to park resources because of this activity suggest that regulations . . . need to be developed to protect park resources."[11]

National discussions on climbing bans also reignited arguments within the climbing community over bolting and climbing ethics. Sides were drawn, with trad climbers rejecting sport climbers' perspectives and vice versa. For trad climbers, their fear was retro-bolting, a process where bolts would be added to existing trad routes to increase the safety of the climb and/or to access new areas of the existing route. Retro-bolting can radically change the climb itself by increasing use (which leads to erosion on holds, for example) while also changing the aesthetic of the climb itself. One could imagine that a route, under this premise, might feel more natural without the metal bolts extruding from the wall. For example, in the Aladağ mountains of southern Turkey, sport climbers retro-bolted "Yeniceriler" despite the presence of a long, easily protected, crack.[12] Bolts were even included in areas where climbers had traditionally moved unroped. A famous example of this in the Red was Greg Smith and Tom Souders's route "Pulling Pockets" at *Roadside*.[13] The route, originally a trad route, was retro-bolted by the time the 1993 Bronaugh guide was released. The retro-bolting reportedly changed the upper part of the route's ending.

In other extensions of the bolting wars, sport routes were occasionally chopped by other climbers, albeit for varying reasons. The most famous case was in Colorado's Garden of the Gods, where a climber placed four bolts on "Credibility Gap." Most climbers there were against the addition of these bolts, leading a climber (famously in flip-flops) to go chop the bolts, fill the holes with epoxy, and cover them with sand so they were hidden. Occasionally, other retro-bolted routes would be chopped, as was the case at "Yeniceriler" in Turkey. In Wyoming's Ten Sleep climbing area, an entire series of routes would be chopped in 2019 over debates about manufacturing holds in the rock.

In the Red, cases of chopped routes were limited and happened many years after the actual 1994 ban. "Eureka," located at *Lady Slipper/Global Village* crag, was chopped sometime in the late summer of 2002. Although there is no consensus on why the route was removed at the time, it may have been related to the issue that this route had clear trad gear placement options and presented a great first trad lead opportunity. "Southern Smoke" at *Bob Marley Crag* would be chopped due to some unclear community disagreements over bolt placement. "The Return of Chris Snyder" at *Roadside* would similarly have bolts chopped. All three were later rebolted to some degree.

Following extensive DBNF examination of the issues at hand, the 1994 ban was soon replaced with the "Rock Climbing Management Guide" (most often described among climbers as the CMG) on January 25, 1996. This Forest Service document shaped how the Red could (and could not) be used for climbing purposes, with the end goal of balancing resource protection with outdoor recreation access. The central purpose was finding balance between climbing use and protecting existing resources, particularly in managing the establishment of any future routes. The DBNF incorporated climber and nonclimber concerns in the CMG through public involvement from "sixteen rock climbers or interested individuals and six Forest Service employees (who) participated in each of two Rock Climbing Task Force meetings." [14] The CMG also considered "100 letters, comments or requests for information about the development of a rock climbing policy," in addition to an unspecified petition with 263 signatures. After the DBNF released a CMG draft for public review, another 33 letters were received.

The CMG made several important statements in its introduction. First and foremost, it recognized rock climbing as "an acceptable way for people to enjoy the National Forests." The CMG later specified that climbing was nationally recognized as an acceptable form of recreation on Forest Service land. This was actually a valuable win for climbers, as their activities could have simply been deemed unallowable. Second, the CMG established that climber populations have grown precipitously over the last five years. The reason for this growth was placed specifically on "several articles in climbing magazines . . . several guidebooks for local climbing . . . and a number of climbing gyms [that] have opened in nearby metropolitan areas." The CMG plainly states that "the increase in popularity of rock climbing was far greater than the Forest Service had anticipated."[15] It further states that, at the time, there was no national or DBNF-wide policy on climbers, but the CMG would be superseded by any future policies that might develop. Finally, the policy hints that climbing management would be further addressed in the upcoming revision of the Land and Resource Management Plan for the DBNF.

The CMG outlined how climbers' presence in the DBNF creates potential issues with two other specific users of the Red: the Virginia big-eared bat and the white-haired goldenrod. Both were defined as threatened and endangered (T&E) species that required special protections. The CMG also listed specific concerns about how climbers could negatively impact the Red. These concerns specifically included "soil compaction, trampling damage to plants at the base of cliffs and the proliferation of bolts on cliff faces," as well as damage to archaeological sites, T&E species, and any other species (plant or animal) living along the cliff line.[16]

The CMG established policy framing future climbing growth. Existing routes (both sport and trad) would be grandfathered into the policy and allowed to stay.[17] This was undeniably huge for climbers, as it legitimized decades of growth in the Red, including its many new sport routes. While no new bolts could be added to these routes, climbers could replace existing bolts as needed, meaning the routes would remain safe. The tradeoff, however, was probably a bitter pill for sport-route developers. Going forward, any proposed new route would need DBNF approval.

Under the CMG, new climbing routes were treated as trail development, or vertical trails, so to speak. Trails are subject to compliance with the National Environmental Policy Act (NEPA), which made its first appearance, by coincidence, the same year the Cumberland Climbers appeared in the Red (1969). NEPA required federal agencies (such as the Forest Service) to conduct environmental assessments and environmental impact statements on all their projects, developments, and changes. Those reports are then assessed by the Environmental Protection Agency to ensure the agency is in compliance. Proposals for new routes required "a map location and brief description of the proposed route or climbing area, stating the need for the proposed development considering the existing routes available."[18] That last requirement could be very difficult given the number of climbing routes throughout the DBNF. Any proposed routes would also be subject to public input. The DBNF estimated (given budget and time constraints) six requests per year. In comparison, recall that Porter Jarrard could bolt that many routes and more at a single crag in a matter of weeks. Additionally, no route proposals would be considered for

Clifty Wilderness, a then-proposed research area in Tight Hollow, nor in any areas where the route posed risk to T&Es or archaeological resources. Similarly, the DBNF would also now regulate developing crags. New crags would require the same NEPA review and possibly a full environmental assessment depending on the size of the proposed area. Moreover, the DBNF could only handle one proposal per year.[19]

The CMG policy allowed an interesting exception to the rule in the form of unpublicized, undeveloped trad routes. A trad climber could utilize natural features and removable protection to climb new routes (for lack of a better term) with the understanding that the routes could not be further developed (e.g., no removing vegetation or chipping holds) or made public (such as being listed in a guidebook or shared with others). Interestingly, John Bronaugh would publicize this very point in a later guide. This did create the opportunity for extensive new exploration of the DBNF, but the routes could not be shared with others—otherwise they would be eligible for NEPA review.[20]

The CMG reiterated seasonal closures already being recognized by climbers at *Sky Bridge*, *Grays Arch*, and *Chimney Top* overlook from April 1 to November 1. Rappelling was specifically prohibited within 100 yards of Nada Tunnel. However, new seasonal closures were recommended as a management option at *Courthouse Rock*, *Haystack Rock*, and *Hen's Nest Rock* to protect historically or geologically important rock formations found at these locations. This would follow the same April–November pattern as other areas. The CMG recommended temporary closures at *Tower Rock* and *Eagle's Point* to allow cliff-line vegetation to recover. The CMG further recommended a camping closure at the base of *Military Wall* to protect sensitive resources found at that location (what is now known to be the archaeological area found at the shelter there). The report also noted that *Military Wall* was a high priority location for monitoring impacts to the crags, perhaps foreshadowing the future dig there described in a later chapter. In what would become an important aside in the coming years, the CMG stated that the presence of T&E species or an archaeological area would not, by default, be automatic grounds for closure. Rather, mitigating measures would be attempted to lessen impact.

The CMG included some additional components looking toward continuing (and perhaps rebuilding) a long-term relationship with climbers. The DBNF agreed they would develop informational bulletin boards at Martin's Fork, Sky Bridge, and Indian Creek listing information about T&E species and forest policies. Likewise, the DBNF sought climber help on regulating trails to crags and curbing user-defined trails. The DBNF valued climbers who could help with cliff-line surveys for T&E species, offering climbers an opportunity to participate in helping the Forest Service identify priority areas for protection and management. When problems were found, the DBNF would collaborate with climbers to find solutions.

Research validates DBNF concerns about the potential impacts of climbing. Peter Clark and Amy Hessl looked at climbing areas in West Virginia's New River Gorge and found a small but negative effect on vascular plants (such as ferns) and no effect on bryophytes (which include moss).[21] However, climbers had a substantial negative effect on lichens. Climbers working on a new route will often use a wire brush to clean moss and lichen away, which can increase the ability to grip the rock and access potential holds. Once there is major traffic on the route, it will generally keep those areas clear of new growth going forward. This impact is also found in other areas like Switzerland, where sport climbing impacted lichen diversity, and in Spain, where climbing impact varied by how often the route was used.[22] That said, the impact will vary by location and approach. For example, Nicholas Walendziak's study on the Red River Gorge found only two of his eight experimental plots showed major damage from climbing over six years.[23] How this impact is measured (and a bit of natural selection on climbers behalf) can also shape results. Kathryn Kuntz and Douglas Larson note the importance of microtopography (microscopic surface features) in the relationship between climbers and environmental impact.[24] For example, sport climbers are often picking places with microsite characteristics of having (and supporting) little vegetation. Overall, these findings showed that some kind of group effort would be needed to address the impacts of climbing over time.

The 1996 CMG overlaps with another major historical milestone in the Red's climbing history: the founding of the Red River Gorge Climbers' Coalition (RRGCC). The RRGCC would be formally founded in November of 1996 by Shannon Stuart-Smith and Kris Snyder (with John Bronaugh as its first president), but its story begins in the transitionary time between the 1994 bolting ban and the 1996 CMG.[25] Shannon recalled a random but important phone call that served as a preamble to the group's formation: as she was leaving the climbing gym in Lexington, the person behind the counter saw Shannon (who at the time was relatively new to climbing) walking by the front desk and said to her, "Shannon, you look like somebody who cares," and held out the phone receiver. Taking the phone, Shannon began a conversation with a regional representative of the Access Fund who notified her that the DBNF was seeking input on the CMG.

At the time, Access Fund was itself still a new organization, having been born from the Access Committee of the American Alpine Club (AAC) in 1985. The committee's purpose was to examine and address closures of climbing areas partly in response to the creation of sport climbing. Rapid growth in the number of issues at hand demonstrated a need for a standalone organization focused solely on access. The Access Fund's involvement in the Red quickly escalated the region to the national stage and made climbing there an early test case for working with the Forest Service. The Access Fund, in talking with Shannon, explained the public input process and that climbers would need to be involved in the public meetings.

Shannon found a strong ally in fellow attorney, John Bronaugh. Christina Bronaugh said she felt that John and Shannon balanced each other out, a sort of yin and yang. Shannon's still limited climbing experience was balanced by John's extensive and respected climbing pedigree. John's dogged pursuit of what he thought right was balanced by Shannon's measured approach to the situation at hand. But before anything could happen with the RRGCC, John suggested that he and Shannon go climbing first. "I felt that it was a bit of a test, to see if I was worthy, so to speak," Shannon recalled. They arrived at *Long Wall* and started up the challenging route. "Boom! Boom! Out Go the Lights." John and Stacy Temple put up this 5.10b sport route in 1992 before the bolting ban began. Shannon's verdict? "I passed the test [laughs]!"

Early participants in the RRGCC included Kris Snyder, Bob Matheny, Hugh Loeffler, Jeff Neal, Shannon, and John.[26] What came out of those early meetings were ideas that remain even today. The RRGCC's purpose was to secure and protect climbing access throughout the Red and to promote conservation of the environment surrounding climbing areas. Their vision statement clearly lists climbing as a privilege that must be earned and carefully maintained. This included working closely with public land managers and private landowners to ensure access, as well as being good guests on those properties.

These were lofty ideals for the time. Recall that climbers had not been organized in any group dynamic since the Cumberland Climbers back when there were far fewer climbers inside the Red. Now, the RRGCC sought to represent an unknown number of climbers among a less tightly knit community and to do so amid divisions over bolting and the future of the Red. Leadership would prove key, much as it was in the day of the Cumberland Climbers, if this were to work. John served as president for two formative years. This allowed him to be directly involved as the face of the RRGCC while also working as an attorney with Becker Law in Lexington. Shannon served as executive director. Shannon had the advantage that she ran her own firm and could set her own hours and handpick projects, allowing her time to work on the important early elements of the RRGCC. She would eventually set up the RRGCC office in her own house in Lexington.

Shannon argued (and still does today) that climbers were *guests* on the Forest Service land. In turn, the Forest Service was a gatekeeper that could legally deny climbers entry to those climbing routes. Part of this was the story of access: "To get to the routes, you need trails. Those trails are on Forest Service land, which makes you a guest on another's land." Shannon agreed that climbers were out of compliance at the time due to bolting, user trails, and the like. Now, she wanted to rectify that and build a new relationship with the Forest Service that would benefit everyone in the future.

Shannon explained that she "didn't see this as incompatible with our quest to get climbing." In fact, if anything, it reinforced why climbers, as users of public lands, should be present at the discussion table and be on healthy terms with the Forest Service. The CMG had made it clear that the DBNF wanted to work with climbers. The RRGCC would put this into practice. This meant working together on issues like trail development, reinforcing desirable minimal-impact behaviors at the crag, and identifying populations of cliff-line threatened and endangered species. Less formally, it even included getting Forest Service employees out to the crags, putting harnesses on them, and letting them learn, firsthand, how those bolts were being used. Shannon and John Bronaugh also worked with the Forest Service's Donnie Richardson to visit many of the crags in the area to identify areas where there might be a problem in the future with regard to natural resources, endangered flora or fauna, or archaeological sites that might require protection through mitigation or route closures.

Amid the RRGCC's early work, climbing continued to grow in the Red. Porter Jarrard and Chris Snyder published a 1997 guide highlighting what they felt were the best routes in the Red. This guide, *Selected Climbs at Red River Gorge, Kentucky*, represented another important milestone: a moment where the Red had so many routes, one could create a guide solely on the selected best routes. One of the biggest additions for this guide was the inclusion of *The Motherlode*, the first major expansion of climbing routes outside of DBNF territory.

At the time, *The Motherlode* represented some of the newest, hardest climbs in the Red. All five parts of the crag were included—*Buckeye Buttress, Warm-up Wall, GMC Wall, Madness Cave*, and *Undertow*—totaling 51 selected routes. (Because this was a selected route guide, there may actually have been more routes, but as this is the earliest listing of routes there, it is not possible to make a comparison.) *Undertow* (at 20 routes) then held the bulk of the routes, and no route listed in the guide at *The Motherlode* was lower than 5.11a.

The highest difficulty route ranking route at the crag was a 5.13d (now 5.13c) by Dave Hume called "White Man's Overbite," located at *GMC Wall*. At *Madness Cave* stood the 5.13c eponymous "The Madness," a 120-foot and 13-bolt sport route first ascended by Jeff Moll using aid and first ascended without aid by Brian Toy.[27] And in the surrounding subareas of the crag were another five 5.13b routes ("Golden Touch" at *Buckeye Buttress*, "Take That, Katie Brown!" at *Warm-up Wall*, "Cutthroat" at *GMC Wall*, and "BOHICA" and "Flour Power" at *Madness Cave*).

This guide also added *Pocket Wall* to the list of southern crags. *Pocket Wall* was aptly named after its many pockets. Pockets varied in sizes (John Bronaugh explained that the pockets ranged from "bullet holes to huge huecos") and offered a place for climbers to put their fingers, hands, or even feet to ascend.[28] The treacherous road to *Pocket Wall* followed an old off-roading and oil access road that led up to and then drove *over* White's Branch Arch. The crag, however, was before the arch, and the Jarrard and Snyder guide notes that if you arrived at the arch, you had missed your turn. The area was a long-standing part of the local (and regional) OHV/ATV community as well as local horse enthusiasts. Climbers similarly fell in love with this area. By this point in 1997, Jarrard and Snyder already describe *Pocket Wall* as one of the most popular crags to get to despite the extreme difficulty in accessing the area. In all, the guide included 19 routes at the crag. The earliest routes at *Pocket Wall* were completed by Eric Anderson ("D-Day," "First Blood," "Friendly Fire"); Neal Strickland ("Lucky Streak"); Tim Cornette ("Tar Baby," "Blackwater," "Mississippi Moon," "Passion Phish," "Dog-Faced Boy"); Porter Jarrard ("Black Flag," "The Mushroom Bruise," "The Cult of Ray"); and Zeb Olson ("Alone").

The guide also included *Torrent Falls*. This crag, which shares its name with the business Torrent Falls, had a very interesting local history before its climbing days. In the late 1800s, Torrent (as it was locally known) had been part of the timber industry, which later led to the development of the L. Park Hotel. The hotel was situated in front of a waterfall (hence the name Torrent Falls), which also included an amphitheater and dance pavilion with seating built to fit 1,000 people. Building such amphitheaters in large crags of this type is not entirely uncommon in the Red River Gorge, although most were not developed to this extent. Natural circular crags sometimes offer very effective acoustics and provide shelter from the rain and a comfy place to relax while being entertained on a weekend.

In 1917, oil was found nearby in the Big Sinking Oil Fields, making the hotel and surrounding area into a boom town. Long after the boom subsided, the hotel continued attracting clients to the Red seeking natural cures and relaxation, until it burned down in 1926 or 1927. Note that torrentfallsclimbing.com includes a picture of the hotel that is worth seeing. John Bronaugh's second-edition guide (discussed later in this book) also provides (on page 295) a picture of ice columns that sometimes form at the falls.

Climbing eventually found its way to Torrent Falls. Climbers visited the crag in the 1980s, putting up a few routes (including "Windy Corner," a 1983 5.11b hand crack FA'd by Tom Souders) before moving on to other areas. Sport climbers revisited the area in 1993 and, finding a blank wall full of possibilities, began bolting the area. The Jarrard and Snyder guide originally split the area into subareas *Torrent Falls Left*, *The 5.12 Wall*, *The 5.13 Wall*, and *Torrent Falls Right*, which collectively included 21 routes. (Looking into the future, a *5.10 Wall* would later be added.) However, an absentee landowner of the property briefly shut down climbing at the site following the early 1993 bolting blitz by Porter Jarrard and Jeff Moll. The property was soon purchased by Fred Martin, who built his home, a bed-and-breakfast, and parking on the property. He allowed climbers to continue using the crag, requesting a $2 donation for parking, making this one of the early examples (if not earliest) of a pay-to-play climbing location in the Red.

Another important contribution of the Jarrard and Snyder guide is that it sets a new standard (at least among sport climbers) for understanding climbing ethics of the era. First, they note the importance of *not* bolting routes in the DBNF: "USFS Stanton Ranger District currently views bolting as an illegal activity, tantamount to vandalism and destruction of public property. Quality sport routes have caused a surge in the popularity of rock climbing in Kentucky. Climbers, unfortunately, are not the only people interested in all the new sport routes."[29] They go on to state that bolting a route on public land would require going through the policies described in the CMG but complain that the CMG itself is "quite restrictive and obsequious in nature."

The authors also note that climbing in the Red (whether on public or private land) is a privilege and that climbers must behave accordingly. Their write-up on *The Motherlode* similarly notes the need to be considerate in working with oil company access in the area. Likewise, the guide includes recommendations on bolting, encouraging planning in creating new routes: "Remember that a new route is like a work of art with your signature on it. Be a craftsman and people will enjoy your route for years to come."[30] Finally, the guide encourages caution in cleaning new routes but not chipping new holds. Chipping involves manufacturing new holds by removing bits of rock, sometimes involving a hammer and chisel, drill, and/or glue.[31] Porter and Chris note there is a "fine line between cleaning a route for safety and chipping. . . . Some climbers consider the removal of any rock from a climb as chipping, just as some climbers consider chalk and sticky rubber as forms of aid."[32]

There are a few useful historical notes in the Jarrard and Snyder guide that deserve special mention. First, the guide notes at this point that *The Motherlode* was now owned by Mother Lode Inc. (slightly different spelling), and the new owners had "recently posted a large warning sign at the lower parking area, advising climbers to obtain permission before going up to the cliff. Permission could be given on sight using a blank liability waiver which could be deposited in the collection box near the sign." [33] Second, the guide included the most detailed maps to date of any guide in the Red, which were the product of one of Jarrard's many skillsets. The guide includes three maps of *Military Wall* and its surrounding region alone. It also includes numerous photographs of some of the era's great climbers on the routes featured in the guide. Third, the guide includes a whole page dedicated to the Access Fund, a national climbing organization then in its sixth year. The page includes the basics of minimum-impact practices (often referred to as Leave No Trace) so climbers could reduce their impact on climbing areas. Interestingly, the description also includes a note to "join or form a local group to deal with access issues," something that was already occurring at that time in the Red via the RRGCC.[34] Despite its youth, the RRGCC would soon prove to be an important part of the climbing community's history.

CHAPTER 8

White-Haired Goldenrod and the Memorandum of Understanding, 1997–2000

In 2018, botanist Thomas Steele McFadden created the first complete inventory of plants in the Red. Thomas shared that this inventory notes over 1,000 known plant species, "which excludes moss and liverworts," but includes many rare species, along with the beloved white-haired goldenrod.[1] The white-haired goldenrod (*Solidago albopilosa, albo* meaning white and *pilosa* meaning hair) grows in the Red River Gorge, eking out its survival in the shady spots along the mineral-rich drip lines of the Red's rockshelters and ledges. Its yellow flowers and the small white hairs on its leaves and stem are a whimsical but mostly unnoticed part of the Red's autumn landscape. Still, to the white-haired goldenrod, this is home. It loves spending all its time in the Red's rockshelters.

The white-haired goldenrod stands out among its family. Thomas explains that "when you drive down the road, look out in a field, and see a sea of yellow, that's all goldenrod, but . . . there's like thirty-four species of goldenrod in Kentucky." It turns out that many of these other goldenrod species are taller with larger flowers. They also are not nearly as finicky about their home turf conditions and will grow wild most wherever they like, including roadside ditches or fallow fields.

This is not true for their mountain cousin, the white-haired goldenrod, which is smaller (only getting a half-meter tall or less), has yellow flowers located in the axis of the leaves, and is decidedly picky about where it drops its roots. It loves the acidity of rockshelter drip lines and the nutrient-laden hydration those seeps bring. "The leaves are markedly different, too," Thomas adds. "A lot of the goldenrods you see in the fields have really long linear shaped leaves and white-haired goldenrod has more of a deltoid shaped leaf [triangle-shaped] with serration around the edge." At face value, the plant does not stand out as a visually stunning plant among the many wildflowers of the

Red. And there are even other forest-grown goldenrods that look similar to the white-haired goldenrod. But this special plant is the only one to bear the visibly evident white hairs that give the plant its name. Thomas notes that it is herbaceous, meaning "there's no wood about it. . . . You could squish it or if you stepped on it, you'd trample it." [2] Based on its genetic preferences, the plant's uncommon choice of territory overlaps with another creature of the Red: *Homo sapiens*. The Red's popular sandstone arches and rockshelters place visitor foot traffic exactly where the white-haired goldenrod would most likely be found, leading to trampling of entire populations.

The US Fish and Wildlife Service listed the plant as endangered in 1988 due to concerns over habitat damage in recreational areas. DBNF and the Kentucky State Nature Preserves Commission sought to identify existing colonies and fence them to prevent walking through the area. They also proposed increased signage to help protect the plant. Undoubtedly, this was an important official step, but government bodies can only do so much given limited resources and insufficient feet on the ground. That's where community partners are quite valuable in protecting resources.

One of the early efforts of Shannon Stuart-Smith, John Bronaugh, the RRGCC, and the climbing community as a whole was to help protect the white-haired goldenrod alongside the DBNF. The 1996 CMG spelled it out clearly: climbers could (and should) work with the DBNF to help protect the cliff lines as a solid approach to maintaining access. Moreover, climbers were regularly in the very crags where this plant was found. Now that they were aware of the plant's presence—through its pictures and descriptions at climbing kiosks and in guidebooks, starting with Bronaugh's second-edition guide—climbers could be part of the solution.

Climbers located and shared several large colonies of the white-haired goldenrod with the DBNF. Shannon herself found one especially large colony that had been previously overlooked. Gradually, multiple colonies were fenced off and protected with signage. This partnership is an ideal example of how outdoor recreation users and public land managers can work together for everyone's best interests.

This unique relationship reached a milestone in August 2015 when Kentucky State Nature Preserves Commission field studies reported that 117 groupings of the plant had been identified (111 on Forest Service land, the rest on private property), with 81 groups listed as stable and, most importantly, 46 listed as stable and self-sustaining. This was enough to support the proposed delisting of the plant from the endangered species list, *a first in the state of Kentucky*. US Fish and Wildlife's report on white-haired goldenrod stated that it could be delisted specifically because "all threats to the species have been eliminated or significantly reduced, adequate regulatory mechanisms exist, and a sufficient number of populations are stable, self-sustaining, and protected."[3] Barring issues in the required five years of public opinion input or unexpected changes in protected colonies, the plant will presumably be delisted in the coming years.

Climbers, including RRGCC executive director Bill Strachan, attended the 2015 Fish and Wildlife Service delisting ceremony at the Gladie Visitor Center in the Red.[4] Later that day, Forest Service officials (among them, the new Cumberland District ranger, Jonathan Kazmierski), climbers, and other attendees hiked together to a rockshelter to examine a white-haired goldenrod plant colony. There, they discussed how the fencing and signage protected the plant colony and how working together had made a major difference in delisting the species.

While climbers were getting to know the white-haired goldenrod in the mid- and late 1990s, the DBNF (and the Forest Service in general) was quietly grappling with another issue: they were being sued over logging practices on public lands. Kentucky Heartwood formed in 1992 and called for a complete stop to timbering (or zero cut) on national forest land. Their mission statement (per their website) is "to protect and restore the integrity, stability, and beauty of Kentucky's native forests and biotic communities through research, education, advocacy, and community engagement." Kentucky Heartwood positioned itself as an independent watchdog agency. In a weird twist of events, their litigation would indirectly change how climbers experienced the Red in just a few short years. The suit also again addresses the difficulties experienced by the Forest Service in balancing different kinds of resources, in this case timbering and the red-cockaded woodpecker.

Kentucky Heartwood embodied three important areas of environmental activism. First was a growing sense of public engagement and environmental activism in the region that followed the Sierra Club's and others' resistance to the Red River Gorge Dam proposals of the 1970s. Second was the Earth First! movement, a direct-action movement founded in 1979. Earth First! has long been celebrated (and sometimes reviled) for its environmental advocacy, including a nationwide call to action against commercial logging in the mid-1980s. Third was regional organizing grounded in a shared love of the forests, such as the DBNF.

A growing regional network of forest activists began meeting at the Lazy Black Bear (home to Linda Lee and Andy Mahler) in Paoli, Indiana, starting in the winter of 1989. Initially called Heartwood, this network of activists from several midwestern states challenged Forest Service approval of logging, mining, and OHV use on public lands. Today, Heartwood includes an 18-state region including the Ozarks, Appalachia, the Ohio River basin, and the Cumberland Plateau. Kentucky would soon form its own chapter as part of the greater Heartwood network.

Chris Schimmoeller served as Kentucky Heartwood's volunteer coordinator. She recalled this was a perfect storm for young environmentalists: "You don't learn about federal law and the public involvement process in school, so going to Heartwood meetings was like this incredibly dynamic classroom. There I was, a young person in this circle of regular people who loved the land and were willing to learn about the law and our rights as the ultimate owners of public land. People willing to stick their necks out to publicly defend, publicly champion protection of our lands. They were all my heroes." Chris had strong ties to the forest and to activism. Her parents were Peace Corps volunteers also active in civil rights in the early 1960s. As a Fulbright Scholar to India, Chris had protested against the construction of a hydroelectric dam in the Himalayas. She would soon play an important part in the story of the DBNF from multiple angles.

Chris led multiple actions against the Forest Service during her decade-long tenure as coordinator of Kentucky Heartwood. She received no pay and worked in primitive conditions, but she had few complaints. "I worked out of my family's log cabin, no phone, no electricity, no running water. I biked to the neighbor's to use the phone and I typed on a manual typewriter for our appeals. It was just an extraordinary time of passionate commitment, hard work, and joy," Chris recalled. "I remember learning clearly, it was in the third grade, that my teacher told me, 'You're getting an education so you can participate in democracy.' And this was just such a rich and immediate example of that. I believed that we were making our country and our world better because we were . . . learning the law and insisting it be followed." Now based in Berea (in Madison County), Kentucky Heartwood recently celebrated their 28th anniversary. Their core concern remains the growing uptick in commercial logging on DBNF land.

A century earlier, the United States was risking a future timber famine because of unchecked tree harvesting. Timbering at the time ran with relatively limited oversight, and commercial timber operations could access forests with relative ease. Presidents from around the turn of the century certainly saw a pending crisis. Benjamin Harrison founded three national parks in 1890: Sequoia, Yosemite, and General Grant (the latter of which would later be included in King's Canyon). He also set aside a million acres of forest in western states, as well as establishing the Yellowstone Park Timberland Reserve to further protect Yellowstone. Grover Cleveland similarly established forest reserve acreage and signed the Yellowstone Act to protect animals on federal lands. Theodore Roosevelt established 150 national forests, 51 bird reserves, four game preserves, five national parks (including Crater Lake, Wind Cave, and Mesa Verde), and 18 national monuments. He also signed the 1906 American Antiquities Act (the first law to establish protections for archaeological sites on public lands) and added land to Yosemite National Park. Roosevelt would also establish the United States Forest Service via the Transfer Act of 1905. At the helm of this new Forest Service was a forester named Gifford Pinchot.

Gifford graduated from Yale (where he would also later found the famous Yale Forest School) and learned European forestry management techniques in France and Germany. Prior to the Forest Service, he served as head of the Division of Forestry under the McKinley administration, established the Society of American Foresters, and served on the National Forest Commission. Gifford participated in a four-month tour of the American West as part of his National Forest Commission work. There, he would develop a friendship with climber and future Sierra Club president, John Muir.[5]

Muir and Gifford shared a mutual life-altering love of nature, but they did not entirely agree on how it should be managed. Gifford took a utilitarian approach to forest management, utilizing tree counting and scientific principles to support timber harvests while also managing forests. Gifford saw value in the use of nature for human advancement yet also the need to preserve this resource for future generations. This idea was summarized in what he often described as the greatest good for the greatest number in the long run. Muir partly disagreed. John could certainly support long-term protections of natural resources. However, reflecting on his early days in Yosemite, John saw the value of the government protecting nature as it was so that humans could experience nature as it was, then letting nature self-manage these wonders. Likewise he felt the nation's grand forests should be preserved in perpetuity by the federal government, limiting timbering to common trees and timbering those sparingly. These two occasionally discordant ideologies remain present in the Forest Service's struggles even today.

Around the time that John Muir and Gifford Pinchot began their intellectual relationship, timber companies like the Red River Lumber Mills were providing vast amounts of lumber to the region. Recall that the mill was the biggest in the state in the 1890s and was reportedly one of the largest in the nation. Over the next few decades, timbering would continue as harvested areas slowly regrew. Perhaps surprisingly, even after decades of active timbering in the area, select virgin timber stands remained in the region. Robert F. Collins reflects on one of these stands at Leatherwood Creek in Perry County, which is near the Red, in his history of the DBNF.

Collins notes that Dr. E. Lucy Braun, a botanist at the University of Cincinnati, gave a talk on March 29, 1935, at a meeting of the Garden Club of Kentucky. In this talk, Dr. Braun described the beauty of virgin forests there, including a gigantic poplar tree with a 24-foot circumference. She noted that this area was now at risk because the Leatherwood Lumber Company held the timber rights to the property and was actively harvesting in the next branch over from Leatherwood Creek. At the time, Cumberland National Forest (although not officially declared yet) was acquiring land that would eventually become today's Daniel Boone National Forest. Dr. Braun encouraged persons attending her talk to rally to have the Leatherwood property purchased by the new national forest. Numerous formal requests asked the Forest Service to step in, and Collins notes this request gained a lot of political and social support, including important figures such as Kentucky governor A. B. Chandler and Tom Wallace of the *Louisville Times*. Nonetheless, Forest Service chief land examiner (Region 7) W. E. Hedges replied to the request that the property was already owned by Kentucky River Coal Corporation and was not for sale. Forest Service records note that the virgin timber harvest at Leatherwood was timbered around 1936. Public anger likely focused on the Forest Service somehow failing to do their jobs even while they were not the landowners or able to purchase or prevent the timbering, which had been contracted long before a national forest was even considered in the area.

Over 30 years later, another timber cut would catch the attention of the Cumberland Chapter of the Sierra Club (CCSC) and news media amid the debate over the Red River Dam. This case further explains the difficulties of timbering national forests. In February 1969, the CCSC inquired about a timber sale at the head of Reffitt's Branch. The forest supervisor explained this was not a timber sale but a selective cut to support the regeneration of hardwood trees in the area by "releasing sprouts of white oak, tulip poplar, hickory, and hemlock through a cutting of the remnants of undesirable trees of poor species, form and defect left by the logging operations of many years before."[6] Much to the dismay of the CCSC (which demanded a full stop of timbering pending a Sierra Club investigation), the project had been in place for over a year and could not be stopped. A later review showed that the DBNF had also followed policies such as the Multiple Use Act of 1960, which balanced multiple uses of Forest Service land alongside sustainable yields from resources such as trees.

The CCSC next tried other approaches. They attempted to stop the cut by buying out the timber company, which declined a financial offer to stop timbering. The Sierra Club then utilized the national spotlight on the Red River Dam to push their requests. This led the Sierra Club and Audubon Society in 1970 to propose the area be removed from Forest Service control and be made a national park or wilderness area. At this stage, the Forest Service realized the power of the Sierra Club at the national level. The Forest Service opted to reexamine all timber harvests at the DBNF while a study of the entire Red could be done to understand how the area could be protected and administered "to render a maximum of service and enjoyment to people."[7] Although this would not be a total pause on timber harvests, it did reduce it and also set a precedent for other groups to challenge the Forest Service.

Jumping ahead two decades, Kentucky Heartwood continued the work of organizations like the CCSC and Sierra Club in the DBNF by examining timber practices. Kentucky Heartwood's goal was to act as a watchdog, ensuring that the Forest Service followed the rules whenever doing logging cuts. As a result, Kentucky Heartwood estimates that their oversight in the region reduced logging by up to 97 percent in the DBNF over time.[8]

In its first decade, Kentucky Heartwood filed multiple legal challenges and suits against the Forest Service, collectively calling for an end to commercial logging over several years. Kentucky Heartwood's first legal action against the DBNF in 1994 (the same year the bolting ban was issued) questioned the legality of the Forest Service's logging of old pines in the southern half of the DBNF. The pines offered an important habitat for the endangered red-cockaded woodpecker. Kentucky Heartwood uncovered an internal memo through the Freedom of Information Act in which a Forest Service wildlife manager had requested a stop to timbering old pines because it was endangering the bird's habitat.[9]

Kentucky Heartwood filed a 60-day notice of intent to sue. Chris recalls, "I remember leading 20–25 media vehicles down into a remote part of the forest for a media tour to show them trees marked for logging." In light of the lawsuit, DBNF voluntarily halted logging efforts and developed a plan to examine and address environmental impacts of the logging activity as it pertained to the red-cockaded woodpecker. The voluntary shutdown stopped logging on the southern half of the forest for nearly a year while the Forest Service worked to ensure compliance with the law.

This shutdown put Kentucky Heartwood on the map but also opened them to criticism. Chris recounts the local resistance: "They had a 70-vehicle caravan in protest of Kentucky Heartwood in McCreary County." The logging halt came too late, as the red-cockaded woodpecker's habitat had already been compromised. Droughts in the area also opened the pine stands to a southern pine beetle infestation. The dozen or so remaining red-cockaded woodpeckers were relocated to South Carolina and Arkansas around 2001.[10]

Following their 1994 legal success in the southern end of the DBNF,

Kentucky Heartwood sued the Forest Service in 1997 to stop proposed logging in the Red. The suit challenged clear-cutting timber on 199 acres in the Leatherwood Fork area (located in Powell and Menifee Counties). This area was home to the endangered Indiana bat. The suit claimed that the Forest Service had again placed the interests of logging over the interests of other mandates (such as endangered species) and had violated the Endangered Species Act in the process. (Recall that bats were also mentioned in the CMG in 1996.) Again, the suit noted a lack of compliance with the US Fish and Wildlife Service to protect listed species when conducting timber sales. While the court case worked through the system, Kentucky Heartwood was ready and waiting on the ground at Leatherwood Fork. Chris vividly remembers the blockade protest there: "We had found out when the Forest Service was going to do their timber cruise with potential timber buyers. We set up a blockade, had signs and people all over the area. . . . Of course the Forest Service changed their plans. They didn't show up, so we didn't get to actually have a conversation. But we won. We won, we stopped it, and it is still protected."

The lawsuit again turned in favor of Kentucky Heartwood. The order required that timbering immediately stop, pending formal consultation with US Fish and Wildlife Service regarding impacts on endangered species, including the Indiana bat. Next, Kentucky Heartwood utilized the specific language in the judge's decision, particularly that logging interests had superseded those of endangered species, to go after logging on the *entire* DBNF. They argued that the entire forest included the Indiana bat's habitat, and if the finding held true in the Red, it should hold true for the entire forest. In effect, if policies protecting species weren't being followed, then timbering had to stop. This challenge in 1998 led to a four-year closure on DBNF logging. US District Judge Karl S. Forester ruled that no further logging could take place there until the Forest Service implemented a legal plan to protect the Indiana bat during management activities such as timbering. Timbering would not restart until 2002.

While Kentucky Heartwood and the DBNF were battling it out in court, John Bronaugh, in 1998, followed up with the second edition of his comprehensive climbing guide. Ray Ellington (author of a game-changing series of guides discussed later in the book) described the importance of Bronaugh's 1998 guide: "John's book, the second edition, was the one that included the sport climbs in the southern region . . . these new areas like *Drive-By Crag* and stuff like that we'd never heard of." John's updated guide now contained over 1,000 routes in the Red, the sum work of climbers in the region. John believed that the discovery of *The Motherlode* had "probably put the Red on the world climbing map for good," arguing, "That one crag alone has the largest collection of the most difficult climbs than any other area in the Red." His guide offered the first comprehensive summary of climbing route difficulties in the Red: it now had three 5.14 routes (a skill level that rivaled most any climbing destination, as no 5.15 had yet been sent (ascended) until 2001's "Realization" in France by Chris Sharma). Moreover, the number of 5.13s had grown from 3 a few years back to a respectable 26 routes.[11]

Bronaugh's updated guide expanded the shared knowledge of the southern region. *The Motherlode* had seen a lot of growth, most notably the addition of a 5.14 rating on a frightening line called "Thanatopsis" at *GMC Wall*. Dave Hume was setting a new standard for strong climbing in the Red. Hume had started climbing young. At age 14, he was competing with the likes of Chris Sharma (also 14) and Tommy Caldwell (17 years old) in national championship events. That was in 1995. In 1996, and only at age 15, Dave sent "Thanatopsis," a top contender for hardest route in the Red at the time, a feat very few climbers have since matched.[12]

More crags were added to the list just down the road from *The Motherlode* on private land: *Bob Marley Crag, Drive-By Crag,* and *Oil Crack Rock. Bob Marley* was originally listed with 14 routes, and the crag was still being developed per the guide. The earliest route at the crag was the only trad line there, a route called "Tony's Happy Christmas Crack," which held an FA date from December 1994 by Jack Hume, Tony Tramontin, Steve McFarland, Gene Hume, and David Hume. The rest were sport routes, some of which were still listed as a specific climber's project. The sport skill levels at *Bob Marley* ranged from 5.11 to 5.13. The 5.13s included Hugh Loeffler's project "Fifty Words for Pump" at 5.13d and Chris Martin's project "Ultra-Perm" at 5.13c. "Ultra-Perm" would stay open until David Hume earned the FA in 1997. "Fifty Words for Pump" stayed open for another decade. That FA would actually be at the heart of a historic 2007 event (and some controversy) and will be described in a later chapter.

Nearby *Drive-By Crag* added another 18 routes, including seven 5.12s and one 5.13. Like *Bob Marley Crag*, several were still projects, including David Hume's open project, "The Nothing," which was originally described as a 5.13c. He would finish the route in 1999 and change the rating to 5.14a, making it another one of the 20 or so hardest climbs in the Red even today. Another nearby Hume route, "Dirty Smelly Hippie," is a common starting route for climbers moving into the 5.13b range.

Meanwhile, *Oil Crack Rock*—so named for a "striking crack which has a slimy ooze emanating from its base"—added two routes then considered to be 5.14s: "Skeletor" (a 5.14b) and "A Clean Well Lighted Face" (5.14a).[13] In all, 13 routes at *Oil Crack Rock* were listed in the guide, including two routes with John Bronaugh's name attached. *Oil Crack Rock* suddenly reflected how valuable climbing in this general region would prove to be, and it also raised a very important issue that would define the coming decades for climbers: how climbers can secure land and guarantee climbing access.

Reflecting on the value of the recent expansions in the southern region, Hugh Loeffler had a realization: all this expansion was on private land and could literally be stripped away from the climbers.[14] Landowners were not always being approached about bolting and climbing on the property. This could result in a situation where an unhappy owner shuts everything down. When Loeffler realized the value of those potential 5.14 lines at *Oil Crack Rock*, he decided he needed to find the owner. He began asking oil workers found around the area (recall that there are even today multiple oil wells in the area), which soon led to the Murray family. Hugh made contact with James Paul Murray, who lived nearby on Fixer Road. Hugh recalled putting all the cards on the table: "Look man, here's the deal: We want to climb on your land, and if we climb there we are going to bolt some routes. You have world-class property. If you let us bolt there, you will have lots of people climbing on your land." Murray acquiesced to allowing climbing, valuing that people would be enjoying the land, but he said he didn't want to know anything about it. The importance of this initial conversation is revisited in later chapters.[15]

One crag developed in the late 1990s that was absent in the new Bronaugh guide was called *Hominy Hole*. The crag takes its name from the bedrock mortars (sometimes abbreviated as BRMs or informally called hominy holes) found in the rocks around the crag. Bedrock mortars were theoretically used as part of Indigenous food production. However, their use is not entirely understood even today. The Red River Museum, located in Powell County, has several replica bedrock mortars created by Johnny Faulkner. Johnny worked with the Forest Service on archaeology digs, including one at *Military Wall*. Fully appreciating both the *Hominy Hole* and *Military Wall* crags requires reflecting on what the past can teach us about human survival, beginning with the bedrock mortar.

Larry Meadows is a respected folk historian and avocational archaeologist in Powell County. Larry is an important part of the Red River Museum, a place that tells the story of the region woven within a quiet narrative about the survival of both Appalachian and Indigenous peoples amid all that nature could throw their way. Along the main building's exterior wall are numerous millstones, many of which came from valleys and towns near the museum.[16] "That's one of my favorites," Larry told me during our interview, pointing at a millstone that came from a river channel field nearby. The conglomerate pebbles in the millstone reflected a glint of sun as we stood in Kentucky's breathless humidity. Larry explained how the sedimentary rock formations in the area formed over time, leaving the unique rock inclusions that make one millstone stand out from another. These millstones were used by locals to create food: "At first, it's a feed. It slowly feeds and radiates, spirals around and it works its way out and out and that's the way the corn is ground into cornmeal."

Larry explained that Indigenous peoples have been using a related process using bedrock mortars by pounding and pulverizing material such as seeds, nuts, and berries against bedrock. The process slowly creates indentions (some surprisingly deep) in the bedrock over time. Faulkner's efforts to recreate bedrock mortars at the museum are an important applied effort to recreate an activity that is not fully understood today. Larry explained, "With all the work Cecil Ison, Johnny [Faulkner], Vernon White, [William] Webb, and [William] Funkhouser [have] done, there's so many unanswered questions. It's all theoretical." Larry is excited about Johnny's work because efforts to recreate these early technologies help archaeologists know more about Indigenous peoples, as well as our own reliance on the resources around us to survive through use of the land.

Nearby, in a log shed behind the museum, is a display about niter mining in the Red and the frontier work of more recent residents. The display includes a rare movable trough used to separate the niter (which is water soluble) from pulverized sandstone.[17] The niter was used as a lower-quality substitute for making gunpowder when French gunpowder stocks were unavailable during the War of 1812.[18] There also may have been other uses, as smaller mines existed other than during wartime. Even though niter mines date far more recently than bedrock mortars, researchers today are still unlocking exactly how niter mining was done. Like the bedrock mortars, the extraction process for niter is mostly theoretical, and efforts to recreate niter mining have not been entirely successful. From time to time, these troughs still pop up, and dozens have been documented by the Forest Service over the years near rockshelters.[19]

Inside the Red River Museum, the story continues: a long history of that important relationship between life and resources, including taxidermies of local animal life (both past and present), common daily tools, food cans and tins more familiar to my grandmother than to me, Civil War woolen uniforms seemingly fresh from conflict, and even old sheepskin diplomas from another era of the academy. In another case is a section of the High Rock petroglyphs from the Nada Tunnel Area.[20] These petroglyphs were carved by Indigenous peoples living in one of the Red's many rockshelters. The museum worked with Dr. Clifton Smith to remove the petroglyph to protect it from vandals. Alongside attempting to recreate bedrock mortars, Johnny Faulkner has also made great strides in attempting to recreate petroglyphs to better understand the tools used by Indigenous peoples.

Preserving resources like bedrock mortars, niter troughs, petroglyphs, endangered flora and fauna, and countless other important resources while also balancing use of the area for timbering and recreation makes the Forest Service's job a truly difficult work. Certain areas, once identified as an area needing protection, can be fenced and signed. For example, fencing off a section of white-haired goldenrod along with signage explaining the plant's protected status is sufficient to keep nearly anyone out of the fenced area. However, fencing archaeological areas can have a deleterious effect: it brings the area to the attention of looters. The Forest Service keeps private lists of known archaeological areas and regularly visits each area to check for impacts and issues. Employees sometimes visit sites out of uniform just to prevent the chance that someone might see them and retrace their hike to the protected area.

Looting is a serious issue in the Red and in many other national forests. It is both illegal and unethical to dig for artifacts in national forests. As the DBNF website points out, "Artifacts include anything made or used by humans including arrowheads or flakes, pottery, basketry, rock art, bottles, coins, and even old cans."[21] Looting permanently disturbs the archaeological record, including its placement amid the structure and composition of the site. Cultural resources like artifacts are protected by numerous laws, including the American Antiquities Act of 1906, the Archaeological Resources Protection Act of 1979, the National Historic Preservation Act, and the Native American Graves Protection and Repatriation Act. Going through rockshelters in the Red, it is fairly easy to identify signs of previous looting. "Once you know what they look like, you'll begin seeing them everywhere in the Red," Mary White, an archaeologist in the DBNF London Ranger District, shared while on an informational walk through Forest Service land. She pointed out the strange piles of dirt amid shelters and the numerous holes around the drip lines. "See those odd piles of dirt? This site has been looted."

While on a visit with Forest Service archaeologists Randy Boedy and Matthew Davidson to document a niter mine in the Beaver Creek Wilderness (in the southern end of DBNF), we found an entire suite of looting tools hidden on site. As I walked along the back edge of the shelter, I noticed a bucket, pry bar, screen, and shovel masked from easy detection in the lee of a boulder. The telltale holes amid piles of sifted dirt were prevalent in the shelter. Bits of chert were noticeably scattered throughout the shelter, confirming this had been an Indigenous use site now thoroughly impacted by looters.

Unmarked areas, while a valid way to protect known archaeological sites, can create complications with climbing. Tim Eling with the DBNF explained why: "Climbing is different from other types of recreation and it's one that land management agencies have really struggled with over the decades. It's not a recreation feature that is put in by the agency . . . they're put in through organizations and individuals. In that way, they're almost like these user group-created recreation features which . . . can provide some challenges." In the case of an activity like hiking, the Forest Service can design the trails so they avoid problematic areas, such as a known archaeological site. With climbing (at least, up to this point), climbers had installed their own routes and created user trails without notifying the DBNF. The rapid growth in the Red since the appearance of sport routes and the flood of climbers into the area had exacerbated this issue. Tim expounded on this issue:

> In the 60s and 70s it was relatively light, mostly trad climbing. It wasn't really a big deal, but when all those sport routes came in, and with that a lot more people, then some of the Forest Service resource specialists . . . became concerned about things like trampling of white-haired goldenrod, an endangered plant that grows nowhere else in the world other than rockshelters and cliff line in the Red River Gorge, right where the climbers like to go. Archaeological sites being impacted by increasing amounts of people going into cliff lines, and so I think that's what happened. . . . It caught them off guard when all those sport routes came in.

A perfect storm of miscommunications led to a major conflict between climbers and the DBNF at *Hominy Hole*. *Hominy Hole* first saw climbing route development around 1997 or possibly even 1998. In all, around a dozen routes were added to the property in just two years. The DBNF realized the rockshelter there held archaeological interest but had not marked it to help prevent looting. Climbers mistakenly believed the area was on private property, not Forest Service land. Adding still further confusion, climbers assumed (wrongly) that nearby logging activity meant they were clear to go. Hugh Loeffler, who developed a route called "Red Headed Step Child" at the crag recalled that someone was "actively logging out there. There was a D-10 bulldozer parked 25 feet from the base at one point, and we were like, 'This place is good to go.'" What they could not have known (as these are not made public) is that this area had seen a Phase II archaeological dig.

Johnny Faulkner described the importance of the area: "We decided to do Phase II excavation there, I think we put in maybe three test units. . . . That particular rock house was very interesting. It's got good preservation. . . . There's really cool prehistoric stuff, especially Late Woodland." Looking around the site, he knew all the evidence pointed to this being a valuable Indigenous site.[22] When he visited the rockshelter as part of annual monitoring, he found the site impacted by climbing. In addition to the dozen or so sport routes at the crag, at least one tree had been cut down, as it prevented a clean and safe fall off the wall.

Johnny reported the violation to Ranger Donnie Richardson. Johnny was quite adamant that he wanted to press charges. "I wrote up an ARPA case to try to pursue prosecuting the people. . . . So I did that and I was aiming to prosecute, really pushing the law enforcement to have the people prosecuted that had impacted the site because the climbers knew [it was important]." ARPA (Archaeological Resource Protection Act of 1979) is a federal law designed to prevent damaging archaeological sites and to penalize those who do so. The law governs activity on archaeological sites on federal land (such as the DBNF) and prohibits removing artifacts from these sites or damaging anything of archaeological interest.

Hugh Loeffler vividly remembers that day: "Shannon called me at work one day and said, '[The DBNF] found out about the *Hominy Hole* and are about to shut down all the climbing, everywhere. We better do something.' And so I cut out of work, I got in my car, I was working in Stanton at the time so it was not a big deal, and I drove out there that morning with Shannon, with Donnie Richardson who was the district ranger." Hugh and Shannon made no effort to hide things. Quite the opposite; Hugh admitted guilt: "We took ownership: 'Yeah, we did it.' "

Johnny similarly reported the event: "We met with [Hugh] down there and [Donnie Richardson] and Shannon [Stuart-Smith], and we asked them about what happened there and they pretty much admitted that they done that, so I really was pushing to have them [prosecuted], because they [were] impacting the site. So then the ranger decided not to pursue that." Hugh recalled that he and Shannon subsequently offered to remedy the situation as best they could:

We were in a pickle, and they were gonna have to hire climbing rangers from western districts to come over and strip all the bolts, to make it right . . . and it was gonna cost them a lot of money, special pay for these guys, and they didn't have it, you know, Daniel Boone doesn't have any money. [Shannon and I] were like, "Look, we're sorry. We didn't know this was your property, but we can make it all okay. We'll make this place go away. It'll be gone in a week." And that's what we did. We got everyone who put routes up out there and we stripped all the bolts. We erased our climbing footprint within a week and a half, probably.

Hominy Hole, as a climbing crag, ceased to exist in early 2000. It has been scrubbed from existence in climbing media, has never been listed in a guide-book, and has almost entirely been forgotten by climbers today. No known listing of the routes established there publicly exists, aside from the name of Hugh's route, "Red Headed Step Child." This closure was the first of more to come. In many ways, *Hominy Hole* represented an early bellwether. It represented a new shift in thinking in progress. Hugh Loeffler considered what this meant for the immediate future: "That signaled the beginning of 'We better do something more than what we've been doing.' No more stumbling around in the dark and drilling on somebody's land. . . . We've got to get organized."

With the issues at *Hominy Hole* as a backdrop, Hugh, Shannon, and John Bronaugh all worked in collaboration with the DBNF in finalizing the historic Memorandum of Understanding (MOU) on February 7, 2000. This document would, for a time, further define and formalize the relationship between the two parties. The MOU officially recognized the Red River Gorge Geological Area for its climbing opportunities and established a framework for the RRGCC and Forest Service to have a working relationship toward common goals.

The MOU lists 17 annual expectations the DBNF has for climbers (as collectively represented through the RRGCC). These include sending lists of potential multiuse projects for funding, maintaining a kiosk that helps inform visitors of Forest Service policies, helping with trail maintenance and limiting user trails, adhering to posted closures of cliffs and trails, providing Forest Service workers a forum in the RRGCC newsletter and through access to the RRGCC email list, and managing "the use of fixed anchors as necessary for climber safety, climber enjoyment, to protect scenic resources and to minimize impacts to cliff top vegetation and rare plant species."[23] In return, the Forest Service agreed to provide information to the RRGCC through the Freedom of Information Act, review projects climbers might like to see funded and provide funding where possible, construct toilets near climbing areas (subsequent to NEPA analysis), participate in annual RRGCC events (such as open executive meetings), and "make the Forest available for furtherance of these joint efforts, subject to applicable Federal Laws, regulations, forest plans, and State comprehensive plans for the affected area, and subject to approval by the Agency head or its designated representative." The MOU also appoints a pair of climber and Forest Service liaisons who, per the MOU, will be regularly available to meet and discuss any issues at hand. The agreement was signed by Donnie Richardson on behalf of DBNF as the district ranger and Shannon Stuart-Smith, on behalf of RRGCC, with an expiration date of February 7, 2002, which could be extended and renewed as needed. Its first test would come from an unexpected source: bouldering in the Red.

Over the last decade, the sport of bouldering had grown across the nation. Bouldering is a style of climbing that focuses on lower-height rocks—

boulders—without using ropes. Instead of roping up, boulderers use bouldering pads, thick pads that can be placed in the fall zone to arrest their fall if needed. In lieu of belayers, boulderers may have friends with hands placed to deflect the boulderer should they fall. Note that bouldering uses a different skill measurement system than climbing. Whereas climbing generally uses the Yosemite Decimal System (YDS), bouldering often uses the V scale. The V scale, named for John "Vermin" Sherman, goes from V0 to V16 (and recently, V17). As in YDS, the higher the number, the higher the difficulty. Recently, boulderers had identified V16 problems (of which there are around a dozen worldwide), and they have since identified V17 problems.[24] Nalle Hukkataival completed "Lappnor Project" in October 2016, which was listed as a V17.[25] In January 2019, Charles Albert proposed that "Fontainebleau" be considered a V17.[26]

The same year the MOU was released, Chris Redmond released a bouldering guide on the Red River Gorge that raised awareness of this unique part of the climbing community. In comparison with climbers, the Red's bouldering community was relatively small but nonetheless present. Brian Clark reflected on bouldering's popularity in the Red: "People still boulder at the Red, but the world-class steep sport routes are the main attraction. That's what makes the Red unique. Boulders can be found in many climbing locations, whereas that crazy steep sandstone of the Red cannot." At the time in the Red, boulder locations were also quite scattered and even remote compared to the many sport crags along the trails and parking lots.

Redmond's bouldering guide listed nine bouldering crags in the Red. They included some familiar names: *Skybridge Ridge*, *Tower Rock*, and *Military Wall*. The boulder problem at *Military Wall* consisted of a massive boulder (called *Military Boulder* in this guide) at the far end of the crag, which, at some point in history, had rolled loose from *Military Wall* itself. It contained seven problems ranging from V3 ("Rainbow Serpent" and "No Smoking") to a V8 ("No Crap") and a V9 ("The Gotama"). The guide had over 130 bouldering problems previously unlisted in earlier guides on climbing in the Red.

Redmond's guide also presented a potential issue involving publishing routes that had not been approved by the DBNF. Looking back, the 1998 Bronaugh guide had served as a watershed guide. It officially grandfathered into legitimacy any existing climbing routes in the Red based on the Forest Service policies at the time. As John Bronaugh explained online, "The routes listed in the latest edition were arbitrarily 'grandfathered in' by the FS. There was no good reason other than the fact that those routes were already 'published' and couldn't be 'unpublished.' "[27] It didn't matter when the routes were climbed, only when they were published. Redmond's guide included vast amounts of material not in the Bronaugh guide. Redmond employed a humorous (at least to climbers) tone in the guide, discussing extensive efforts to scrub routes of any vegetation. One section is locally famous for its wit:

> Once a boulder has been found, moss must be removed along with any trees that would inhibit a safe landing. A fundamental tool in this process is the wire brush, since the moss can be nightmarish. The rhododendron bushes in the Red are also a problem around many boulders. Unfortunately, Agent Orange is not readily available to combat this threat and its use is often looked down upon. However, anyone with access to an F-4 [Phantom military aircraft] should use his or her own good judgement.[28]

The sarcastic tone, meant to be humorous, changes later in the guide, with Redmond admonishing climbers to erase chalk tic marks, minimize chalk use in general, avoid chipping holds on boulders ("If you can't reach a hold, I can assure you it's not the rocks' fault"), and pack out all trash.[29] Although the guide's recommended use of Agent Orange has come up in conversations with the Forest Service, there's no evidence it necessarily impacted relations between climbers and the DBNF, and there's no record of Chris having been formally reproached for publishing the routes. However, the routes are not listed in subsequent climbing guides today.

Meanwhile, the DBNF was also experiencing a new transition, altering its activities as a result of Kentucky Heartwood's legal efforts. Recall that a 1998 lawsuit had paused timber operations while the Forest Service designed a plan to fully address timbering impacts on endangered species. By stopping timbering, Kentucky Heartwood inadvertently shifted resources used in the DBNF to look at other compliance issues, such as impacts at archaeological sites. Red River Gorge archaeologist Johnny Faulkner also felt that the DBNF changed their foci as a result of Kentucky Heartwood's legal efforts: "At the time, our main emphasis was toward timber sales surveys." However, after Heartwood's lawsuit, the DBNF began looking at other aspects, such as monitoring archaeological sites.

Johnny saw a valid opportunity for growth in the archaeological knowledge of the Red but also a chance to protect those sites: "We had a chance to . . . start working on the district," Johnny noted in a conversation with Cecil Ison, then forest archaeologist, where he raised this issue after Kentucky Heartwood's suits and the subsequent changes to timber policies. "We really need to get out, see what's going on in the Gorge because the recreation was blossoming. More people coming in. Rock climbing was becoming an issue. I started doing more monitoring out in the Gorge, just getting a perspective of what was going on." Johnny described that the increase in use was "highly impactful [to] the rockshelters," and it was "not just the climbers."

At the time, Johnny shared concerns about fires in rockshelters, trampling deposits (such as artifacts), and digging latrine pits in archaeological sites. Johnny said that he asked Donnie Richardson (with Cecil's backing) to better protect archaeological sites with the help of the State Historic Preservation Office and Heritage Advisory Council. *Military Wall* was one of their early targets. Why *Military Wall*? Recall that it had already been on their watch list in the CMG, noting concerns over camping at the site. Moreover, Johnny noted the growth of sport routes, and the proliferation of information caught their attention, too: "It became known at that time there [were] climbing books being put out, there was internet advertising of climbing areas, and we said, 'Well, we really need to look at those areas first.' And so *Military Wall* was one of the favorite climbing areas, so Cecil Ison and I went up there."

CHAPTER 9

The *Military Wall* Archaeological Dig, 2001–2002

It is perhaps ironic that a place with a combat-oriented name would be home to a conflict that would change climbing in the Red forever. It is at *Military Wall* that the relationship between climbers and the DBNF would be put to the test in partnering to conduct an archaeological dig. For decades, the two had collaborated to support climbing access in the Red while also protecting its natural resources. In recent years, that relationship had been strained by unauthorized sport-route development on DBNF land. The DBNF rightly had to take a stand, offering both the Climbing Management Guide and later Memorandum of Understanding to outline how climbing should function at the Red while also protecting resources. The lawsuit by Kentucky Heartwood, however, somewhat changed the context of history by offering a rare opportunity for the DBNF's archaeologists to shift resources toward protecting archaeological sites from climbing impacts.

Metaphorically speaking, this dig represented a clash of the Titans among deeply respected members of the archaeological community (Johnny Faulkner, Cecil Ison, and Eric Schlarb) and the climbing community (Shannon Stuart-Smith). Each fiercely held stalwart beliefs quite relevant to the DBNF's long-standing purpose: finding a balance between protecting resources on public lands while also providing access to public lands. The wounds from this clash would remain with both sides for years to come. Even today the dig at *Military Wall*, much like the Red River Dam, is a very delicate conversation topic. This chapter, in part, hopes to heal some of those wounds by documenting the event's history while also placing it into its historical context.

Johnny Faulkner took a trip up to *Military Wall* with respected DBNF archaeologist Cecil Ison. "I'd been up there and told Cecil that particular site, it looks very dry," he recounted, with clear evidence of a cattle pen and niter mining use. Johnny's experience told him this shelter presented a great opportunity to examine prehistoric cultural artifacts at the site. He asked Cecil, "I would like you to go with me to record that." They performed a Phase I examination with three shovel probes. The results confirmed what was already clear: the deposits were very dry, which hinted that this site probably had high potential for preserving anything early humans might have left behind. "That is a site that, one of many, we chose to look at, that we considered, we really need to start looking at these rock-climbing areas first," Johnny explained, reflecting on the importance of the site: "It's an overhang. If I were writing a report or doing survey work, I would classify it as an overhang as opposed to a shelter. A lot of the shelters will go deeper into the cliff. Another thing about this overhang, if you've got these hearths and you're doing cooking and all this kind of stuff, you're going to get a better smoke release out of an overhang than you are a shelter." That smoke release, it turns out, was exactly what Indigenous peoples were thinking, too, and the analysis would eventually trace it as far back as the Late Archaic (as early as 8000 BP) or Early Woodland (as late as AD 1100). In fact, that hearth would prove to be far more important than was expected.[1]

The recent results of the Kentucky Heartwood lawsuit had inadvertently thrown a spark for reassessing archaeological areas throughout the ranger district. It leveraged pressure against Ranger Donnie Richardson to protect the sites. Others (including the Advisory Council) also placed pressure on protecting the sites; Richardson agreed. Johnny coordinated early archaeological surveys at multiple other areas on Forest Service land. "We didn't just look at the climbing area. We looked at a little broader spectrum of the cliff outside the boundaries of the climbing area so we could . . . compare the impacts of the climbing and camping." As one might expect, the impacts were there: issues with erosion due to user trails, trampling of vegetation, and compacting soil are common even today at climbing areas, and it was certainly the case back then. This was also the case at *Military Wall*, even beyond the initial area under the shelter that interested Johnny so much.

While out at *Military Wall* for the Phase I examination, Johnny and Cecil's report also noted a campsite right in the middle of the archaeological site. Unidentified climbers from Ohio had chosen an inauspicious time and location for their neon-glow tents. Shannon Stuart-Smith confirmed that they were, indeed, climbers camping at *Military Wall*. She qualified their campsite selection in that they had arrived the night before in a light rain and were unsure exactly where they were. They pitched their tent directly in the lee of *Military Wall*, which was then photographed by the Forest Service.

The encounter reinforced a long-standing local belief that climbers here generally camp where they climb, something that for the most part does not prove true today. Relatively few climbing areas in the Red (that *Military Wall* location being a great exception) present decent options for camping. The surrounding forest, where camping is allowed with a permit and under specific distances from water and trails, would have been a much more suitable area for camping. In the early days of climbing in the Red, camping near the crag might have been modestly more prevalent, but early guidebooks directed campers to established campgrounds in preference to dispersed camping in the DBNF. As climbing became an increasingly social activity in the 1990s, climbers generally flocked to Miguel's to be with other climbers.[2] More recently, cabins and RV parks have entered the fray, with some climbers renting out RV spaces for the entire year. Throughout the Red there is a distinction between where climbers go to climb and where they choose to stay: they venture to the crags for solitude from the world, whereas the campground is for socialization.

Based on the evidence of the test probes and the subsequent evidence of camping, Shannon recalled that Cecil had recommended that the district ranger should close the *entire Military Wall* site to climbing. He reportedly argued that the test probe evidence showed the site was important and likely contained more archaeological data. The tent use, user trails, and active climbing put the site and its archaeological resources at risk. The only way to protect it was to shut down climbing altogether at the site. Recall that the 1996 CMG had already noted concerns about camping at the crag. Now that they had evidence, it made logical sense not to risk further erosion or compaction at the site.

Shannon and the RRGCC went directly to Donnie Richardson to plead their case. Shannon asked what it would take to keep *Military Wall* open. Richardson deferred to Cecil's expertise, whose archaeological data from the Phase I dig had already supported closure. So Shannon asked Cecil: What has to happen to keep it open? Per Shannon, Cecil said that performing a Phase II dig could keep *Military Wall* open—but open *only for the time being*. A Phase II dig would allow the area to be excavated beyond the test probes. But this would be costly, as it would require bringing in an external archaeologist to perform the excavations, as well as a review of the resultant report by the state historic preservation officer. However, if climbers could get the funds together to cover the costs, it could hypothetically prevent the full closure. Still, the results of the dig would not guarantee that the entire area would ever again be open.

It is not clear if the entirety of *Military Wall* was really of interest to the DBNF. Climbing, hiking, and camping had gradually changed the area. The shelter held far more archaeological interest and was far less disturbed. Johnny explained that the rest of the sites were recorded in the reports, but there was no plan to do further examination beyond that. Their primary interest was in the rockshelter. Climbers didn't realize they were probably predestined to lose access to the rockshelter area and the routes above it. Johnny Faulkner recalled that climbers "proposed to pay for the Phase II if they could believe that through the Phase II, they could continue climbing. . . . We just wanted to protect that site."

Interestingly, another form of use at the site had protected the area. Much of the site was sheltered underneath a compacted layer of manure from logging oxen or mules that had once been kept there. In my visit with Shannon, she showed me this unexpected attribute in the soil: "One of the first things I dug [she pointed at an odd, earthy-colored object that slightly resembled a stone] . . . you know what that is? Hardened manure." The manure had been packed down hard and thick by both human and hooved feet, laying a protective barrier over the already dry soil composition. That upped the preservative qualities yet another notch.

Shannon went on a mission to secure the funds needed for a Phase II dig and could clearly recount the historic moment it happened: "That day I called up the Access Fund . . . I need $10,000! If you guys can get the $10,000 today by 2 p.m., I can guarantee that we can keep Military [Wall] open." Access Fund called back that day and agreed that they could secure the funds. Shannon then notified Donnie and Cecil that she, in fact, had come up with the money. "They didn't see that coming," Shannon shared with a laugh. The die was now cast for what would become a watershed moment in the Red: Access Fund had selected to put their resources and mission statement behind this dig, making it a very big affair for the climbing world.

The next step was to contact Kentucky Archaeological Survey (KAS) to schedule the logistics of the dig. KAS worked with state agencies and private landowners to protect archaeological sites while also educating Kentuckians about the state's extraordinary archaeological history. Eric Schlarb was establishing his career in archaeology when the opportunity to work at the Military Wall dig occurred: "I was about five years in" when he worked with David Pollack on the Military Wall dig from November 17 to 20, 2000. "For me, it was just this exciting thing . . . me and Dave get to work with Cecil and Johnny, we get to dig in a rockshelter, just my love of being in the forest and getting to work with those guys. That was exciting back then, just to get to work with them."

Eric vividly remembered his early days of archaeology in the Red. "When I started volunteering back in the early to mid-90s, I got to work with Cecil and Johnny and a guy named Bill Sharp out on the Forest . . . working on different excavations, and surveying these rockshelters. It was a great experience for me." Eric remembers Cecil the way that so many others do: "The guy is a really highly intelligent, really bright man who was very dedicated to his job over there in the Forest [Service]. . . . Cecil was just one of these people you just don't forget. He's a character, but again, but he's very, very bright and a very capable archaeologist." And Eric remembered Cecil's strong fashion sense: "I've been to weddings where he's married people, and he's wearing high-top Converse tennis shoes with wings on them, kind of like Mercury. . . . Very entertaining person, but very knowledgeable."

As a scientist, Eric went into the dig with no preconceptions of what might be found:

We're going [to *Military Wall*] to collect data, but there was no foregone conclusion going into the dig, at least from the perspective of the archaeologists participating in the dig. Prevailing theories may guide what is to be expected—and in the Red, it could be expected that most every shelter has a good chance of showing signs of past use—but we don't know what that's going to tell us until we do our analysis. A lot of times, you go to a site, you have a research question. With archaeology, once you get in there, you have way more questions than answers.

Eric felt, like Johnny did, that the conditions in this shelter could make it a perfect spot for preserving artifacts:

The beauty of a rockshelter is that dry environment, and it's similar to a cave and that's what enables the preservation of these materials. And when you get a lot of ash, you get ash deposits in these shelters, that changes the pH of the soil and it enables that preservation even more. Things like bones and wood and plant fibers, and of course, these carbonized plant seeds, that kind of preservation's really what makes these special because they're essentially time capsules.

There is also a magical element of time involved with archaeological digs, as one site can hold artifacts from multiple eras of activity.

Another thing about these rockshelters, none of them are exactly alike. . . . You can dig four shovel probes and not one of those shovel probes looks alike, because a lot of times [Indigenous people] are utilizing these things in different ways, so a group of early archaic people . . . utilized the front of the shelter or the middle of the shelter to refurbish or recycle their stone tools, camp overnight like they're at a Motel 8 and move on because they're hunter-gatherers. But by the time we get to this period where they're more intensively using them, they're producing these hominy holes and they're processing plant use, they're utilizing these locales in different ways.

Eric mentioned that in early digs in the Red, researchers would sometimes find moccasins made out of woven plant fibers, something that would generally decay in the wetness of the forest but would last for millennia in the dry conditions of an overhang. Likewise, Johnny Faulkner noted that parts of wooden niter mining troughs from the 19th century were also fairly frequent finds in these dry areas. Thus, until those shovels got into the dirt and analysis began, it was quite uncertain what might be found, if anything.

Jumping forward in time, standing at the *Military Wall* dig site in 2016, Shannon pointed at a small spot near some rocks that once housed a test pit. "I dug right there. You can see the remnants of it." That spot is also marked in the archaeological dig report as Feature 1. From the archaeological report: "Feature 1 was first identified in the southeast corner of [Test Unit] 1, at a depth of 18 cm below the surface. [Test Unit] 4 was excavated to expose more of this feature." A pH analysis would hint that this location had been used as an earthen oven and later had caught debris from cleaning out hearths after the feature itself was no longer used. Shannon continued pointing out the remaining test pits and then named all the important climbing routes right above the pit.

In all, the archaeological dig report listed 226 lithic materials (rock fragments created by humans), 13 of which were tools or tool fragments. The tools included two projectile points (one Lake Erie Bifurcated Base point from 8300 to 7800 BP and the other a Stanly Stemmed point from 7800 to 6000 BP) and eight point fragments. Faunal remains were also present from the consumption of 92 animals, including deer, raccoon, squirrel, woodchuck, rabbits, rodents, turkeys, birds, box turtles, and mollusks. They also found what Shannon described as an old fire pit. She remembered her time there in a positive light: "I learned a lot. It was very fascinating." But there was also foreshadowing of what was to come," she remembered. "They were very excited about the fire pit part."

Johnny remembers the site was packed with help—"We had the climbers, Shannon and other people come out and help us"—but their unfamiliarity with archaeology may have been an issue from the start. Eric remembered the lack of excitement at what was being found:

> So when you go and you do a dig, people are looking for all the "ooh, ahh" stuff. They're looking for arrowheads, pottery . . . tools, those are the things that grab people's attention. Well, when we were doing the

dig, we weren't finding a lot of that stuff. We weren't finding a lot of weapons, we didn't find any pottery, so to the outside viewer's eye, like Shannon Stuart-Smith, she's like, "Well, crap, you know, they've only dug up a couple of arrowheads, they're not really digging much up. I don't see what the big deal about this is."

Climbers were confident that the lack of major findings (from a nonarchaeological perspective) was a good sign. Shannon remembered that at the time, "We thought we had a green light and we were going to reopen this area, and Access Fund did [as well]. It's a great win-win for everybody."

Once the actual results came in, the dig at *Military Wall* took on a new and perhaps unexpected importance. The overhang had, indeed, been used, and all those perfect conditions played a pivotal role in preserving the area. This was no surprise. When asked about the importance of the findings and the site overall, Eric explained, "Just the sheer number of plant remains—the botanical remains in there." As it turns out, *Military Wall* held important early evidence of crop domestication in the area. Eric explained this further:

So you have these hearths of domestication, and you know, of course when you think about the Tigris and Euphrates Rivers and all that kind of stuff, early agriculture taking place over there, well these folks started doing horticulture and domesticating these wild plants in this area in the Red River Gorge like 4,000 years ago, and that's the earliest evidence we've got on the North American continent. Now as archaeologists do digs in other places, that could change, but right now it's one of the earliest places that we know of in North America where they were actually domesticating these plants.

Eric remembered the moment they dug into that feature: "We found that earth oven, and the soil was black." He was shocked by the contents. "We had no idea what that one pit would produce. There were complete logs in there . . . significant tree branch size pieces of wood in there." Johnny Faulkner was also working on that earth oven and was equally amazed by the analysis of the contents. As he recalled, "It pretty much [included] the whole Eastern Complex of what was grown [in the region]." This was now a *major find*, as one rarely finds a site with so many cultigen data points.

As it turns out, early residents in the Red were actually engaging in an evolutionary process with their selection of plant life, and *Military Wall* was a small but very significant part of this history. For example, when selecting seeds for planting, Indigenous peoples selected the healthiest and largest seeds. The same process happened in successive generations. This favored the growth of larger and better fruits from these newly domesticated plants. Archaeological research in the Red supports the fact that Indigenous peoples established garden plots on cleared hillsides and banks.[3] The purpose of the gardens was to supplement a diet of protein from animals. "And we didn't know until we sent our flotation samples in and had those analyzed, and then the results came back to us, we didn't know until we got the results," Eric recalled of his findings.

Back in the lab, flotation samples work on the principle that buoyancy helps raise particulate matter that might go unnoticed amid all the dirt. First, a feature, such as an earth oven, is excavated, as was the case at *Military Wall*. Part of the dirt removed from the feature goes through a sifting process to help find larger items such as arrowheads. Another sample is sent for a flotation examination. The sample is added to a flotation tank with water and is agitated. Heavier material such as rock goes to the bottom of the tank, while "the light fraction, like charcoal and carbonized seeds, they float to the top," Eric explained. Archaeobotanists can then examine and identify the material that has floated to the surface, such as nutshells.

The Schlarb and Pollack report lists 513 nutshell pieces among the samples, as well as plant seeds and evidence of squash and gourds.[4] There were multiple native eastern cultigens present: maygrass, chenopod, erect knotweed, marsh elder, and sunflower. Wood charcoal found in the flotation process, which dominated the list of plant remains, can also be used for carbon dating. Eric stated that the carbon-dated material from *Military Wall* all came from wood from the flotation samples. Collectively, the botanical remains were described as a "well-preserved collection [that] strongly suggests a terminal Late Archaic/ Early Woodland occupation that utilized a variety of both domesticated and wild plant resources."[5] In the end, it was carbonized plants that were the defining find at *Military Wall*.[6]

With this finding, the DBNF, the Kentucky Archaeological Survey, and the Forest Service in general had all the reasonable evidence needed to effect a closure to protect the site from public use. Eric clarified who made the decision to close part of *Military Wall*: it was not KAS. "[Kentucky Archaeological Survey] writes a report and then we make a recommendation. So if we're recommending that this thing is eligible for the National Register, then it needs to be protected and I don't think you could protect a site like that by impacting it through recreational use. It was a decision [the Forest Service] made." The Forest Service elected to enforce that closure only at the overhanging portion of *Military Wall*, leaving the remainder of the crag open.

Those arriving at *Military Wall* on April 23, 2001, found it markedly different from the weeks before.[7] Kris Hampton remembers it like it was yesterday: "I went up there the very first day when they put the fence up and they put the sign up that it was closed. I went up and took a photo of the sign with 'Revival' blurry in the background, and you can see the chalk up the wall." That image remains burned into Kris's memory. "I still have that photo around somewhere. . . . Climbing was this, like I just said, it felt more like an art, and it was definitely a lifestyle and it just seemed, at the time, that because of the history of the archaeology that's in the area and the Forest Service trying to protect that archaeology, what it seemed to me was that they were completely ignoring the fact that this was important to us as well, and only focusing on the importance of the archaeological history that was there." Kris further recalled that " 'Revival' was like the popular sport route if you wanted to make your name in Red River Gorge. You had to go do 'Revival,' and they shut it down."

In all, seven routes were officially closed, a mix of sport and trad routes spanning over a decade of development and two overlapping generations of climbers. The closure hit two trad routes from the 1980s: "Blade Runner," a 5.7 completed by Martin Hackworth and Harvey Johnson in 1982, and "Beenestalker," a 5.10d by Tom Souders and Jeff Koenig. "Beenestalker" was a big loss given its ties to the multiple Beene Brothers' routes by Souders and Koenig and its difficulty rating. The remaining five routes all linked to Porter Jarrard's extensive development here in his early days in the Red. These included two 1991 routes: "Hurricane Amy" (5.11c with Mark Williams) and "Revival" (5.13a with Steve Cater). Along the eastern-facing end of the closure were three more 1990 Jarrard and Mark Williams routes: "Thirsting Skull," "Jac Mac," and "Rad Boy Go." Several of these routes had both symbolic and cultural attachments for climbers, so the loss was especially difficult for climbers to accept. Although signage at the closure noted the area was closed because it was an archaeological site, there was no noted effort to explain the closure's rationale at the time and the importance of what had been found. Today, climbers remain largely unsure why the closure existed, with reasons ranging from arrowheads to bedrock mortars to bones being found at the site. Very few are aware of the carbonized plant material found at the hearth feature and its historical significance.

Quite commendably, the DBNF had considered other options that might allow the site to remain open beneath a protective layer. There had been early conversations between Donnie Richardson and climbers about alternatives to the fenced-off closure that were never fully pursued. Two early suggestions were either a protective material that could be poured over the area to preserve the contents below or the construction of a deck over the area. Eric recalled those conversations: "I remember them talking about a material that they could actually pour over the shelter and encase it, protect it, but that was probably cost prohibitive." Likewise, "the deck, that would have been another alternative, but I don't think the Forest Service has a lot of money. They're just like everybody else, all stretched for money . . . and I can't speak for them [but] somebody made the decision we're just gonna close this off. We're gonna fence it off."

Shannon agreed that following word of the pending closure there were, indeed, discussions with the Forest Service about that protective layer. "It was a geotextile mat and the Forest Service was really excited about it. [Donnie Richardson] brought it out, showed me samples and everything. I mean they were really down with it!" In other cases, DBNF has put interlocking concrete pavers into action to create a protective layer over archaeological sites, placing value on leaving the materials safely underground and sealed by thick stones that also create a durable layer for activity above ground. Again, pavers are an expensive effort, and for unclear reasons, it was never pursued by either party.

The partial closure had long-lasting effects. Climbers largely did not know or did not understand why the closure happened. This fomented a distrust of the Forest Service, DBNF employees, and archaeologists in general that occasionally still resurfaces even today. Following the rapid expansion of routes in the early 1990s, a select few climbers rejected being told where they could and could not climb, although the closure at *Military Wall* has certainly been respected by these climbers, and violations of this closure are unheard of. Further, a contingent of climbers rejected Shannon's work with the DBNF and felt disenfranchised by the whole process. And certainly a few climbers handled themselves very poorly following the closure, creating individually selfish events that would undermine generations of relationship building between climbers and public land managers in the Red.

One factor complicating the scenario was the DBNF's limits on what they could say about the closure. There were public presentations explaining why areas in the Red would sometimes need to be closed, but these presentations were limited in scope as to precise reasons why part of *Military Wall* was closed. Tim Eling with the DBNF explained: "It's a challenge because that information is often protected. It's one of the few things that we don't have to release even to Freedom of Information Act requests because of the protections of various federal laws related to heritage resources." Being specific about what is present can open these areas to looting issues, especially when dealing with cultural resource sites like the closed section of *Military Wall*. As a result, Forest Service employees are put in the difficult position that they "often can't say what was there." This same issue can hold true for any Forest Service action. Tim explained it this way: "When we do our environmental analysis plans for anything, a timber sale, a new road, there's an archaeological survey that's part of that, but it is usually sealed up as part of that report, and not part of the information that goes out to the public." What may feel like oversight or avoidance on behalf of the Forest Service could actually be a decided effort to protect cultural resources sites.

The desire to place blame for the closure (again, likely without fully understanding the reason for the closure) created palpable tension in the Red, and it occasionally boiled over. Eric Schlarb recalled a run-in at Miguel's: "I was just in there with a crew one day doing another [archaeological] survey and somebody made a comment . . . , 'Hey, that's the archaeologist who wrote the *Military Wall* report.' And a couple of them started making snarky comments. . . . I had a crew there I was responsible for, and I decided to just pack up, put our pizza in aluminum foil, and get out of there." Johnny Faulkner has similarly had run-ins at Miguel's, but with different results. "I'd go to Miguel's. I still do. [I get] these looks [motions with head]. 'Hey, that's him. He closed *Military Wall*.' It still goes on." He still gets requests from climbers to talk about *Military Wall* and the dig, albeit more friendly now than in the years immediately following the closure, searching for the exact cause. Perhaps this chapter, then, will help bring that issue to a conclusion.

After the completion of the dig, Shannon and the RRGCC continued working with the DBNF on a number of fronts. This reflected Shannon's belief that climbers needed to work with the DBNF, as they were the gatekeepers who controlled access. Shannon began offering seminars at gyms on minimizing impacts. She and other climbers helped identify white-haired goldenrod colonies, built trails to climbing destinations, spotted possible niter mines, and notified the DBNF about potential areas that might need to be protected. Shannon guided archaeologists and biologists to several climbing areas on Forest Service land to point out additional sites that were likely of interest. This included two small archaeological sites at *Long Wall*, a huge niter mine, and several populations of white-haired goldenrod. The result was the closure of around a dozen routes, nearly all trad: "Better that they close off a small section than either the whole wall or all climbing altogether," she said. Looking back, Shannon felt that "if we'd had a different [Forest Service] archaeologist, they'd probably said, 'Yeah you'll probably be fine, there would be no harm done' " based on the hardened layer of manure at the overhang. This point is debatable but unlikely given the importance of the findings at the site. Nonetheless, the archaeological dig site remains closed today and will likely remain closed forever.

As part of her work to spread accurate information about climbing, Shannon took local Forest Service employees out to the crags, put them in harnesses, and showed them the ropes. She explained that those bolts in the walls were there to keep climbers safe and to keep the Forest Service from potential injury lawsuits. She wanted to work with the gatekeepers who were truly in control of whether or not climbing would happen on the DBNF. Shannon recalled one such day where a Forest Service employee asked her how long climbing would last in the Red. "Well Shannon, is this just a phase? How long do you think this is going to last?" Shannon flatly explained the new reality of things in the Red. "Well, I think this is a tsunami, and you're just looking at the wave rising up."

Only a few more routes appeared at *Military Wall* after the dig. In 2001, Terry Kindred completed "All Things Considered," a 5.11d. The following year, Dave Hume contributed an astounding 5.13d called "Nagypapa." Terry had equipped "In the Light," which was FA'd by Brian Maslyar in 2002. Terry is also listed on "Parting Gift" in 2006. The last route established at *Military Wall* was, perhaps fittingly, a trad route ("Gullyneering," a 5.9 completed by Dustin Stephens and Patrick Miller in 2012 that works up a natural crack system located between two Porter Jarrard sport routes, "Reliquary" and "Mule"). While *Military Wall* remains one of the most popular sites on DBNF land, new route growth would soon turn attention elsewhere in the region.

Following the partial closure, Shannon left this epoch with an idea that would define the status quo of climbing in the Red for the next two decades: "The surest way to protect climbing is to get out of this guest status that we've always been in. [As a lawyer], I knew enough about American property law to know that if you own property in America, unlike other cultures, you're given absolute, near absolute control over it . . . and the only way to ensure continuous, uninterrupted access to climbing is to buy it." The phrase "If we buy it, they can't take it away" began to circulate among climbers in the Red and beyond. Reflecting back today on five decades of climbing history in the Red, *Military Wall* was a tipping point that changed climbing here forever.

CHAPTER 10

Transitioning off Public Land and into a New Era at the Red, 2002–2004

John Nowell shared that "Mississippi Moon" at *Pocket Wall* was probably his favorite all-time route in the Red. "The route itself is fantastic, and the first time I did it, I fell in love with it, and the second time I did it, I actually strapped a lawn chair onto my back, climbed up there, set the lawn chair down . . . [and] sat in a lawn chair in this six-foot-tall hueco 60 feet off the ground, smoked a cigarette, and just checked out the view." [1] Others soon followed suit, making this hueco a private thinking spot for the Red. "Have the belayer tie you off to a tree and just hang out in the hueco for a couple hours or whatever." "Mississippi Moon" was just one of many early routes developed at *Pocket Wall* during that rapid era of growth in the mid-1990s involving expanding onto private land with unclear permission to do so. In an ideal world, *Pocket Wall* is one climbing area that would be open to climbers. Despite active work by the RRGCC and climbers, Kentucky State Parks have declined to reopen it to climbing as a result of its designation as a state park and nature reserve.

In 2001, Access Fund's newsletter notes issues not with climbing but OHV access to *Pocket Wall*. The area surrounding *Pocket Wall* had long been part of the OHV/ATV community, and even horse community members utilized the trails found there to enjoy the southern region. Climbers also reported that Natural Bridge State Park employees had made multiple attempts to block road access to OHVs by building earthworks (most likely either large dirt piles or impassable trenches). The land was acquired in 2002 by Kentucky State Parks, which did not allow climbing on the premises. Today, the only place one will find a list of climbing routes at *Pocket Wall* is in the guidebooks from that era. The online guidebook and newer print guides have long since stopped listing *Pocket Wall*. Like *Hominy Hole*, it has essentially been scrubbed from existence, the bolts have been chopped or removed, and the routes exist only in the burning memories of the climbers who loved them. It does not mean it must remain that way, John Nowell argues: "The state park is saying 'never ever ever.' And we've heard 'never ever ever' before, and 'never ever ever' has changed. And my hope is that that 'never ever ever' will change as well. Not just for that area but the whole mindset, and that they'll realize this *is* a meaningful sport, it's a meaningful area, and there's a lot of people who love it just as much as they do. So I'd love for that route to get opened back up again."

There are some possible inroads in that other comparable areas have taken a different stance to climbing. One big example was Carter Caves State Resort Park, which opened an area specifically for rappelling and rock climbing in 2015. Visitors must register for a free permit at the lodge front desk and follow basic rules, such as climbing only during daylight hours, not climbing alone, and using the existing anchors. Another important example is Breaks Interstate Park, located partly in Virginia and Kentucky, which has now opened to climbing. Here, park managers are working closely with climbers to ensure the natural areas are protected while increasing access to new and potential routes. Similarly, in Ohio, the John Bryan State Park (not far from Dayton) had initially been closed to climbing before eventually allowing climbing in select areas. They later allowed new climbing crags to be developed. Both provided new proving grounds for collaboration between climbers and public land managers beyond Forest Service land. One important start to reopening *Pocket Wall* would be first proving that climbers could be land management partners, and this would take time. For now, it remains closed while other changes in the Red have taken precedence.

As a young trad climber, Ray Ellington was detached from the sport-route growth of the 1990s. "I was kinda anti sport climbing. Like my second edition of John's book has all the sport climbing ripped out of it, which is stupid now. I wish it didn't . . . that's just a weird phase I was in." Ray remembered that at the time, "I was going around with my friend Kris Hampton, and we were . . . seeking the backcountry and looking for new cool cracks to climb because there was a lot to be had still." He would soon become one of the central figures in the Red's climbing community by transitioning John Bronaugh's guide online.

Around 2002, Ray approached John Bronaugh about adapting John's second-edition climbing guide for online use. Ray remembered that he asked, " 'John, can I take your guidebook and put it online?' Which at the time, it wasn't really a normal thing to do, but I wanted to learn some SQL, so John was like, 'Yeah, go for it.' " Hosting a Red climbing presence online wasn't in and of itself new. Climbers were already online at this point in the Red. Probably the first online forum specifically focused on the Red was kywilderness .com, which included a section on climbing and route beta. Next, climbky.com (managed by Jason Burton) created an online forum entirely dedicated to climbing in the Red. Later, redriverclimbing.com offered an online forum for climbers to communicate and discuss everything from climbing partners to gear to issues in the community.

What Ray was discussing here was something even bigger. While beta on routes was present online, Ray was about to make information about all the routes in the Red available to everyone. Ray's effort probably marks the biggest innovation of the decade. "I put it online and made it available to print PDFs. People were walking around with three-ring binders of the online guidebook printed out." An early version of the online guide was announced on redriver climbing.com on November 19, 2002.

There were potential risks in making this transition. The most common concern was that broad, easy online access to a guide would further increase the crowds. Previous guidebook authors had worried that their guides would bring a wave of new climbers. A cadre of climbers worried that the guide would now be accessible to the world, including some of their favorite lesser-known crags, which meant crowds might soon be coming to these places as well. And then there was the DBNF, which could now see every crag development in real time, which might not be appealing to the climbers' perspective at the time. Moreover, publishing trad routes in the DBNF without NEPA examination technically violated the language of the earlier 1996 CMG.

Ray saw it differently: "There are a lot of locals who are anti-guidebook because they think it creates unnecessary crowds and stuff, but I always thought it just kind of dispersed the crowds. You know, because it lets people know, 'Oh, look. This place looks cool!' Where they only may have known about 10 places, now they know about 20 places."

Continuing on Ray's approach, the online guides allowed for revisions to existing routes to happen immediately. This had a desirable safety component. If a route had a bolt in need of replacement, this kind of information could now be easily shared. Moreover, with the southern region (beyond the Forest Service borders) now experiencing rapid route development, new routes could be immediately shared. Likewise, route and crag closures could be made public without delay—the word could go out within moments rather than waiting for the next guide. There was also risk. In debates on redriverclimbing.com, climbers pointed out issues with posting projects, routes on private land, and proposed routes currently under review by the DBNF. Climbers found themselves in a scenario where they needed to police themselves in terms of which routes could be shared and which could not.

Tim Eling arrived for work on the DBNF in late 2003. His first major task was to run and facilitate a public planning process specifically for the Red called

Limits of Acceptable Change (LAC). LAC was designed to find balance between allowing recreation on public lands and maintaining existing resources found there. The LAC identified key features of the Red and placed them within the current context of human use in these areas to identify where management might be needed, where alternative activity areas might exist, and where closures (permanent or temporary) might be needed to allow an area to recover. As part of this process, Tim had to understand recent bans on climbing and how these fit into protecting the DBNF, along with catching up on a lot of history in the Red. He learned about early climbing history from none other than Don Fig, who was still working with the DBNF and nearing retirement. (Recall that Don had worked with the early climbers like Ron Stokley, Dieter Britz, and the Cumberland Climbers.) Tim was also charged with running many public meetings, because public input is a central part of the LAC process. Interestingly, he noted that two of the biggest groups who would attend the LAC meetings were archaeologists and climbers. Tim felt that over time, "they gained a better understanding of each other," even though they may have still disagreed over climbing access.

Climbers' behaviors were also evolving in the Red. As route expansion in the southern region increased, climbers sought new places to stay that were closer to the new crags. Moreover, a generation of climbers who had willingly crashed at Miguel's amid all-night parties in their 20s now were aging. Many had more disposable income, as many climbers are well-educated professionals and were looking in their 30s for a softer place to sleep at night, along with a 10 p.m. quiet hour. Just down the road from *The Motherlode*, two nearby landowners, Linda and Doug Black, were also looking for a new gig after giving horse riding lessons to the Bear Track Community's kids had provided only limited income. Enter Lago Linda Hideaway, where climbers could camp back then for just $5 a night. The campsite earned its name from the lake on the property and the beloved Linda Black.

Growing up in Liverpool in the UK (not University of Kentucky, but the other UK across the Atlantic Ocean), Linda Black found her way to America. While working in Washington, DC, she met her future husband, Doug. "I met him at a sail club. I wanted to learn how to sail, and he had a sailboat and was looking for a crew." Doug worked for the US Geological Survey and, in 1969, had scouted and purchased a wild tract of land in Lee County, Kentucky, with plans of retiring and building a cabin there. Linda remembers her first visit vividly: "He brought me here to show me his log cabin, and it was an okay place for a brief spell, but I yearned to get back to Washington, DC." Doug retired officially in 1991, and he eventually convinced Linda to come live with him in

Lee County. They married in 1992 at the cabin. Having given up her work in DC, Linda remembers asking Doug what came next: "I said, 'Well, what are we going to do now? Sit on the porch and the swing and look at each other? That's not my scene at all.' "

Linda began offering horseback lessons to locals, "which in this area, of course, didn't go down a bit well because there wasn't money [here]. I mean it was really cheap, and I gave a lot of kids free lessons, and of course I was paying out a lot of money for insurance." She later expanded the lessons and molded the land into a horse camp with stalls and rental cabins. The horse camp eked out a living, but when Doug was run over by a tractor in 2001, things changed. "He was never really able to help me physically from then on, and it was very hard to get help in this area, and so I was cleaning all the [horse] stalls . . . cleaning and renting [the cabins], and even with the horse camp there was a huge insurance [cost]. . . . It was just too much for me. I made myself really quite sick." Linda gave up on the horse camp in 2003.

Linda's first steady climber resident was probably Columbus, Ohio, native Kenny Barker, who left his camper at Linda's around 2003. Kenny is much respected for his route development and his bolting in the Red. His work includes bolting a route that is considered one of the hardest in the Red, a 5.14c called "The Golden Ticket." Although Kenny was not the first ascensionist (that honor went to Adam Taylor in 2009), "Golden Ticket" has remained a respected route since its creation and stays steadily in the limelight. Internationally famed climber Adam Ondra onsighted the route in 2012, bringing renewed attention to the Red five years after the Petzl RocTrip in 2007, which is discussed in the next chapter. The route again returned to climbing news when Michaela Kiersch became the first female to ascend the route in fall 2016, breaking a long-lasting belief in the community that "Golden Ticket" was a male-dominated route due to the large distance between key handholds. Conveniently, "Golden Ticket" is not far from Linda's.

Word quickly got out that Kenny was leaving his camper at Linda's, and other climbers wanted to do that.[2] Soon, Linda added bathrooms, a café, and an air-conditioned public shakeout room ready for her visitors. She also turned the horse camp stables into a picnic shelter. Before long, Linda was an important part of the climbing community. Linda reflected on this:

> It was so interesting because a lot of them were just sleeping in the back of their SUVs . . . and then I saw them grow. I saw them get a girlfriend. I saw them move in together. I saw them get a dog and some of them even got married, and a few have got married here, and now, a few of them have babies. . . . It's lovely to see them from young climbers sleeping in

the back of a truck or the back of a car, and now . . . with [their] tiny house.[3]

Climbers feel the same way about Linda. Linda shared that she was diagnosed with cancer in recent years, "and I was very sick and in hospital for a long time, and the climbers were so kind. Several of them managed my place last fall while I was in hospital." Climbers even improved on some of the money collection systems at Lago Linda's to help increase cash flow and reduce the odds of campers (both climbers and nonclimbers) leaving without having first paid for their spot. They visited her in the hospital, bringing flowers and cards, "and once I was out of the hospital, I was pretty much bed bound for a while, and they would come down on a Saturday evening to visit because they were camping here, and it was very, very nice. It was like, 'Wow, they do think something of me, because I'm kinda bossy with them when they make a mess' [laughs]."

The southern region offered a desirable dispersion of climbers to new areas, but crowding farther north continued to be a problem, particularly at *Roadside*. For example, climbers had frequently used parking (and sometimes camped) at a public park in Wolfe County dubbed Roadside Campground among the climbing community. (Local residents instead referred to the area as Green Thumb.) Due to increased use, the county had installed a dumpster at the site, replacing the oft-overflowing trash cans previously used there. However, this had the unintended consequence of also being used for illegal dumping by community members. In March of 2003, Wolfe County installed no camping signs there to deter overnight use. The dumpster was removed soon after the closure. The end result was climbers looking for more camping options in the area, forcing a mixture of nondispersed camping on Forest Service land, private land, and certainly crowding at other campgrounds, like Miguel's.[4]

Car break-ins also became a common issue at locations at the crags, such as *Roadside*. Voicing their concerns online, climbers argued a range of options.[5] Several suggested that the RRGCC should take an active role in the situation, whether this meant keeping records of the break-ins to establish a pattern, patrolling the lot via community self-policing, or getting involved with local officials. Over time, climbers (partly with the help of the climbing forums) began to notice a pattern of break-ins, often involving parking at *Military Wall/ Left Flank*, *Roadside*, and *The Motherlode*. Throughout this period, climbers suspected locals were involved, and for some, this strained already stretched relations with local residents.

A climber outed a potential local resident as the culprit by name in 2003 on the forums. Vigilante justice was suggested as another option to the RRGCC's involvement: "I say we get about 10 people, a junk car, fill it full of stuff, hide in the woods, wait and then kick the shit out of em [*sic*] when they strike." In several posts on redriverclimbing.com, a local resident (or possibly transient) was mentioned as either living in the parking lot or hanging out there most days. Some of the climbers found him to be a vigilante concerned about the break-ins and helping to police the neighborhood, others thought him another potential thief. By June 2004, climbers intercepted persons while they were breaking into cars and recorded the accused's license plate. The license plate was later tied back to a resident in Owsley County, and that individual's information was publicly listed on the forums, but it is not clear if it was reported to the police. The thefts continued relatively unabated for years and still occur occasionally even today. This added further impetus for climbers to move away from public lands and establish their own climbing areas.

Sitting in her immaculate vacation home perched on a cliff line overlooking Muir Valley in Wolfe County, Liz Weber, when asked about a framed first-place state fair ribbon on the wall said with a sly wink, "That's one of Rick's prized possessions, a blue ribbon for watermelon seed spitting at the Indiana State Fair." Liz and Rick created Muir Valley, a renowned climbing destination located in Wolfe County. The home's huge windows look directly over the *Solarium* off in the distance, one of the many popular crags at Muir Valley. "We can hear the climbers from the house," Liz said, pointing at a group of climbers working the cluster of great 5.11 and 5.12 routes at the crag. Rick laughed that "you can hear people making and missing their moves" from the living room. The two are more often found guiding visitors to parking lots designed to maximize the use of space, working on one of Muir Valley's many miles of trails, or having a friendly chat with first-time visitors. This work leaves little time for them to climb, but they nonetheless remain passionate about what they do.

Rick and Liz first saw Muir Valley in 2003. Liz remembered that "we just happened to stumble onto this property. In fact, we were actually with a friend who was looking at property around the rim of [what is today] Muir Valley." After seeing the unpolished gem that would soon become Muir Valley, they went down into the valley and "just fell in love with the place." "We saw only a small percentage of the rock, but we could tell from what we saw that it was going to be, not only phenomenal climbing, but a huge variety [of climbing] and incredible natural beauty." They bought the property "almost on a whim," negotiating a purchase agreement that same day and officially closing in January 2004 on this first of six contiguous land purchases from 14 different property owners. Liz and Rick soon considered the place "too great not to share. We've got a lot of friends who are climbers. If we open it to the public, we'll probably get a couple hundred people a year, and we can handle that. . . . We had 42,000 people last year. It felt sometimes like having the tiger by the tail."

Liz carefully reminded me that "the Muir Valley that you see today is nothing like what we saw when we came here 15 years ago." Instead, it took a lot of investment and work to turn this into a climbing destination:

> There were no roads, no trails, no belay stations, no parking lots, no restrooms, culverts, bridges, signage . . . and in fact you couldn't walk from one end of the valley to the other because there were briars higher than your head and swamp. The last half-mile leading to the entrance was a single-lane logging trail. We bulldozed a road from that, eliminating the blind hills and curves, and creating ditches for drainage. We also put in the road that runs the entire one-mile length of the valley so that we could do maintenance to the valley and as an emergency rescue road.

Along the way, the Webers have poured their own money, and the majority of their waking hours for 10 years, into planning and making this climbing destination from a dream to reality. The land here is literally soaked with their sweat equity.

The amount of improvement and development at Muir Valley is excellent, especially given that it has no fiscal return. Rick countered with a laugh: "Many people think we are somehow making money off of this property. In fact, there is no write-off. There is no financial gain to us whatsoever. It's essentially a big hole in the ground you throw money into." Rick and Liz spent their own funds in improving the property to make it more hospitable to climbers. Along the way, they have also been mindful of the precarious balance between development and destruction of the environment and have worked to reduce environmental impacts, such as erosion, trash, and soil compaction. Liz explained: "We've tried to have the philosophy of good trails and belay areas so that we don't damage the environment by a lot of erosion, so we've spent a lot of money on trails, stairs, bridges . . . things like that."

Rick and Liz did not want to attach their name to the property because they wanted it to be available to climbers beyond their lifetimes. Instead, they dubbed it Muir Valley in honor of naturalist and climber, John Muir. By midyear 2004 they had developed and documented a strategic plan under which they planned to make a gift of the property to a not-for-profit so that it could be available to the climbers and nature lovers in perpetuity. They also reached agreements with owners of other contiguous property to purchase additional land, which became the northern part of Muir Valley.

Rick helped organize and finance Friends of Muir Valley (FOMV), a group of climbers who wanted to give back labor and talent. Karla Hancock (then Karla Carandang) was one of the prolific route setters in the early days of Muir Valley and became the first chairperson of FOMV. That same year, in the fall of 2004, Friends of Muir Valley organized their first volunteer trail day. Over 80 climbers gathered and worked all day on trails and other maintenance tasks. Muir Valley continues to hold a trail day every fall. Participation reached over 200 volunteers the final year that Rick managed the day in 2014, before the Webers gifted Muir Valley to FOMV in 2015.

When they bought the property, Rick and Liz quickly discovered two cultural uses local residents had assigned to the space: it was an illegal community trash dump and an unofficial OHV trail network. The first year they owned the property, Liz and Rick, along with some friends, had spent an entire vacation just digging out and removing trash from part of Muir Valley. Annually, Wolfe County made highway trucks available to local residents to remove large amounts of trash. Liz was in the county judge executive's office when she overheard a phone conversation about this. Although all the trucks were already spoken for, Liz convinced the county to send a huge gravel truck to Muir Valley and filled it five times with trash. "The more we dug, the more we found," Liz reminisced. She continued,

The northern part of the valley, in particular, had been a generations-long trash dump. It wasn't just small items. It wasn't throwing your garbage out. . . . Mattresses, cars, washing machines . . . I found a fellow working in county government to work with me and we got a superfund grant because there was close to $100,000 spent just trucking to haul trash out of there. It was very hard to access because of the steep cliffs. . . . Rick and I actually taught some of the people who were coming in to do the heavy work how to rappel so they could get down to hook on to the trash.

Today, Muir Valley has a network of trails clearly leading climbers and nature enthusiasts from the parking lot to the climbing areas. Rick says, "Now it's pretty pristine." Liz also shared that climbers are really good about picking up smaller trash that someone else had dropped and minimizing trash left at the crags. Rick said that he feels "more and more climbers are following a Leave No Trace ethic today." And the OHVs, once a major concern, are now absent. Liz recalled, "We had an issue with that initially because people felt if the property wasn't guarded, it was public property, and we had a couple confrontations with ATV users doing a lot of environmental damage." It is still somewhat common to see OHVs traveling on local roads in the area on any given day, but they are no longer allowed in Muir Valley.

While the Webers finalized things at Muir Valley, the RRGCC was also working out exactly what to do about another historic climbing location to the south in Lee County. In recent years, climbers had developed new crags on the Murray family's property along Bald Rock Fork Road. Recall that RRGCC president Hugh Loeffler had originally secured permission in the mid-1990s for climbers to climb and bolt in the area. Now, something more permanent seemed possible and perhaps even necessary.

Landowner Mattie Murray (née Pendergrass) was born in nearby Beattyville in 1920. Mattie operated (with her husband R. L. Murray) a local grocery store in Beattyville for over 50 years. Mattie inherited that property in 1963 from her family lines to Daniel Boone Pendergrass, who had originally purchased the property in 1908. By the late 1990s, however, there were reasonable concerns that the family's agreement to allow climbing was tenuous. Mattie was in her late 70s (she lived to be 85 and passed away January 10, 2006) and had recently relocated to Harrodsburg to be closer to family. Mattie's eventual death risked the unknown. What could be done to address this?

Buying the land outright was certainly a viable option. The idea of buying climbing land was not entirely new at the time. Access Fund had, at the time, worked on 22 land acquisitions (today, the total is over 70). These projects often included working with local climbing organizations to purchase and maintain the land. Attorney and conservation activist John Myers served on the Access Fund board of directors and had been a vocal advocate for purchasing land to protect access. John called Shannon Stuart-Smith, who was serving as the executive director of the RRGCC at the time, and they talked about the idea of purchasing climbing areas. Soon, John Myers volunteered to help guide the RRGCC on purchasing the Murray property. John came to the Red, and Hugh Loeffler took him to the many exciting crags in the area. The next step was to learn the boundaries of exactly what would be purchased, which was easier said than done.

Property lines in rural eastern Kentucky can be problematic. Family land lines and land use are often based as much on tradition as property plats. As the RRGCC lacked the thousands of dollars that might be required to get an official survey completed, John Bronaugh took the lead on identifying the property lines with the Lee County Clerk's Office. He outlined his work in a post on redriverclimbing.com explaining the property purchase:

Property in rural areas like this are based on deeds that were written in the 1800s which have only vague descriptions of boundaries. It's not like in cities where every piece of land has been surveyed. It has taken me many trips to the Lee County Clerk's Office to try to sort out all the neighboring deeds and deeds that have been sold and are within the boundaries of the original Murray property. Only a few small tracts have been surveyed within the boundary. Based on my research, it appears that the Murray tract extends from Sore Heel Hollow (the big valley on the right aka Big Dick Lick) to the Arena and on around a bit to the north. It also includes all the land on top of the cliff where Charmane Oil Company is located. There is probably some land on the south side of Bald Rock Fork Road that includes the Getaway Crag. The land probably does not include where the Ashland Oil property is (Cave Fork). There is a separate tract that includes Coalbank Hollow (Solar Collector and Dark Side).[6]

Two crags assumed to be on the property and that the Murrays felt would be included in the sale held particular interest to several climbers: *The Arena* and *Oil Crack Rock*. Recall that *Oil Crack Rock* had seen work in the mid-1990s. It held two 5.14s ("Skeletor" and "A Clean Well Lighted Face") and had partly been the impetus for Hugh Loeffler seeking clearer approval from the Murrays, which eventually led to this proposed purchase. *The Arena* (or often simply called *Arena* among climbers) sits just across from *Oil Crack Rock* but did not see development until 2003. Much of that early work included a lot of bolting by Terry Kindred.

Terry had already extensively worked through the nearby crags (*Oil Crack*, *The Gallery*, and *Shady Grove*) and gained a deserved reputation as a steadfast route equipper. Terry was a pilot, and his profession's interest in safety and precision overflowed into his climbing. Stephanie Meadows shared that Terry "added a lot of flavor to the community. . . . He was very meticulous in his work. He was a perfectionist." Like John Bronaugh, Terry would not hesitate to speak his mind. This made Terry occasionally unpopular with some members of the climbing community, particularly when he argued that a route was unsafely bolted. Terry was actively involved in the anchor replacement effort in the Red that replaced outdated (and often less than safe) bolts on older routes with cutting-edge technology. This interest later led to Terry's appointment as the first chair of the RRGCC's Fixed Anchor Replacement Committee in 2004. This committee would later develop into an informal group called Team Suck, comprised of climbers who wished to help with replacing aging hardware throughout the Red.[7]

The Arena quickly grew to hold almost 40 routes in 2003 alone. Terry had several to his credit, including five routes in the 5.10 skill range and likely a number of other higher-skill routes. Blake Bowling, who would also become an integral member of Team Suck, worked alongside Terry on route development at *The Arena*. He later joined several other individuals who would come to be important members of the climbing community leaders in the following years—Yasmeen Fowler, Jason Burton, and Ray Ellington—as well as route developers in the southern region—Jesse New, Scott Hammon, and Ryan Adams. John Bronaugh also worked on a route at *The Arena* (with Jason Burton) called "Chocolate Waterfall," as did Mark Jackson with Bob Matheny on "Through the Turnstile." In all, *Arena* held thirteen 5.10s, five 5.11s, eight 5.12s, and a 5.13 ("Power Play"). This crag simply upped the ante for the RRGCC to secure the property for climbing.

The next steps for the RRGCC moving forward on the property were difficult and contentious. On one hand, the RRGCC simply did not have the funds to purchase the property, period. On the other hand, this was an extraordinary opportunity to preserve the climbing and avoid a massive closure. John and Hugh were both on board with purchasing the property. Shannon realized that an extensive fundraising effort would be needed to get the ball moving. As executive director, Shannon empowered John to negotiate a deal. In September 2002 the RRGCC obtained, reportedly for $100, the rights to purchase the property by September 30, 2003. As purchase negotiations continued, the Murray family agreed to owner-finance part of the funds, meaning the RRGCC would need around $40,000 for a down payment and annual payments of around $20,000, with the condition that a missed annual payment could default the loan. RRGCC officially purchased the property on January 20, 2004, with the financial help of Bob Matheny, who made the initial down payment of $35,000. He continued to make payments on the property for the coming years, as there was no clear funding source on hand. The property would soon be called Pendergrass-Murray Recreational Preserve (PMRP), named after the two families historically linked to the property.

With both Muir Valley and now PMRP up and running in the Red on climber-owned property, this created an interesting new dynamic between climbers and the DBNF. Growth at both properties effectively acted as a pressure release valve for public lands. Climbers who had once been crowding parking lots and roadside parking spots throughout the DBNF were now gradually visiting new areas. Likewise, the pressure to develop new routes on the DBNF winnowed as climbers had extensive room for growth in the south. Having the chance to become their own land managers also pressed climbers to better understand their impacts on crags. This is discussed further in later chapters.

The Murray purchase also altered how RRGCC looked at fundraising. One big issue was language in the purchase stating that if the climbers missed one annual payment, the Murray family could default the loan. RRGCC had held Derby Fest each spring as a fundraiser at Miguel's Pizza. Prior to the Murray purchase, Shannon said the event would "raise a few hundred dollars" for the RRGCC. Derby Fest, over time, would merge into the Red River Reunion event, which is still held today by Miguel's Pizza. Proceeds from this event support the RRGCC. Bill Strachan, executive director of the RRGCC from 2004 to 2016, recalled that in 2001, Shannon came up with the idea of "Rocktoberfest" as an October educational event for climbers. This event fit in well with Shannon's interest in educating gym-to-crag climbers in everything from outdoor ethics to minimizing impact and preserving access, which also harkens back to the earliest efforts by the Cumberland Climbers to hold educational events encouraging safety at the crag. Soon, Rocktoberfest took on an increased organizational fundraising role.[8] Rocktoberfest will be revisited in a later chapter.

Amid the bustle of the PMRP purchase, myriad other issues were running in the background regarding the property. First, there had been conversations about the RRGCC reselling the land to the Forest Service to be included in the DBNF in order to pay for the purchase. At the time, ties between the two groups were tense following the archaeological dig at *Military Wall*. John Bronaugh noted that a RRGCC task force assembled to handle the land purchase "doesn't feel that climbers' privilege to climb on FS property is secure enough at this point to see that as an immediate option. Private ownership by the RRGCC seems better in the short run. We can always revisit this idea down the road if things change."[9] Here, a chance to expand the DBNF was potentially lost as a result of the distrust that had grown out of previous encounters at *Military Wall*.

Second, the RRGCC was not the only organization interested in purchasing the land, something climbers would not learn until several years later. Stephanie Meadows shared some important insight on this. Stephanie spent her first day in the Red climbing at *Military Wall* in 2001 and would move to Lexington in 2004 to be closer to climbing. Stephanie joined the RRGCC board in 2007 and served as interim treasurer from summer 2010 through late 2011. As part of her role as interim treasurer, Stephanie met with James Paul Murray, Mattie's son, in a Starbucks in Lexington in 2010 to make a final payment to the family. The final payment used funds from an Access Fund loan that the RRGCC would later pay off in 2012 (more about this arrangement in the next chapter). She recalled, "I made a big fake check . . . and a real check [laughs]" to commemorate the purpose. Then, six years after the purchase, James Paul told Stephanie that the RRGCC had not been the only group wanting to buy the property. In fact, the local oil company, Charmane, had offered the Murray family $100,000 more than the RRGCC, but the family had declined. "He wanted the climbers to have the property." Stephanie acknowledged how extraordinary this decision was for climbers: "They could have had $100,000 dollars more, but money wasn't the issue. They knew what climbers wanted to do for the area." Likewise, Whitney Boland's article "(There's no place like) The Lode" notes that the RRGCC actually did miss a payment during the loan process, but the Murray family chose to be forgiving: "The RRGCC, penniless when compared to Charmane, missed the original deadline to make a payment for the property, and the oil company stepped up and told [James Paul] Murray that it not only had the down payment, but was ready to buy the land right away. Yet because climbers had shown such congeniality to Murray, he told Charmane, Over my dead body, and moved the deadline back."[10]

Third, leases on oil rights complicated the purchase. Even though the Murray clan owned the land, Charmane had leased the oil rights for many years. The lease provided them reasonable access to the property to claim that right. Separated land rights is relatively common in resource-rich areas like eastern Kentucky. Land purchases can separate surface land rights (e.g., to build and reside on the property) and mineral, timber, and oil rights. Those rights can be sold or leased separately from the surface rights, meaning that there are, in essence, multiple interests in a particular plot of land. Right to extract resources allows access to the property to obtain that resource, which can include building roads, putting in equipment, and accessing extraction areas round the clock. That was the story of a handful of oil wells located throughout the Murray property. And some of those, like the one at the top of the Bald Rock hill on the way into the property and another at the foot of the hill, created immediate issues. The PMRP purchase did not exclude Charmane from the property, as they purchased only the surface, mineral, and timber rights, but not oil, which was still held in a long-term lease to Charmane. Climbers could not block access to these wells, and this briefly became a point of contention because of parking.

Before the purchase could even be finalized in 2004, conflicts and miscommunications between Charmane and climbers boiled over. A lack of parking in the PMRP resulted in climbers blocking access to oil wells. This meant Charmane could not access their pumps and enact their rights under their oil lease. In October 2003, Charmane began having cars towed that blocked access to wells and attempted to gate off access to the property. Bob Matheny explained that RRGCC took Charmane to court over the matter and received an injunction preventing future towing, gating, or other adverse behavior. The clash was further brought back from a fever pitch by the RRGCC, which worked with Charmane on behalf of climbers. The RRGCC brokered an agreement that climbers would be informed to steer clear of the pumps and right of way, something that would be self-policed in the community.

Finally, the exact dimensions of the property remained unclear. The RRGCC was unsure of exactly what they were purchasing. Bob Matheny reflected on how confusing the plats for the purchase were: "I was in the Lee County Courthouse looking at property plats because of this property . . . and the lady down there, we were just talking, and I said something about what I was doing and what I was looking at, and she started laughing and said, 'You know, nobody knows anything about that property down there.' She says, 'We have full plotted deed descriptions but as far as where the lines actually are, there are only a couple places that are referenced well enough to be able to identify them in this day and age.'" Most of the crags in this hollow were clearly in the property, but two were up for debate, and they were big ones: *Oil Crack* and *Arena*. The RRGCC felt they had purchased both in the Murray deal:

> The original understanding when the purchase agreement was entered into was that the *Oil Crack* was included in the whole property and what we purchased from J. P., Mr. Murray, and his mother, Mattie, quote "All of the unsold lands of," not "you're buying this." It's "everything that has not been sold of this." And there were some descriptors and so forth and we thought because no one could find any other deeds that said this wasn't the case, that the property included not only what we currently own, but the *Oil Crack* and the *Arena* area, which turned out to be two separate tracts.

Arguably, John Bronaugh had his concerns that both crags were not owned by the Murrays going into the purchase. While sharing news of his research to ensure that crags *Dark Side* and *Solar Collector* were on the property, John shared this on the redriverclimbing.com forums on January 10, 2003, a year before the purchase was finalized:

> I'm doing research for the RRGCC on ownership of the Dark Side/Solar Collector. It is not clear yet who owns that property. The deeds are so confusing that even the Lee County PVA (who assesses property taxes) has that land as labeled "unknown" as to ownership. Nobody pays taxes for that land currently. Before the RRGCC will exercise an option to purchase on the Murray property, we'll have to determine what crags their land encompasses. Preliminary indications show that the Murray's own

from the Motherload (not including the Motherload) west to Drive-By. They probably own Oil Crack and the Arena, but I haven't confirmed that yet. There is clearly a dispute from another landowner as to ownership of the Dark Side/Solar Collector. As such, I would recommend not publishing those routes yet.[11]

In the end, both *Oil Crack* and *Arena* were effectively closed to climbing by the actual property owners soon after the Murray purchase was finalized. Bob Matheny thought that "it was effectively closed from the point of first purchase, or very shortly thereafter, due to frictions with Charmane Oil." He noted, as was outlined above, that the lost crags included quite a few midrange routes, which made the area a very desirable part of the planned purchase. Due to a blurry history of unclear deed language, lost and refound plats, an intestate ownership, and eventual sale to Charmane Oil, these crags were no longer part of the deal. And then things got even more confusing, as Charmane would dissolve as a company. Bob explained: "Charles Hatfield died. He was the head [of Charmane Oil]. . . . His widow attempted to restructure things when oil was selling quite well 12 years ago or so." Hatfield's widow tried to restructure things so that Charmane would become primarily a servicing wells company, servicing wells as opposed to drilling and recovery. As oil prices sank, this changed, and she sold out to Triad. Later, to further complicate issues, Triad's owner, too, died suddenly and intestate, reportedly causing the land to be purchased by American Natural Gas in probate. They hold it still today, and the land remains closed to climbing. *Oil Crack* and *Arena* both remain on the wish list of crags to be reopened in the region.

Crag losses did not hold back growth in the Red. That year, Muir Valley saw over 100 new sport, trad, and mixed routes added to the list of routes in the Red. In 2004, "Prometheus Unbound" was completed by Greg Martin, Bryan Boyd, Jeremy Stitch, and Tommy Wilson. To the south, Bill Ramsey sent "Golden Boy" at *Gold Coast*, a route bolted by Chris Martin. And Kenny Barker completed "Paradise Lost" at *Purgatory*. Those three routes now added to the 30-plus 5.13a or higher routes now in the Red. At *Gold Coast*, Jeff Moll had also equipped two open projects, which, when combined in 2010 by visiting climber Jonathan Siegrist, would become 5.14c route "Twenty Four Karats." At *Rebel Camp Hollow*, the *Bruise Brothers Wall* had 19 new routes, while its next-door neighbor *Sunnyside Wall* saw five new routes.

Meanwhile, the southern region saw over 50 new routes. The new spot called *Purgatory* attracted the attention of Kenny Barker, who, in addition to his "Paradise Lost," crafted "Fallen Angel" and "Dracula '04." Although it had not been sent, respected 5.14c "Lucifer" (FA'd by Mike Doyle in 2006) was most likely an open project in 2004 at *Purgatory*, as well. At *Shady Grove*, several famous Red climbers had created 10 routes since PMRP's open season on route development. Shannon Stuart-Smith established "Citizen's Arete," "Coming Out Party," and "Irreverent C." Also in 2004, Terry Kindred completed "Girls Gone Wild . . . WOO!" and "Crucify Me." Blake Bowling sent "Who Knows?," "Who Is Who?," and "False Idol." Chris Martin also bolted and sent two routes there: "Which Is Which?" and "Far from God."

John Bronaugh had a keen eye for potential lines and developed multiple crags in the southern region in 2004. At *Left Field*, John equipped and FA'd four routes: "Lowered Expectations," "Apoplectic Chick from Missouri," "Autograft," and "Hop Scotch." Just around the corner, he developed *The Playground*, bolting and sending eight routes. At nearby *Volunteer Wall*, he placed red tags at what he thought were the best lines that could be bolted. Several were completed in 2004. Wes Allen finished "Darwin Loves You," while Bill Strachan FA'd "First Time." John and Ryan Adams completed three routes: "Swap Meet," "Helping Hands," and "Nice to Know You." John's son Alex Yeakley also completed "Family Tradition." John planned to have a so-called *drill fest* in which volunteer climbers would spend a day bolting even more lines at the crag. But this did not come to be, at least not how John nor anyone else in the climbing community envisioned it.

On Sunday, August 22, 2004, climbers were doing what they do all throughout the Red: climbing. But as the day progressed, news that John Bronaugh had suffered a heart attack while climbing broke the serenity of the Red. He died later that day in Lexington at the hospital. He was 44 years old. One of the most important climbers in the Red's brief history was lost.

News of John's unexpected death quickly spread through the Red. John's former climbing partner, Ron Snider, laments John's sudden death: "Well, we had families, started having kids, I wasn't climbing as much as I used to be, and I'd met some different guys to climb with when I did get out, and then John got back from California and [had] just started climbing again. We crossed paths once in a while and I always would say, 'Yeah, we need to get out again, man. We need to get . . . ' Just never really got together, and then he was gone." Memories soon poured in on redriverclimbing.com, where John frequently posted route beta. User Wes remembered the moment as "a great loss for our community and a great loss for many people personally." User roots wrote, "Johnny definitely left his mark in the Red and will be remembered in the most high." User tsparks commented, "Johnny did great things for climbers in the Red." User hamsco remarked, "The Red will never be the same." Nearly everyone had a John story to share, and they consistently found him a hero to the climbing community and a bitter loss to accept. Many climbers stated in online discussion boards and in conversations that they "climbed for Johnny" that day.[12]

Climbers held a celebration of John's life at Torrent Falls on August 28, where they mourned both the loss of a dear friend and climbing partner and an advocate for climbing access. John's time on earth would soon be commemorated in several ways in the Red. Muir Valley added *Johnny's Wall* in 2005. At PMRP, a wall called *Inner Circle* between *Shady Grove* and *Purgatory* was renamed *Bronaugh Wall*. In his work in the surrounding crags, John, along with his son, Alex, had also completed routes here. John had put up "Collision Damage" (a 5.11d sport) and "Crumblies" (a 5.12a sport) the year he died. Likewise, in 2004, Alex had put up "Jingus," a highly regarded 5.11b sport route.

Prior to the name change to *Bronaugh Wall*, *Inner Circle* had yet to appear in the guidebooks. After John's death, the trailhead sign marking the crag mysteriously disappeared. The trail also had tree limbs pulled across it. As it turns out, Shannon Stuart-Smith was quietly completing two routes in memory of her friend and colleague: "Belly of the Beast" (a 5.12c sport) and "Take the Scary Out of Life" (a 5.10d originally trad route retro-bolted in 2011). Others would later join Shannon in 2005 in adding routes there, including Blake Bowling and Julia Fain. And following John's suggestions, a group returned to *Volunteer Wall* in 2005 to continue bolting the lines above the red tags John left there the previous year.[13]

In his time in the Red, John's son Alex had also become a respected climber. Alex developed a very popular 5.8 route called "27 Years of Climbing" at *The Gallery* and attached his name to five other routes. In the online guidebook, "27 Years of Climbing" has maintained a strong reputation as an excellent starter route. Recall Alex had also collaborated with John on "Father and Son" in 1993 back when Alex was not even a teenager. And in 2004, Alex had conquered "Family Tradition," possibly paying homage to the fact that both of his parents were climbers. Heartbreakingly, tragedy struck yet again. Alex Yeakley died December 4, 2004, following complications from a car accident in which he was a passenger. Alex was only 20 years old.

Today, both John and Alex's names are regularly spoken in the Red not only because of their routes, but because of Johnny and Alex Trail Day. In 2005 the RRGCC elected to change their annual trail development day—a day of service in which members put down their climbing shoes and pick up shovels and hammers—to commemorate two cherished members of their community. That first year (2005) it was called the Johnny and Alex Crag Day rather than Trail Day because it also included a focus on getting first-time route developers into mentorships with experienced bolters. The trail work aspect that year also focused on getting better access to *Gallery* and *Volunteer Wall*, two locations where John had worked as a route developer. Since then, this annual event is simply called Johnny and Alex Trail Day, or JATD, by climbers. JATD had initially included route development but would later come to focus solely on trail and crag infrastructure growth. It represents one of the major homecoming events for the community.

CHAPTER 11

The RocTrip, Growth, and Impact Issues, 2005–2010

The years immediately following the two large climber preserve purchases, Muir Valley and PMRP, represented a period of transition and growth unparalleled in the Red's history. Climbers were now in the process of focusing the bulk of climbing routes off Forest Service property and onto climbing preserves at Muir Valley and PMRP. This dramatic change called for a new printed guide. Recall that Ray Ellington (with John's blessing) transferred Bronaugh's guide listings into an online format. This development had been a wonderful tool for climbers sitting in their living rooms, where they could find and print routes. However, it was not nearly as convenient in the field. A printed guide, therefore, still held a lot of value for climbers. In 2005, Ray published his first print guidebook, *The Red River Gorge: A Rock Climbing Guide*. It represented a comprehensive list of over 1,300 routes in the Red. The 2005 guide summarized the history of the Red's climbing community in around four pages. It also offered several full-page profiles on important characters in the Red's climbing community story, including a story about John Bronaugh, dubbing him "King of the Red River Gorge."[1]

Two major additions to the Ellington guide were Muir Valley and PMRP. As the first of the climbing preserves, Ellington noted that this approach "represents a powerful new tactic in the struggle for access."[2] At the time Muir Valley was rapidly nearing 150 routes, with the bolting team of Jared Hancock, Karla Carandang, Mike Susko, "J. J." Jones, and Tim Powers averaging three new routes per weekend according to Ellington's guide. In effectively a year's time, Muir Valley had developed six crags on the property. Several of the hollows also contained multiple walls that had been developed. Meanwhile, PMRP had grown to include 10 new crags in the guide.

At Muir Valley's *Rebel Camp Hollow*, the *Bruise Brothers Wall* held 24 routes in the Ellington guide, while *Sunnyside* held 11. *Joe Ponder Branch Hollow* included 12 routes, including a very uncommon (for the Red) 100-foot-long bolted route called "Heard it on NPR." This crag also held the official first route recorded at Muir Valley: Rick Weber's (2003) "Bad Dentures," a 5.9 top rope. At *Lower Tantroft Branch Hollow*, Muir Valley's developers had added a notable 54 routes since 2004, at the time the most routes of any Muir Valley area. This location also included numerous 5.12 and 5.13 rated routes and held six walls: *Indy Wall, The Sanctuary, Inner Sanctum, The Stadium, Tectonic Wall*, and *Johnny's Wall*. Nearby, *The Great Wall* (a standalone crag) had 31 routes, including the popular "Boltergeist." *The Solarium*, at 10 routes, remains popular today for its numerous 5.12s, and it was still being developed when Ellington's guide went to print, as was *The Great Arch,* with six routes.

Climbers also continued to develop new routes at PMRP at a blistering clip. One important area of growth was *The Dark Side*. This new crag saw growth starting in 1999 and 2000 (Rob McFall's "Small Fry" and "Mama Benson," a 5.9 and 5.12a, were completed just after Bronaugh's last guide) but soon gained notoriety for its many hard (5.12–5.13) routes. Several big names in the Red were active, too: Chris Martin, David Hume, Hugh Loeffler, Neal Strickland, and Bill Ramsey all attached their names here. Chris Martin's "Shanghai" (a 5.12d) and Rob McFall's "Tuskan Raider" (a 5.12d) both got special mention in the Ellington guide. *Gold Coast* and *Purgatory* also demonstrated important high-skill route growth, as previously mentioned.

The Ellington guide included the most comprehensive list of closures in the DBNF to date, and this deserves a bit of explanation. The DBNF had asked to include information on specific areas that were closed to protect resources found there. According to Tim Eling, "Ray Ellington was good about putting information in the front of the book." Working with the DBNF, Ray "put in there information about white-haired goldenrod, info about archaeology. We put in those climbing crags that had some sites closed off with those woven wire fences. We had a list of them in there and explained why we were doing that. And it was right there in the front of the guidebook, which I thought was great for them to do that, to help address [the issues at hand]."

These closures included two routes at *Lower Small Wall*, three routes at *Dip Wall*, the archaeological dig routes at *Military Wall*, three routes at *Tower Rock*, "Flashlight" at *Funk Rock City*, bouldering problems at *Grays Wall* and *Jewell Rock*, user trails at *Long Wall* and *Woody's Wall*, and five routes at *Western Sky Bridge*. Also noted were several proximity closures where climbing within 300 feet of a particular landmark would be closed. These included "Sky Bridge Layback," routes at *Spring Wall* and *Tunnel Wall* (near Nada Tunnel), and several climbs at *Chimney Top Crag*. The guide explained that closures were due to archaeological sites, proximity to endangered plants (such as the white-haired goldenrod pictured on page 30 of the guide), the creation of user trails, or other important areas. Additionally, the guide included a notice from the DBNF adding that climbers could not camp in rockshelters or build fires (or even use stoves) within 100 feet of the base of any cliff. As well, RRGCC included a one-page ad explaining minimal-impact approaches to climbers and the importance of responsible climbing. Learning to adhere to these principles would prove critical in the coming years, most notably starting at Torrent Falls.

Mark and Kathy Meyer purchased Torrent Falls in 1998. Their initial business was a bed-and-breakfast and two rental cabins on the property beside the area where the L. Park Hotel had previously stood. Mark and Kathy would later also purchase the neighboring area (probably around 2004; the year is not certain) to establish a *via ferrata* and Mark's Mountain BBQ. Via ferratas (or *iron paths*) utilize established cable systems to allow clipped-in users to safely and quickly cross a natural feature such as a rock face. They were previously used to transport expeditions up mountaineering routes in the Alps. The idea was later used by military forces to move goods and troops in the Dolomites in World War I. Today, via ferratas are part of the adventure tourism industry and allow everyone to experience heights without actually climbing.

Torrent Falls had recently gone through an unclear series of changes in terms of climbing access. Recall minimal route development had started in the 1980s, but it was the bolting blitz of the 1990s that created rapid route development at the property. This led to a temporary closure until Fred Martin purchased the property and allowed climbing again with a $2 parking donation. Climbing access was again closed at Torrent Falls when Mark and Kathy initially purchased the property, but they subsequently reopened access. They allowed climbers on the property for a donation of $2 per climber. It again became a central fixture among climbers. This, however, would not last. On March 14, 2006, Mark posted on the forums that Torrent Falls was officially up for closure to climbers as of May 1, 2006. To be even more specific, Mark noted that he had planned to close Torrent Falls to climbing immediately but had been convinced to wait by the RRGCC.[3] The crag would stay open only if climbers could follow specific conditions outlined in his post.

Mark's post began by noting that this land was purchased as part of a business. Recall that several cabins are present at Torrent Falls and were rented out to those visiting the Red. Mark's complaints originated around the popularity of the site amid the rapid growth of the Red's climbing community. Increasing use had worn down the trails and created parking overloads in which climbers parked their cars in reserved cabin rental spots (or even at Torrent Church's parking lot just down the road). Although a public bathroom was available at the BBQ restaurant, certain climbers had urinated and defecated on the property, creating major issues. Some climbers also brought dogs and left them off leash, allowing the dogs to roam around the property. And then there was an issue with language use, which ranged from the foul and offensive to simply loud. Remember, the Meyers lived on the property and were firsthand witnesses to the issues. Effectively, climbers had, from Mark and Kathy's perspective, behaved very poorly at Torrent Falls, and things would clearly need to change if this relationship were to continue.

Climbers' responses on the forum to the threatened closure are quite interesting and telling. There were those who pledged full support behind the effort, reminding climbers of other closures and reiterating the importance of Mark's requests. User SikMonkey confessed to his occasional use of strong language while climbing and promised to fine himself an additional dollar for every swear word uttered while at Torrent Falls on top of his entry donation of $2. Several climbers thanked the Meyers for allowing climbing to happen on the property and identified ways that word of the issues could be spread to other areas. Still, another common response was that it was only a handful of climbers actually causing the issues. Rick Weber (from Muir Valley) wrote, "We feel your pain. Most climbers are terrific. But, it takes only a few bad eggs to ruin things for all the good folks. We are starting to encounter similar problems and hope that peer pressure from other climbers will solve some of them. If not, the consequences are obvious." [4]

User Wes also made an important point common to the sport: climbers have a reputation (occasionally rightfully earned) for breaking rules: "I think it has always been an issue with following the rules by climbers, the problem now is that there are just so many of us out here. I personally climbed at pocket wall after the no trespassing signs went up, because 'they don't apply to climbers.'" [5] Wes also suggested concerns about what this meant for the future of climbing as things stood:

Maybe I am a bit jaded, but I really don't see much hope of real change. It will continue to be a very small percent of people that go over and above their fair share of work to keep things going, while the majority just keeps its collective head in the sand. Personally, I am strong enough and diverse enough in my climbing, that I can still climb for years at the Red and other places without much trouble, even if a few or even many places get shut down. It is the people that only get out a couple times a month (or year) at the most that are going to suffer, so those are the people that need to step up.[6]

Wes's concerns were not heeded. By November, Torrent Falls was closed.

Mark's rationale for the closure included "a dog tied up all day beside the van under the No Dog sign" and numerous other dog visits, "a female [climber] to the left of 'Paranoia' pissing in my yard, under the rock house, in front of [my family]" despite a nearby portable toilet, and unauthorized guiding on the property.[7] The general sense was disrespect of the rules. Mark felt that "there is a great community out there. Maybe, this community can or maybe they cannot educate young, inconsiderate people. I do not have to [worry] about it, I tried since this spring."[8] This closure, however, excluded climbers who were customers paying to stay in the cabins and rooms on the property.

The Meyers kept the property closed to climbing until a surprise announcement by Ray Ellington on March 15, 2007: the Torrent Falls property was being purchased by none other than Bob Matheny. Due to size constraints and the popularity of the site, limited public access was allowed through a daily allotment online waiver system and subsequently a security gate. At the time, the parking area fit no more than three cars and allowed only three parties to enter. It was also only available on Thursdays through Sundays from 8 a.m. to 8 p.m. Access to the crag would also be granted for those renting cabins at Torrent Falls or through Red River Outdoors. While keeping access an option, this greatly limited the number of climbers who could climb at Torrent Falls.

One important component of Torrent Falls was that it was fully owned and managed by climbers. Bob owned the property, while Matt and Amy Tackett managed the cabin rentals. In January 2005, Matt and Amy had shared the announcement that they had purchased Red River Outdoors. Red River Outdoors (previously owned by the Chaney family) had been offering a variety of services to the outdoor recreation community, including kayaking, shuttling, cabin rentals, climbing guiding, climbing lessons, and more.[9] The storefront also offered snacks, pizza, and climbing gear. Matt and Amy purchased this store with the idea of continuing its strong ties with the outdoor recreation community. Climbers made their café part of the usual trip into the Red, and the store became a central part of social activities in the community. Matt continued to establish new lines throughout the southern region and had also started guiding in the region.

Not long after the initial closure at Torrent Falls, the climbing community experienced another loss. Terry Kindred died on May 28, 2006. Before his death, Terry had completed one last route at *Military Wall*, a 5.11b route, but he had not publicly declared a name for the route. After his death, Lee Smith suggested naming the route "Parting Gift" to commemorate Terry's last climb, and the name stuck. Several climbers held a Terry Kindred Day in May 2008 in which climbers would spend time on Terry's many routes in the Red.[10]

Climbers again turned to the forums to post their memories, this time of Terry. In one post, user the lurkist described Terry as "the most ardent and colorful champion of the Red. He believed in the Red and the value of the climbing there and saw the potential of climbing there more than anyone else in the community." User Artsay also had a poignant post, noting Terry's unwavering, "motivation to educate climbers, his obsession with developing quality routes, and his passion to preserve climbing in Red River Gorge. His love for RRG climbing speaks for itself." User merrick described Terry as an "institution," adding, "He was always at the Red, he was always psyched to climb, he was always so psyched." User Spragwa noted the importance of Terry's role as a frequent critic within the community: "In life, we need a dissenter. Terry was at times my greatest critic and my greatest supporter. I felt honored to have him as a friend. If nothing else, Terry knew that I wasn't one of those 'literal' people." And user campusman aptly summed up Terry's contributions to the Red as a teacher and doer: "I met him at Pocket Wall, easily, I found out Terry was one of the big dudes. There, he taught me a little about anchors which goes a long ways. Later I saw him replacing at Torrent Falls, he was real, a hard worker, and someone we needed while we had him. . . . Go Team suck go." It should be noted that Team Suck continues their important work today, replacing aging gear throughout the Red.[11]

Southern region development continued at a rapid clip, and Ray Ellington released a second edition of the climbing guide in 2007. In just two years, the new guide added nearly 300 routes to the Red. At PMRP, climbers had several new crags in the Sore Heel Hollow: *What About Bob Wall, Courtesy Wall, Chica Bonita Wall, Curbside, The Shire, North 40,* and *Rival Wall* all held exciting new routes developed by newer names in the community. Matt Tackett, Jason Hass, Jeremy Egleston, Jared Hancock, and Ron Bateman worked on dozens of routes in these areas in 2005 and 2006. One new name, Kipp Trummel, quickly appeared alongside many of the new routes.

Kipp moved to Lexington in 2005 and soon created many impressive sport climbs. His first route had been at *Sunnyside* in Muir Valley, where he and Eric Heuermann completed "Suppress the Rage," a 5.12a. In the southern region, Kipp's name was on nearly every route at *North 40*, including the visually stunning "Amarillo Sunset," a 5.11b. The route rose along a water-stained wall that offered a particularly gorgeous view around sunset. Kipp also found himself busy at *Curbside* along with Ron Bateman. *The Shire* offered many new climbing opportunities (bolted by Josh Thurston, Ron Batement, Matt Tackett, Betsey Adams, and others) for beginner climbers transitioning into lead climbing. In the coming years, Kipp's work as a route developer would be an important part of the quickening pace of route growth off DBNF property.

Muir Valley also continued to grow, and Kipp, Eric, and others worked on several routes there during this period.[12] *The Arsenal* offered a sunny-facing crag for cool weather climbing and included six routes in the 2007 guide. "Bathtub Mary," a 5.11a by Kipp Trummel and Karen Clark, and "Reload," a 5.12c by Brad Weaver and Eric Heuermann, both stood out as popular additions. Nearby, *The Boneyard* added 15 routes to Muir Valley, including Craig Luebben's popular 5.11c route, "Renegade."[13] *Midnight Surf* represented a crag in development offering a huge section of wall that looked very little like the rest of the Red, as well as desirable 5.12 routes (like "Cell Block Six" and "Iniquity") and a 5.13b ("Shiva"). In winter of 2007, Rick Weber brokered a deal with Kipp Trummel: Rick would provide the hardware if Kipp would develop the routes at *Midnight Surf*. Kipp took the job, creating several highly skilled routes. Kipp allowed other climbers to take a shot at the first ascents, however, as his central interest was in the route development itself. New crags *Coyote Cliff* and *Slab City* similarly offered new growth to the valley.

On April 24, 2007, a different kind of tragedy struck that again showed the strength of the climbing community: much of Red River Outdoors burned down. Amy and Matt lived above the store, and Amy had noticed smoke coming from the side of the building around 5 p.m. She went out to investigate. Two explosions, which the local fire marshal suggested may have come from the gas tanks of a pickup parked near the building, engulfed the building in flames. Their dog, River, died in the fire. Matt and Amy also effectively lost everything they owned in the fire.

Morgain Sprague opined that climbers felt Red River Outdoors "was our home away from home," and it is quite remarkable how climbers jumped in to rebuild that connection. The climbing community responded almost immediately with resources like clothing, food, and cash. They organized efforts to rebuild Red River Outdoors. In a post on the forums, Matt and Amy wrote, "We have had people drive from Ohio, Michigan and further just to hug and offer their help. The climbing gear scene has reacted with amazing efforts. I have enough gear to continue my guide/instruction services. The local businesses have gone all out. Amy had shoes on her feet within 10 minutes of the blaze from Miguel's, food from Miguel and Mark and many man hours from True North."[14] The Tacketts soon began rebuilding the shop.[15] Meanwhile, the RRGCC prepared to host its upcoming Rocktoberfest, an event that would bring international attention to the Red.

The 2007 Rocktoberfest became a legendary event here in the Red and, to some degree, to the entire world of climbing. It was held at Natural Bridge Cabin Company Campground, just off the Slade exit and down the street from Natural Bridge State Park, Red River Outdoors, and Miguel's Pizza.[16] It was certainly a moment that fully put the Red out there as a sport-climbing mecca. That year, Rocktoberfest (October 12–14) coincided with a major climbing event called RocTrip. RocTrip, in its sixth year, was a traveling climbing event that highlighted the best of climbing around the planet. It brought some of the premier climbers of the era—Chris Sharma, Dave Graham, Emily Harrington, Lisa Rands, Joe Kinder, Chris Lindner, Danny Andrada, Steve McClure, Tony Lamiche, and Said Belhaj—to Lee County, Kentucky, where they would climb at *The Motherlode*.[17]

Bentley Brackett explained that RocTrip happening in the Red may have inadvertently begun with a pair of shoes bound for Rocktoberfest. As part of Rocktoberfest, climbing gear is often given away as prizes for winning numerous competitions. Morgain Sprague had contacted Bentley, a sponsored Red climber, to see if one of his contacts might be willing to contribute some free climbing shoes as a prize. Bentley made a few phone calls. Greg Houston, a sales rep with Petzl, was fine with sending swag, but then the ball started rolling that would make this something much bigger.[18] Morgain Sprague recalled in an interview with Christophe Migeon that John Evans at Petzl moved forward with the idea to have the RocTrip overlap with Rocktoberfest to show support for the RRGCC's land purchase and "bring the attention of the world climbing community to the threats against the crags."[19] As a result, Bentley felt that the RRGCC's annual Rocktoberfest "went from a very small local grassroots event to the best of the best." Morgain hoped the event would "promote our cause to all the people in the climbing community around the world. At the beginning of 2007 at the large Outdoor [Retailer] trade show event nobody had heard of us. In February 2008 when I went there, everybody asked me what the situation was. I would say that we have 80 to 90 percent more donations compared to 2006."[20]

RocTrip also proved more than just a celebration. Using recent conflicts with oil company workers as an example, Petzl came to make a statement about access to climbing areas and private land purchases: "The only solution for maintaining climbing is the purchase of the land itself."[21] Petzl gave all proceeds from the event plus additional funds to the RRGCC—in all, generating just over $30,000, per Bentley. Petzl raised awareness of the RRGCC and increased the visibility of their work.[22] This was a major help in keeping the Pendergrass-Murray property open to climbing but also for setting the stage for future land purchases. It fomented the idea that local climbing organizations could and should take a strong role in pursuing climbing access. And interestingly enough, local residents showed up to watch. Once media word got out about all these famous climbers being in the Red, Bentley recalled that local folks made their way down the road to see for themselves.[23]

During this RocTrip, one of the Red's long-lasting open projects, "Fifty Words for Pump," was sent by Michaël Fuselier, and the route stood as a 5.14c.[24] Others remained unclaimed, particularly "Golden Ticket," a 5.14c and potentially the most difficult sport route in the Red at the time. Many of the great climbers visiting the Red during the event gave it a try, including Chris Sharma, but the route was not solved. Ellington's 2007 guide questioned, perhaps in jest, if the route was even possible.

Immediately following Rocktoberfest, a founder of climbing website 8a.nu shared their perspective on the Red, and this note was later posted to a redriver climbing.com post: "This is the founder of 8a speaking. I want to officially state that Red River Gorge is the best sport climbing area in the world. Just book a flight and you will find more and better quality routes than in any other area in the world. Then again, scenery and bolting is not so good and rest days are spent waiting for the next climbing day. But climbing wise RRG is way better than any other climbing destination I've been to."[25]

The full effects of the rising popularity of the Red following Rocktoberfest 2007 were evident in Ray Ellington's third edition of his climbing guide. Released in 2010, it is most notable for two things: its *exclusion* of numerous less-visited crags and the rapid growth at Muir Valley and in the southern region that made this exclusion a necessity. This guide represents a turning point: because there were now so many places to climb, largely due to expansions at Muir Valley and in the southern region, the guide began gradually winnowing out less popular and less visited crags.[26] This includes a massive list of crags: *Tarr Ridge, The Dome, Buzzard Ridge, Coffin Ridge, Clearcut Wall, Minas Tirith, Willie's Wall, Brighton Wall, Jazz Rock, Bear Wollor Hollor, Between Wall, Backside Wall, Board Wall, Asylum Wall, Blackburn Rock, Bee Branch Rock, Buzzard's Roost, Wildcat Wall, Rough Trail, D. Boone Hut, Haystack Rock, Auxier Ridge, Courthouse Rock, Star Gap Arch, Double Arch, See Rocks,* and *Friction Slab.* Rationales for being less visited generally included long distances to the crag and/or the presence of only a few (generally low-quality) routes. In lieu of being listed in the print guide, these crags were made available in an online downloadable guide from the publisher, Wolverine Publishing. Note that most of these crags are located in the DBNF. This represents a gradual transition away from climbing in the Red proper and into climbing destinations around the Red.

Meanwhile, the southern region continued offering up difficult, classic routes, particularly at *The Chocolate Factory*.[27] The crag's route names frequently related back to Willy Wonka references, including "The Golden Ticket," "Violet Beauregarde," "Chocolate River," "Augustus Gloop," and in later years (2012) "Pure Imagination." The overall reputation of this crag was for its intense and difficult climbs. Recall that Kenny Barker, a prolific route developer, had put up "The Golden Ticket" in 2007 for the RocTrip, although no one would climb it for another two years. In 2009, Lexingtonian climber Adam Taylor was the first to send it, and he did so with much fanfare. That same year, Kipp Trummel, Jeff Neal, Russ Jackson, and others completed another 16 routes at *The Chocolate Factory*. In the coming years, *The Chocolate Factory* would continue to represent some of the great climbs in the Red.

Muir Valley added several crags in the 2010 guide. The valley included more climbing in the Calvin Hollow area, which now included *Bibliothek*, *Persepolis*, and *Animal Crackers Wall*. *Bibliothek* was notable in that it was a themed crag where every route was a book title. *Persepolis* was also another Kipp Trummel crag with five routes. Nearby, several of Kipp's late 2007 Muir Valley routes at *Midnight Surf* were now in the guide for the first time. *Boneyard* also saw new route growth.

In addition, the 2010 guide captured a period of rediscovery. Even as some of the less popular crags were being excluded, a handful of southern crags visited and partially developed in the 1990s were now experiencing a second look. Prior to 2010, *Beer Trailer Crag*, aptly located behind the Beer Trailer, had only a handful of routes. In 2009, it added eight routes, two of which remained open projects. Dario Ventura equipped at least three of these routes. *Crossroads* was another example located at PMRP. In 2009, Jeff Neal, Matt Johns, Theresa Neal, and others recorded 12 first ascents at *Crossroads*.[28] *Crossroads* was originally visited by Brian McCray (and likely Roxanna Brock) in the mid-1990s.[29] Both were talented climbers who were also among the first climbers at *The Motherlode*.

While the new 2010 guide began circulating, the RRGCC refinanced the PMRP purchase using a loan from the Access Fund. This allowed the RRGCC to pay off the balance due to the Murray family and remove any risk of a default on the property, while also saving on interest. Access Fund would now hold that debt through their land loan and acquisition program, and the RRGCC would pay off the loan in a few years. Up to this moment, paying the mortgage on the PMRP had been a concern several times. Often the RRGCC relied on its members to foot this bill (particularly Bob Matheny), but this expectation was unsustainable.

Changes in the latter part of this decade would see the RRGCC adapt their approach to land purchases. Rick Bost served on the RRGCC board just before RocTrip and would later serve as RRGCC president (July 2010–December 2011), and he saw a very real issue in RRGCC land purchases at the time: "If we can't afford this, we can't own it." However, the newfound success of Rocktoberfest alongside international exposure created by RocTrip increased economic support for the RRGCC. Rick envisioned this as "a transition from one person taking care of everything to the community taking care of everything." This was especially buoyed by the Access Fund land acquisition program. To date this program has offered a total of $3.2 million to 27 climbing areas across the country. At this moment it was clear to the RRGCC board and its leadership that paying off the PMRP was soon to be a reality, but that raised a very important question: What comes next?

Rick remembered that "by this point, we knew [the RRGCC] could pay [PMRP] off because we'd seen from RocTrip and Rocktoberfest that we could raise money." He and upcoming president Paul Vidal both felt a growth mindset could expand the number of climbing opportunities available in the southern region and make available new climbing areas. Rick shared that he and Paul steered the RRGCC toward expanding its land ownership: "We wanted to pursue acquisition. We wanted to be more involved in the community, as well, and so that was where we started looking at different properties." The recent years' events would collectively prove to be a watershed for the RRGCC and all climbers in the Red. As landowners in the region, they now sought to become part of the Red's local community.

CHAPTER 12

Learning to Be a Red River Local, 2011–2019

The Red River Rockhouse (locally called the Rockhouse) is a farm-to-table restaurant frequented by both locals and climbers. Watch for the big wooden bear in the roadside gravel parking lot. The restaurant's model favors using locally and regionally sourced ingredients whenever possible, ranging from cheese to beef to coffee. They also feature the farmers and artisans who create these ingredients on the restaurant's website. In 2016, they were ranked in the top 51 farm-to-table cafés across America.

Owners and business partners Tina and Aaron Brouwer are both climbers. Tina has strong family ties to eastern Kentucky, and those ties shaped her choice in colleges: "I actually chose to go to the University of Kentucky because of the Red River Gorge." At the time, Tina was just getting into climbing in northern Illinois and described herself as a weekend warrior climber. Her grandparents lived in eastern Kentucky, which guided her back to the Red. "Well, this will be perfect! I can live with them and go climbing in the Gorge and I'll go to school at UK, and so that's what I did." Aaron was a self-trained cook and conceptualized a personal dream of opening a restaurant right there in the Red. Tina recalled that the restaurant and location played central roles in deciding their next steps: "We decided we wanted to be down here in the Red. We were working and living in Chicago and driving down to the Gorge during the weekdays and then driving back home and working on the weekends." Both Tina and Aaron embody the strong attachments to the Red that many climbers here experience. Negotiating this identity among local residents has, in the past, been difficult, but it has steadily become easier with time.

In the recent decade, a central difference at the Rockhouse, Koops, Miguel's, Bear Track Grocery, and many other locally owned businesses is the prevalence of out-of-state tags belonging to climbers intermixed with Powell, Lee, Wolfe, and Estill County tags in the parking lots. On many days, under the dining awning of Miguel's, local residents intermingle with and outnumber climbers. Inside the Rockhouse, climbers chat with their local neighbors. Over time, the two communities are building friendships. Tina shared that this blended crowd has "been really an important part of our vision for the Rockhouse. . . . It would service a need for climbers" while also "supporting local farmers and the local people."

Still, blending the two communities of climbers and local residents hasn't gone perfectly. At least some local residents remain unsure about climbers. Tina reflected on that: "We [have had] some people come out of the woodwork and say, 'You have no idea what it's like [to live here]. You don't know any locals, you only know climbers and that's who you're here to service. Climbers who are going to come here and take our jobs, and take our money.' That's the opposite of what we're trying to do. We eagerly seek to employ local people and bolster this economy.'"

Tina felt that climbers and locals do share a strong love and attachment to this area, including a shared interest in its well-being, and "we're trying to show that in a multitude of ways. If you haven't come there, and you haven't met us, and you haven't talked to us, and you haven't read the stories about our farmers, we encourage you to do so." Tina noted that "being suspicious of outsiders is common in Appalachian communities, as I have learned from my own family experiences. However, we hope to show that we love this place and we are here to give to it, not take away."

Linda Black (from Lago Linda Hideaway in Lee County) similarly vividly understands how perceptions of climbers have changed pointedly in a matter of years. When Linda talked about courting climbers to local businesses, local residents' comments were quite contrary: "What are you doing? You'll close down!" Linda described the local feelings about climbers in the early 2000s, long after the growth of sport routes in the Red: "When the rock climbers started coming in and they started going to tourist meetings . . . the political atmosphere towards them was not good. [Locals] would say, 'Oh, they're just tree huggers, they're dirtbaggers. They won't spend any money.' And that now makes me kind of chuckle because the same people are now saying, 'Let's bring the rock climbers in!'"

In recent years, Linda feels that minds have changed about climbers as their expenditures in the region grew: "They were going to the grocery stores, they were filling up with gas . . . [now] everyone's building cabins. In Bear Track, you've got several people that have built cabins. You've got the Bear Track Grocery that was sold to somebody and they've done a lot more business. They're selling gas, they're selling wood, they're selling ice, of course, and they're selling snacks. . . . Everybody has benefited. . . . It's a rock-climbing mecca." Local gas stations throughout the region have taken to selling climbing-related items, such as finger balm and guidebooks. Linda noted that the fall of 2016 was the busiest year on record for the campground, showing that climbers are coming in increasing numbers.

While trying to make inroads into the local community, climbers still struggled with balancing impacts and access. *Roadside*, located in Wolfe County, was a major pivotal point and learning experience for climbers. Recall that it had been in the climbing community since 1984 and was a favorite climbing location. Its ownership, however, kept it at risk as a crag that could be lost at any moment. Two respected climbers, Grant Stephens and John Haight, set about securing this crag. They purchased the property in 2004, probably just in time. Grant, in a post on climbingnarc.com, explained that the property was of interest to both cabin developers and Natural Bridge State Park, effectively placing the crag at risk of being lost. Grant and John had been able to sort out the complex landownership and buy the property first.[1] Renaming the area Graining Fork Nature Preserve, the owners allowed climbing to continue with fairly minimal rules, limiting route development and permadraws on sport routes (which can aid less-skilled climbers in ascending routes beyond their skill level) and minimizing human and crag dog impacts.[2] Everything seemed fine. However, climber impacts, still a hotly debated issue with limited solutions, almost immediately created problems.

The eventual *Roadside* closure at Graining Fork came in stages.[3] The first issue was the crowding. *Roadside* remained a highly visible, easily accessed crag, and for a time it offered more parking than other crags. It also stayed fairly dry on wet days. The glut of amazing routes piqued climbers' attraction to the area. "Roadside Attraction" (the eponymous Greg Smith and Ron Snider trad route from 1984) still brought the crowds two decades later. Located in a wicked dihedral (where two portions of rock meet to form a corner much like a vertical open book), the subsequent crack leading up the wall remains a fan favorite and classic route for trad climbers. "Ro Shampo" (a 5.12a sport route by Jamie Baker and Jim Link in 1992) also sees long lines. As mentioned, parking availability also helped, along with long-standing ties between the crag and the climbing community. But when the crowds arrive, so do the problems.[4]

Jason Burton spoke out in the community about the negative impacts of the crowds at *Roadside*. User trails and trampling killed plant life and created erosion that removed topsoil. Trees had been removed, while others were dying due to impact to the roots and topsoil. Jason posted his remorse about the issue on redriverclimbing.com: "This is a fault of mine. I climb there. I contribute to the problem. I am sorry. I am not even sure what can be done about this at this point. I personally am putting a self-imposed restriction on climbing there. I won't be heading up to do those climbs any time soon. That's fine for me . . . I've done the routes. I don't know what to say to those who haven't."[5] Moreover, what could be done at this point? Jason knew no solution aside from his self-imposed climbing restriction: "I know the land is now privately owned . . . but [I] would not know what to recommend to the landowner."[6]

Multiple complaints were on hand—in fact, the very things that the owners had been concerned about from day one: unauthorized bolting, perma-draws, crowding (which fomented erosion and impacts), crag dogs digging around the wall, litter, human waste, and not adhering to staying on designated trails. The RRGCC's website and the forums announced the perhaps antici-pated but still dreaded announcement that *Roadside* was closed as of May 24, 2011. Eric Cox (who would later do some carpentry work for Land of the Arches campground) posted a fitting picture of *Roadside* with the words "REST IN PEACE" tacked onto the rock face on the climbing forums.

Access Fund ran a particularly telling announcement about the closure on their website, noting that "it is a privilege to climb on private land" and that "our behavior plays a critical role in keeping climbing areas open."[7] The closed sign at *Roadside* was stolen several times, which did little to encourage the owners to reopen. The closure stayed in place for nearly four years, until April 3, 2015, when John Haight announced on the forums that Graining Fork would allow a set daily allotment of permits to access the site. This continues even today, with rules in place to minimize impact.[8]

Torrent Falls, although reopened to climbers in 2007 by new owner Bob Matheny, had a very similar fate to *Roadside* for nearly identical reasons. Since 2008, Torrent Falls and Bob had dealt with several frustrating climb-ing impact issues. In the online forum, Bob recalled his experiences: "In the past 8 months I have deconstructed 3 fire rings under the 11 wall, I have picked up a lot of trash and people continue to use the rock houses as their bathroom. . . . It smells like the back end of a questionable bar in New Orleans (I've been there) and the social trails between the 11 and 12 wall continue to wear down."[9]

Bob made it clear that if these issues could not be remedied, a closure was imminent. It was announced around April 9, 2011, that Torrent Falls would close to those not renting a cabin on the property. In the preceding days, Bob had shared his perspective on the issues with leaving Torrent Falls open to all climbers:

> Bottom line . . . it costs me a fair amount of cash to keep Torrent open to climbing (insurance costs, property maintenance costs, etc.) on an annual basis and all of these costs would simply increase with unlimited access

and they would go away with closure. This is an issue that should be of some concern to all land owners with cliff on their property and to anyone wishing to climb anywhere in Kentucky. I am not as concerned about my cash outlay as I am about the air of entitlement that seems to exist in and among the climbing community (please see the comments section for Torrent in the online guidebook). The least expensive and troublesome route of dealing with these issues is to simply close the property to climbing. It has been suggested that I create further signage, greater web presence, etc. to address these issues; however, I feel that anything that I have to "do" is an imposition on me and should not be a part of allowing general access to my property.[10]

Today, Torrent Falls remains open on a limited basis using an online registration system that curbs the number of climbing parties and climbers per party on the property. The number of available days is also restricted to when someone can be on-site to oversee climbers and reduce friction with renters.

Bob's 2011 announcement included an inauspicious warning that aptly defined a critical need for climbing conservation, land management, and impact minimization in the Red: "In a nutshell the climbing community should realize that the easiest way to deal with access issues for private property owners is to close all access and that the response from every climber should be 'WE CAN POLICE OUR OWN' in an effort to prevent closure."[11]

Environmental impact, at this stage, remained one of the greatest threats to climbing areas. The rising popularity of climbing would only make this worse. Amid historic purchases like Pendergrass-Murray was a much larger looming issue for the RRGCC and for climbers in general. What role should climbing organizations play in teaching both climbers' etiquette and outdoor climbing ethics, and what limitations were necessary to protect climbing destinations? Examples of etiquette include how one handles parking one's car in a climbing area, bringing (or not bringing) crag dogs to the climbing area, brushing off chalk tick marks, and not spreading out gear. Outdoor climbing ethics center on preserving a location through minimum-impact practices, such as packing out trash, used toilet paper, and feces. Although separate, the two ideas overlap, as having a solid outdoor ethic is part of having an environmentally friendly climbing etiquette.

For the growing number of indoor climbers turning to the outdoors for their first trip—and likely future trips—climbing outdoors presented a problem. There is a general consensus (albeit one never examined via data) that the growing popularity of the Red—and really any outdoor climbing destination—now attracted an influx of climbers who were largely experienced in gym climbing but not how to handle themselves outdoors. In an interview with *Climbing Magazine*, Chad MacFarland, director at an indoor climbing gym, summed it well: "Gyms are the conduit for new climbers, but they may also present someone's first experience outside, beyond a trailhead, ever. For a lot of folks climbing outside for the first time, it's also outdoor education from square one. Realize this and be compassionate."[12] An entire generation of climbers had learned to climb outdoors when gyms were either nonexistent or rare. That mentorship process instilled how to handle certain behaviors, like how to urinate outdoors, and what was expected (e.g., not urinating at the crag). How would a gym climber who has never experienced the outdoors handle the same experience? Without some kind of community reinforcement of desirable outdoor ethics, it could spell trouble for the climbing community.

Access Fund also created an early nationally organized effort to remedy climber environmental impacts. In a partnership with Black Diamond, Access Fund began a new initiative called ROCK Project in 2014. That program aimed to minimize climber impacts in climbing areas. In a news release announcing the project's inception, Brady Robinson, then Access Fund executive director, reflected on the importance of inspiring good behaviors at the crag: "It's vital to educate the climbing community on minimizing impacts at climbing areas and to inspire behavior that will ensure continued access to the places they love."[13] In later years, the program would be more commonly called the Gym to Crag Movement, and numerous documents detailing minimum-impact behaviors at climbing crags proliferated through climbing media.

An important component of this project focused on the rise of climbing gyms. At the time, Access Fund estimated there were over 1,400 indoor climbing gyms in North America. The concern was that many of these new gym climbers may have little to no awareness of outdoor impact or minimum-impact ethics. Advice on minimizing impact covered numerous facets in this transition. For example, where music playing would be normal at a gym, it disturbed wildlife and other climbers outdoors. Excess chalk use could be easily swept away at the gym, but in the crag, the climber should be mindful of preventing chalk spills and overuse. Other ideas, like not spreading one's gear all over the crag, minimizing group sizes, and being mindful of the best way to deal with bathroom use in varying biomes, became important knowledge for climbers making the trip to the crag. Information about Gym to Crag was prevalent, ranging from kiosks at climbing areas and climbing gyms to expert talks and training sessions at crags around the nation. The early hope was that this would, over time, reduce impacts at climbing destinations, which in turn would make climbing access to these areas possible.[14] This was going to be important, as the Red was about to experience a dramatic uptick in climbing routes.

Yasmeen Fowler served as president of the RRGCC in 2017 and was on the board when they began in earnest scouting out climbing properties to purchase in the area. Yasmeen noted that the RRGCC had used a somewhat different approach to their second purchase compared to the PMRP purchase: "Paul Vidal, the president at the time, had started going to Beattyville and Lee County Tourism meetings, so he was able to really make a presence for himself, climbers, and the [RRGCC] there amongst the local community." This would lead to landowner Libby Roach getting in touch with Paul about some potential climbing areas on her land. Interestingly, Libby envisioned climbers as being good for the region's economy, and setting the property as a climbing area would continue those benefits. As Libby explained, "I care very much for Beattyville and Lee County. It is my hope that our decision to sell this beautiful land will only bring positive things to all." [15]

Yasmeen remembered the RRGCC board's group visit to the property: "In January 2013, we went and walked it. All the board members walked it, and we got some of the local route developers whose opinions we trusted to go out there and look at it." Everyone favored acquiring the property, as it held a great deal of potential for climbers, even though this meant going back into debt. Early estimates were that perhaps 200 routes could be added as a result of the purchase. That estimate, it turns out, was very conservative. The RRGCC closed on the property in May 2013.

At a public meeting at Miguel's, RRGCC soon announced that they had purchased 309 acres in Beattyville and Lee County for $245,000. They again used Access Fund's loan program ($200,000), an Access Fund improvement grant ($10,000), and self-funded the remaining balance due. They announced that the property would be known as Miller Fork Recreational Preserve (MFRP), named for the Miller Fork Creek that flows through much of the property. Paul Vidal, then president of RRGCC, discussed the property as a representation of the growing ties between the local community and the climbing community: "Acquiring this property illustrates the strength of the climbing community in this region and its importance to the area. Without the community of climbers and businesses supporting us and pushing us to look to the future, we wouldn't have been able to secure this climbing." [16]

MFRP, in some ways, harkens back to the earlier days of climbing in the Red because it represented a rare, wide open area for route development. The site is placed along multiple hollows adjoined by a somewhat treacherous gravel drive. A stream occasionally blocks access to certain entry points and the hikes to most of the routes are longer than those found in other areas of the Red, making the area feel quite wild and remote. It is somewhat similar to early experiences of Ron Stokley and Dieter Britz bushwhacking through the Red or John Bronaugh scouting potential crags in the fall and winter months. Like PMRP, there is an open policy on individuals setting up new routes, allowing many newer developers to put up first ascents here and even develop crags here. When first opened, MFRP had only a small portion of climbing routes in the area, with the remainder open for climbers to develop. This opened the door to both familiar and new faces in route development, such as Dustin Stephens, Kipp Trummel, Blake Bowling, Art Cammers, Scott Curran, Mike Wheatley, and Andrew Wheatley, to name a few. Yasmeen Fowler added that it was "really cool to see all these people come out and be so excited about this fresh, new, empty land. . . . They came out and started putting up crags, not just one line here or there." This rapid growth soon led to a new guide focused on MFRP.

Ray Ellington released an MFRP guide in November 2015, filled with Elodie Saracco's photographs, with Steve Isabell's artwork, and with Michelle Ellington and Yasmeen Fowler serving as editors. This guide added 21 new crags spread across two forks (Bowman and Miller) that flow into Hell Creek. Along Bowman Fork are *Cloud 9*, *Infirmary*, *Cooper's Cove*, *Serenity Point*, and *Deep End*. Along the Miller Fork are *Corner Pocket*, *Pharmacy*, *Scotch Wall*, *Highlands*, *Nursery*, *Vine Wall*, *Portal*, and *Fruit Wall*. Hell Creek includes *Record Shop*, *Morgue*, *Graveyard*, *Laboratory*, *Chaos*, *Alcatraz*, *Monastery*, and *Secret Garden*. MFRP's early grades largely concentrated in the 5.11–5.12 range. Five routes were listed as potential 5.14s, including "Biophilia," "Booyah," and "Matrix," along with two open unnamed projects at the *Record Shop*. Utilizing recent developments in mapping software, the guidebook now upped the crag map game by including three-dimensional maps. One somewhat humorous issue with this guide is that so many new routes were being established, it was difficult to include them all in one guide. Thus the guide could not fully document all the routes at the time.

The guide included 11 illustrations by Steve Isabell. Two stand out in capturing the early feel of MFRP. First, the cover, entitled "Chaos," depicts the flood of route developers coming into MFRP to create new climbing routes. Again, this area was effectively new territory open for development. Following word of the new property, developers began staking out areas where they wished to work. This in itself created some conflicts between developers, which the cover treats in good fun. Second is "Secret Garden," which, Steve explains, depicts "caricatures of what some dubious locals might look like to out-of-town climbers." Prior to climbers being on the property, it was used as an OHV area, local hangout, and shooting area (the first two of which continue today). Early developers encountered locals there, perhaps surprising both sides. Local gas and construction crews would later help climbers create a stable parking lot there in summer 2014, with ATS Construction donating their time and effort to the road and parking lot in 2015 after the spring floods.[17]

At this stage, the presence of climbing became more noticeable in the local residential community (perhaps as opposed to being noticed *by* the local community) as climbers increasingly trickled into nearby Beattyville businesses for supplies. Beattyville, the seat of Lee County, is a small city with a population just over 1,200 and is locally celebrated as the birthplace of the Kentucky River. The downtown stands alongside the North, Middle, and South Branches that combine to form the Kentucky River. Each year on the third weekend of October, the festival celebrates its official symbol—the woolly bear caterpillar—along Main Street. Climbers are familiar faces at the festival, as well as at local business like the Chocolat Inn and Café, which completely renovated a dilapidated motel in the downtown. Climbers also visit the grocery store and sometimes swing by the county library just outside of town.

Beattyville's fortunes have ebbed and flowed over the years, but it offers great potential for the future of the region. Economic transition in the region, including the decline of manufacturing and decreasing stability in extraction industries, has hit hard. As of 2019, Beattyville ranked third nationally in terms of poverty for cities in its population class. Dedra Brandenburg, director of tourism for Beattyville and Lee County, feels her city and county are on the upswing. "Right now we're starting to see a change in the tide. We're starting to see people turning away from the big box stores . . . which really helps our small towns. We've got a couple of neat places that have opened in the past two years."

People's Rural Telephone Cooperative is addressing infrastructure issues in Beattyville by offering vastly improved phone and internet capabilities for residents and businesses alike. Teleworks established a business hub in Beattyville in 2016. This hub offers online digital literacy, tech support, and customer service workshops to train prospective teleworkers. The hub created 83 telework jobs in 2019, and this speaks directly to a strong desire for community members to find work while remaining within their home communities amid a transitioning economy.[18] A nearby mountaintop removal site has also been transitioned into an impressive community park, playground, and performance area, taking available resources and turning them into something valuable for everyone. In short, Beattyville has great potential.[19]

In terms of location, Beattyville is uniquely poised in the southern region within a short drive of PMRP, MFRP, Muir Valley, DBNF, and *The Motherlode*. Historically, climbers traveled more frequently to Stanton when in the Red proper. Stanton includes a Kroger grocery store and more shopping options. This is the difference of traveling 30 minutes to Stanton versus perhaps 10 minutes to Beattyville. That tide is slowly changing. As new businesses develop in downtown Beattyville, climbers are increasingly found there on rest days and rainy days. Beattyville has room to develop within the city, where there are still vacant lots and unused buildings, and there is room to grow in the greater county, as well. This includes a number of unused houses in the area left vacant by people who moved away.

Travis Estridge is a Jackson County native and Berea College graduate. Today, he works for Save the Children in Kentucky, addressing childhood poverty in the region. Earlier in his career, he worked with local communities and local government to identify and rebuild homes with mold or major repair issues through community development block grants. Projects included Powell County along Nada Tunnel Road (not far from *Military Wall*) and the outskirts of the Red in Ravenna in Estill County. Travis is aware of the impact the region's homes have on regional and multigenerational poverty in eastern Kentucky:

> When folks think of poor people, they think that they may not be home-owners. Well, there's a lot of homeowners in Appalachia, and people might think that's a great statistic. The thing is they may own a dilapi-dated mobile home . . . or they will live in grandma's house that grandma handed down. Well, you know, grandma's house might have been good 50 years ago, but the thing is when folks are on limited income, particularly older folks, they can't afford to maintain their home. They don't have 2,000 bucks to replace the roof. If they don't replace the roof, it's going to cause the whole house eventually to fall apart.

Travis recalled with a cringe, "We'd crawl up under these old houses and they'd be held up with railroad ties." In another case, Travis was "under this hundred-year-old house, and it was held up by boulders" in lieu of more current (and up to code) options.

Grant funds supported making these homes energy efficient and ADA compliant, which is ideal in supporting residents in the region. The houses also helped contribute to the tax base in the region. This is a great thing for those who could take advantage of it. But there are not enough resources to address all the homes that need it. As Lee County's economic options dwindled over the last decade, unused homes became an increasing issue. However, Beattyville's closeness to multiple climbing opportunities triggered an increase in climbers moving into Beattyville or Lee County.

John Nowell is one climber who has settled into the community. He knew of several others in the area, too, even as far as Powell and Wolfe Counties, who were living in the area at least some portion of the season in a home they purchased. John felt that they were not concentrated in any one space, but rather dispersed over the entire region. Still, the tax benefits are clear: these are newcomers (if not locals) now investing in the community's long-term viability. On the flipside of this argument is, of course, concern about gentrification as new people enter the housing market and potentially impact rents and selling prices. This issue is taken up in the final chapter.

The presence of climbers also began creating subtle changes in the community's social capital. For example, climber and Microsoft employee Audrey Sniezek began working with Lee County High School to begin a new technology education initiative. As part of the Technology, Education, and Literacy in Schools (TEALS) program, Audrey arranged for Lee County students to take online programming courses taught by Microsoft employees. Likewise, teachers in Lee County would be taught how to teach programming classes in the future so that the training could continue for future generations. After graduating, students then had a chance to do internships with Microsoft, potentially leading to jobs in programming. Audrey also worked with the Lee County Recreational Center (located just down the road from *The Motherlode*) in constructing a climbing gym for local kids with a goal of improving community health.

Tina Brouwer has continued this outreach to children in the region through Red Oaks Forest School. In 2014, Tina and cofounder Melissa Rudick created the school as a nonprofit organization designed to get kids in the woods. The idea is that letting kids have time in the woods develops confidence, a sense of risk management, a strong environmental ethic, and ties to the region. How better to teach the next generation of kids the value of loving the Red than to have them build those ties early on? Today, the school is open to all students and has expanded its programming to include families and adults. The school is located on 60 acres in Stanton and is representative of the diverse habitats and ecosystems found throughout the region, making it a perfect place for nature education and exploration. There, Red Oaks schedules campouts, hikes, and more throughout the season, including a weekly event in the spring and fall.

Red Oaks started by scheduling one day a month that kids would meet to go into the woods together. Those early events went well, despite the weather, per Tina Brouwer: "We had some beautiful days and we had some rainy days, but we stayed committed to it, and the kids loved it!" This led to adding additional days in the first two years: "We went from once a month to twice a month and we grew . . . but we still kept it very loose." In later years, they applied themes to their events (such as flowers or mammals) while maintaining that unstructured wild play that was so important to the overall framework of the program.

Red Oaks is bringing local children from throughout the Red to play and learn in the woods. Kids living in the Red are attending the events alongside kids from Lexington, Richmond, Berea, and beyond. As their vision clarified, Red Oaks realized that this was an important part of developing an environmental ethic and sense of place attachment in the next generation of our region's residents. Tina added, "Even though you might live in this area, it doesn't mean you're getting out into it. Local teachers have shared with us that many local, especially underserved kids, spend little to no time outside exploring and playing in the woods." By putting these kids together in the woods, it brings about an entire array of new experiences that make wild places special.

Climbers in the Red are also working together with local business owners. Located on the back end of Muir Valley in Wolfe County is David Terrill's campground. David owns Land of the Arches, an iconic campground often used by climbers. It is home to a building nicknamed "the Hangar" because, best described, it resembles an aircraft hangar tucked at the end of an impossibly short runway. "This building was built on speculation," David recalled. He explained that his original plan was to open a dance hall and saloon, but a trip to West Virginia's New River Gorge offered an entrepreneurial spark that resulted in Land of the Arches. Realizing tourism was booming in the New, he felt something similar could happen in the Red. He purchased the land in the 1990s, right when the first growth period of climbers was brewing in the Red. Today, the property is home to Rocktoberfest, but it was a long pathway to get there.

David's history in the region ties back to the Appalachian Great Migration. This period, roughly the 1940s to 1970s, marked a time when Appalachians relocated to major cities for work as the American manufacturing sector boomed. As a baby, David was moved with his family to Ohio. David remembers that "Dad wanted to stay. . . . He didn't want to leave. He wanted to stay here and farm." His father wanted to sharecrop back home. "And, Mom told him, 'Well, let's go up there, let's get a job, let's make enough money to buy the team.' Of course, [she meant] a pair of mules, the plow, the disc and the mowing machine, and the lay-off plow, and the cultivating plow. . . . You know what you had to have to barely make a living." Both of David's parents worked at the General Motors factory. Sadly, his father died of Hodgkin's disease at age 29, leaving four-year-old David, his mom, and his four siblings to find a new path together. David was sent back home to Kentucky to help his mom make ends meet: "I got farmed out simply because the grandparents [back in Kentucky] would take me and get me in school a year sooner," which often made him the youngest kid in the class.

Something clicked for David back home in the summer of his fourth-grade year. "I came back for fourth grade for the summer, and I think they had this planned out." David's grandpa had farmland and cows and David remembers that "Grandpa said, 'Let's go up there and see that calf. Let's see how it's doing.' So we got up there and I like went crazy for the calf, I guess. Grandpa said, 'I tell you what. I'll make you a deal.'" That deal would change everything for David's path. "'You come stay down here this winter and help me feed these cows, and I'll give you that calf.' Boy, that was hard to say no to, and I didn't. So long story short . . . he gave me the calf. He was always good for his word."

While there, David learned how to run a farm and work with livestock. "I learned a lot by staying here. I was showing cattle by the time I was a freshman in high school, and by the time I was a junior I had several head of my own." Working with his grandparents, David remembers, "We were self-sustainable on that farm. . . . We used to raise bedding plants, like tomato plants, cabbages, sweet potato plants, and such. . . . I don't know if it's entirely possible to be self-sustaining [today]. It is, but you really have to work at it. But there's a lot of things that would make it so much easier than what we had it." For example, "Something as simple as a container, we don't even think about. The container that we put the salt in to carry it out to the field was a gourd. Was a big ol' gourd . . . and it grew in a shape that made it conducive to that, and you drilled a hole in the top, put the leather strap in it, cut out a big hole, and you put your salt in there." But life on the farm is obviously difficult. "Every time [grandpa] said, hey, let's hit the floor and go feed the cows, or fork manure, or whatever it was, we did it. I did it. You know, these people are feeding me and putting clothes on my back, I'm gonna help them all I can."

At 18, David returned to Ohio for work at General Motors. He would not return to Kentucky until he retired at age 48, when he came home looking for property. He ended up buying land about three miles down the road from where he grew up. His wife at the time was from the region, so coming home made sense. They both referred to the area as "down home" and had been thinking about going there after retirement. The land that now holds Land of the Arches belonged at the time to David's great-uncle. David remembered seeing the property as a child the day after his uncle had purchased the land. This was a time when Appalachian cultural norms dictated inviting the greater family over for their blessing after a big land purchase. "In those days, if you bought a farm, you showed certain members of the family, everybody if you could. You were proud of that." After purchasing the land, David kept with tradition. There was good and bad: "Not much was said. . . . It was mowed good

... had a house on it," but David laughed that his grandfather noted "it was too steep" for farming. As luck would have it, farming was not the end goal for the property.

David began work on Land of the Arches in 1992. He built a camp to provide lodging for visitors riding horses from Cliff View resort down the old railroad grade to the Kentucky River. He built a barn, purchased eight horses, and took visitors on trail rides across his property to see its rural beauty. David named this new camp after Robert Ruchhofts's book, *Kentucky's Land of the Arches*. The book highlights the graceful arches prevalent in the Red.

David began building the now famous Hangar around 1993, utilizing insulated panels to frame in an office and kitchen space. The Hangar would briefly hold the Line Dance and Saloon. After it was clear that the saloon and dance hall weren't panning out, the building sat unfinished. It temporarily held a horse show, the floor covered in sawdust and entertainment coming from a local resident's truck tape deck. David added a concrete floor, which led to it becoming a roller-skating rink. "That worked about three months. Probably had 20 people [who] actually came." He was then approached about holding wrestling events there, "three, four times. They set up a big ring in the middle there." Next was a flea market, which completely filled the space for about six years.

Rick Weber from nearby Muir Valley paid David a visit around September of either 2006 or 2007. Rick thought that David could make something of this new influx of climbers, noting cautiously that it would be two years before he was on the map, but after that things would go well. David recalled he had several things that made this a good fit, including parking, a bathhouse, electricity, and a flattened area for camping. Climbers were packed at Miguel's, and many looked for other places to camp, including an area near Muir Valley. Then the gentleman leasing the Hangar as a flea market decided to go out of business. When that happened, David upgraded the Hangar, including a sink, cooking area, and tables so campers could sit and eat indoors. He also renovated the bathhouse from the horse camp and added an outdoor picnic space under an old shelter previously used by vendors. News of the campground's opening was moving through climber forums.

David set the price to camp at $5. Eric Cox, a climber, built the payment kiosk where campers self-registered and paid to camp. Now, on most any given decent weather day, you'll find a large number of climbers spending the night at Land of the Arches. Meanwhile, David continues to expand his offerings inside the Hangar, including private rooms, indoor bunks, apartments, and even a business incubation space that could eventually double as a telecommuting work site for climbers staying at the campground. The sky is the limit: David stated that he's all in for "sponsoring events that we think will draw tourism and be an annual thing." Thanks to a connection made by Eric Cox between David and the RRGCC, in 2016 the RRGCC announced that Rocktoberfest would be held at Land of the Arches, where it has remained since.

In 2017, new climbing developments in Lee County were also bustling. Atop a gorgeous overlook in Lee County sits the Cathedral Church of Saint George the Martyr. The church and its surrounding children's camp, called Cathedral Domain, are located on a limestone formation that stands in contrast to the region's sandstone. They had already had rappelling available for camp attendees for decades, thanks to route development by camp counselor Mark Arnold, but the camp was a seasonal affair restricted to summers. Climbers, on the other hand, were absent from the Red during the months when campers were at Cathedral Domain. Cathedral Domain decided to add climbing routes to their existing property and open Rock Domain. Rock Domain, for the cost of parking, provides camping options and a lot of climbing—23 crags designed by climber Troy Davison.

What would become Cathedral Domain got its start back in 1913. Alexander Patterson was not your typical Kentucky clergyperson. He started in the priesthood in his 50s. He was Scottish and probably was supported by family money. And he liked to walk. In fact, he was known as the *walking man in the mountains* because he walked everywhere he went. He also shared farming techniques as he went from holler to holler. "He saw his mission as helping to save the mountain people," said camp director Andy Sigmon. He traveled as far as Hazard in his work—that's 60-plus miles of mountain bushwhacking and hiking. He arranged for local residents to receive medical care and dentistry, he created a free library available to everyone, and conducted seminars on farming. Alexander used Cathedral Domain—then Girl's Friendly Society Farm summer camp and later Patterson's Friendly Farm—as his base of operations and used his funds to purchase the land, as well as land across what would eventually become the highway leading into the Red.[20]

World War II changed the camp. "After Pearl Harbor, the camp was shut down," Andy explained, until navy cook Glen Adkins was hired by Lexington Diocese Bishop William Moody to restart the camp. While stationed in the Boston area, Glen, a certified SCUBA diver, worked with a local summer camp to build a dock. That sparked Glen's interest in summer camps. Glen returned to his home in Pikeville, where Moody learned of him, called him in for an interview, and asked him to run the camp and be in charge of a diocese church in Beattyville as a lay reader. Glen examined the land included in the Patterson farm and found that its closure had left it in ruins, with local residents scavenging the house for resources. Glen decided to open the camp on the second property, where he laid plans to build the church. Glen's work (and indirectly, Alexander Patterson's work) continues today in the form of the Cathedral Domain Camp.

Andy Sigmon works in a small cabin near the cathedral itself, where he has gradually accrued a lifetime of memories: photographs, awards, painted rocks, mementos, history, and paperwork to run a successful camp. When he became director in 1991, Andy had been at this camp for nearly 25 years, and he and his wife Cindy have been there for more than another 25 years now. He first attended Cathedral Domain as a camper in 1967 when he was nine. He was born in North Carolina but moved to Harlan when he was eight or so. "My family was in the coal-mining business. . . . I wasn't born in eastern Kentucky but I very much call it home. It's where I grew up. All my formative things were there, good and bad. [Laughs] It's a tough way to grow up." He soon fell in love with the camp. "I wouldn't go away, so they soon gave me a job," he chuckled. As a counselor, Andy enjoyed working with kids from all backgrounds and helping them build ties to being in the outdoors.

Presently, the camp holds multiple sessions on reading, environmentalism, and more. This includes bereavement camps to help kids who have lost parents. Death of one or both parents is now a common event given the region's opioid addiction. The counselors use rappelling and climbing as part of the growth process: Andy explained that "the rappelling was time and time again something [attendees] mentioned because it taught them to trust again. That portion of 'I can do this' and overcome things, and they tied it in really well with [the idea that] bad things happen in your life, but you can overcome fears and anything else." The camp continues to bring students from all across the region regardless of their ability to pay. All attendees have the same opportunity to experience getting in touch with nature and their faith, regardless of resources back home. Their work in the region is also creating a new generation of climbers from all across the state.

As more and more climbers have come to the Red—and the many other climbing destinations across the nation—minimizing environmental impacts on crags has remained a foremost issue for land managers. In 2017, Access Fund began the Climber's Pact, an organized effort designed to place the responsibility for maintaining public climbing areas squarely upon the individual. Climbers were encouraged to sign up for the pact and make an agreement that they would follow minimum-impact behaviors—minimize chalk use, minimize group sizes, and respect wildlife, to name a few—and help reinforce positive behaviors among other climbers or, in the terms of the Climber's Pact, "be an upstander, not a bystander." The campaign was also paired with a concentrated effort to put minimal-impact awareness in the hands of climbers.

In 2017, the RRGCC also announced an important new effort to ensure climbing areas remain accessible forever. On September 7, 2017, RRGCC president Yasmeen Fowler announced the signing of a conservation and recreation easement on the RRGCC's properties, including the recently purchased Bald Rock Recreational Preserve (discussed in chapter 2). This agreement ensures that Access Fund will hold a permanent easement to the three properties, "preventing any use of the properties that would significantly interfere with or impair their recreational and conservation values, which includes providing for public access and recreation with no cost or fees, specifically rock climbing, so that present and future generations may enjoy these preserves in their open space condition."[21] The easements also allowed for other types of outdoor recreation, such as hiking and mountain biking, but prohibited residential developments. "The RRGCC is committed to preserving the legacy that the climbing community and its supporters have all helped build over the last two decades," Yasmeen noted in the press release on the easements. "We hope that all organizations who are able to will also partner with Access Fund to strengthen permanent protection of climbing access across the country."

Two interesting facets of this momentous agreement stand out. First, as has been the tradition in the Red's climbing community history, an attorney who also climbs volunteered their time to make this happen. Attorney Melissa Bellew donated her time and expertise to the RRGCC during the approximately nine months it took to complete the conservation and recreation easements project. Melissa grew up in Kentucky and had spent many years climbing, cycling, and hiking in the Red. Her inquiry about whether she could assist the RRGCC with any projects was perfectly timed, and her legal assistance was integral to completing the project. Melissa, thus, stands with many other attorneys in the Red's land acquisition and protection history, including Shannon Stuart-Smith, John Bronaugh, Grant Stephens, Dan Chandler, and John Myers to name a few. Second, announcing this easement on September 7 was an auspicious date. Recall that on September 7, 1969, Dieter Britz and Ron Stokley established "Tunnel Route" at *Chimney Top*.

With Access Fund's help, the RRGCC would make comparatively short work of the MFRP mortgage. Alongside a matching grant from the Conservation Alliance in 2014 ($35,000), the RRGCC would make the final mortgage payment in 2017. On June 29, 2018, the RRGCC announced the opening of a new crag at MFRP: *Camelot*. Today, this Monty Python–themed crag has 31 routes, including seven 5.10s, five 5.11s, and two 5.12s. There is something very important about *Camelot*'s opening in that it represents a continuing approach to climbing and land management. Rather than open the routes to climbing as they were equipped, the RRGCC instead opted to develop sustainable trails and infrastructure to preserve the area. Ashlee Milanich, then RRGCC executive director, explained that "last year we announced *Camelot*'s opening, which is essentially what we want the model for new crags opening to be. . . . The trails were built as the climbs were developed, belay bases were built. . . . It really essentially built a sustainable climbing area that is full of moderates." In fact, the crag had been under development since 2016 and kept unpublished until it was publicly announced.[22]

Over the last decade, new information on the region was also being rapidly shared through a seemingly nonstop series of new guides on the Red. First, the Red's size now warranted delineating guides between the northern and southern regions, with Miguel's operating as an unofficial middle point between the two. Ray Ellington, Blake Bowling, and Dustin Stephens released a two-part guide focused on the northern (volume 1) and southern (volume 2) regions. Ray Ellington also released a fourth and fifth edition of the *Red River Gorge Climbing Guide*. Brendan Leader released the *Best of the Red* guide in 2017, as well as a more comprehensive guide in 2019. Likewise, Dario Ventura, Mike Williams, and Ray Ellington released a select guide highlighting outstanding routes in the Red. In 2017 alone, climbers recorded 50 new route listings, mostly in the southern region and in MFRP. And in 2018, 54 new listings were added, which now included Foxtown, a bouldering area that has opened farther south in Jackson County. Chris Chaney released a guide capturing outdoor recreation stories from the Red's recent history in 2019, reflecting on the Red's storied past and the people who were part of it.

In 2019, at Rocktoberfest, the DBNF and RRGCC announced that a new MOU had been signed between the two groups, reaffirming a 50-plus year relationship for the coming decades. At the announcement, Bill Strachan, who had worked on this project for the RRGCC tirelessly for decades, was visibly overjoyed. The MOU recognized that climbers and the DBNF had mutual interests in being public land stewards and protecting the Red. The agreement includes climbers in identifying mutually beneficial projects, such as trail and access improvements, recreational use studies, and educational programs. It also notes that the two organizations will confer on potential projects that could be authorized in the future (which could potentially include new climbing opportunities) and collaborate in sharing informational, educational, and interpretational materials on climbing in the Red. In discussing the current status of climbers and the DBNF and their relationship going forward, Tim Eling with the DBNF felt that the DBNF's relationship with climbers was very strong, adding that the RRGCC had been an excellent partner since his arrival in 2003.

In a mere half century or so, climbers had gone from a small cadre of climbers and cavers working through a handful of routes to a small army visiting over 3,000 routes spread across several counties in eastern Kentucky. They had gone from a band of not-quite locals (being from Lexington) to working with local businesses, landowners, schools, and towns like Beattyville to ensure climbing access and mutual economic growth. And they had grown from depending on public lands as their main source of climbing to now owning the bulk of climbing routes themselves. Climbers had also gone to great lengths to ensure that those climbing preserves would remain open to climbing through conservation and recreation easements, whatever may come. All the groundwork now supports climbers and ensures ongoing access to climbs, regardless of what may happen in the future. The question left unanswered is plain, yet deceptively complex: *What comes next?*

CHAPTER 13

What Comes Next? Climbing in the Red and Beyond, 2020–2050

Climbing could continue as is and unchanged in the Red for the foreseeable future. Between the multiple private climbing preserves available and the new MOU with the Forest Service, access to climbing is predictable and protected. In their quest to become Red River locals, climbers are now being increasingly accepted in the community as economic partners, welcome visitors, and, in some recent cases, local residents. Some climbers are also giving back through programs such as Technology, Education, and Literacy in Schools described in the previous chapter.

Additionally, climbers are becoming part of the local community in important cultural ways. Climbers are depicted upon select cans of the locally made soft drink, Ale-8-One, or as the locals (and climbers) call it, Ale-8.[1] Climbers and DBNF have cemented a strong commitment to work together in the Red. Climbers are also improving relationships with local businesses and residents. However, there is another variable at hand happening far beyond the Red: climbing has become a mainstream activity featured in news and media around the world. Tom Cruise goes free soloing (via movie magic) in the new *Mission Impossible* movie as he did back in *MI II*.[2] Tommy Caldwell and Kevin Jorgeson were featured on NBC's *Today Show* in 2015 for their free-climbing assault on El Capitan's *Dawn Wall*.[3] Likewise, Alex Honnold's 2017 free-solo ascent of El Cap and the documentary that followed had people around the nation talking about climbing.[4] Most every episode of *American Ninja Warrior* features climbing-related obstacles, and an abundance of the participants are themselves climbers making easy work of the impossible.[5] Climbing was selected as a new sport for the 2020 Olympics.[6]

Kids are also seeing climbers. Revered mountaineer Conrad Anker takes kids climbing in the Smithsonian Museum's *National Park Adventure* IMAX film. Indoor climbing walls are a regular find in gyms and rec centers, complete with kid-friendly starter walls. LEF, the local Lexington climbing gym, has an entire youth training series to get kids roped up and climbing. Even Pete the Cat, a children's book character, is talking about climbing: he thoughtfully constructed an indoor climbing gym in his treehouse for all his friends to use.

In recent years, climbers have turned to national lobbying to protect climbing access. The designation of the Bears Ears National Monument and the subsequent revisions pressed climbers to the forefront of a legal challenge to retain its original borders.[7] Access Fund, in 2017, filed suit to prevent this change. American Alpine Club and Access Fund's mutual efforts (dubbed *Climb the Hill*) sent a team of 50 globally renowned climbers to Capitol Hill to meet with Congress, the Forest Service, and the Department of the Interior.[8] The Red has been present in this conversation, as well, with climbers meeting with Kentucky representative Hal Rogers to discuss the Red's climbing community. Alex Honnold similarly wrote about the economic impact of climbing and the importance of climbing access in *Outside Magazine*, using the Red as one example.[9]

One might argue that the Red itself has also been under the spotlight in recent months. In mid-October of 2019, news broke of a proposed destination resort development in the Red River Gorge. The concept, as presented by Red River Economic Development, LLC (RRED), included adding a privately developed, state-maintained facility including a 150–175 room lodge on 891 acres adjacent to Natural Bridge State Park, a 20-acre themed commercial village designed as a gateway to the Red River Gorge, and a transportation connection to Natural Bridge State Park and potentially other locations throughout the region. The concept also included a long list of other smaller, state-themed developments (such as a brewery), destination visitation buildings (conference space and wedding space), and recreation opportunities (including a human-made lake, indoor climbing wall, and linkages to hiking trails).

The proposal's initial details were vague, as a full concept was not yet completed. Instead, the report concluded with the next step of securing a professional masterplan. The call for proposals was soon made available with a deadline of July 31, 2019, with the masterplan to be completed by April 30, 2020. In January 2020, project manager Dave Adkisson, then president and CEO of the Kentucky Chamber of Commerce, announced movement forward, with a contract for the study to be done with a deadline of July 31, 2020.[10]

Although the lodge was news to many, it had actually been in the works for nearly a decade. Dave Adkisson reported leading an informal group in discussing what tourism options could be open amid the decline of coal in 2011 or 2012. The conversations were held via the Kentucky Chamber Foundation (KCF), a wing of the Chamber of Commerce focused on economic development in the state. RRED, which would eventually release word of the destination resort concept, is a charitable group founded under the KCF.[11]

KCF hired firm AECOM to study all of eastern Kentucky and explore the options available. AECOM noted that "eastern Kentucky is well-positioned for tourism growth" and they believe that the "region's natural beauty lends itself easily to outdoor recreation."[12] The report offered several next steps, each built on the idea of finding ways to keep existing visitors in the area longer while offering reasons for new visitors to come to the area. These included partnerships with state parks (e.g., Natural Bridge), encouraging commercial lodging growth, utilizing public incentive programs to attract private developers, developing worker training programs to create a "tourism workforce," increasing awareness of tourism benefits to businesses and local residents, and conducting a feasibility study on any specific projects. Later, KCF hired HVS Group to do an early study of creating a destination resort in the Slade area. The report, completed in April 2017, conducted a tourism market assessment of the region.[13] This assessment would eventually lead to the lodge proposal being worked on by engineering firm Stantec.

Early local resistance to the plan focused on the lack of information in the plan. For example, it isn't yet clear how the lodge proposal would impact archaeological, floral, faunal, and other resources in the area. Local news station WKYT reported that the initial plan does not include any effort to examine environmental impacts. Gerry James with Explore Kentucky Initiative questioned why the $800,000 funding for the proposal was not instead used to support existing tourism in the region. The proposal also purportedly included a rule preventing other businesses from being built or operated within 10 miles of the resort as a step to protect investors, even while this impinges local business development. However, David Adkisson soon refuted this claim at the project's next public meeting.[14]

On June 30, 2020, John Buchar (with Stantec) and David Adkisson held a virtual town hall meeting to discuss updates on the proposal. Approximately 80 people attended. David noted that Stantec was approximately one-third of the way through their study. The meeting shared some of the early analysis and provided an opportunity for attendees to ask questions. Perhaps the singular main point from the presentation was that no site has been officially selected at this time, with a full report arriving in September 2020.

Although no location has been selected, John did share some of the process for how Stantec has approached the resort's location. Presently, Stantec is considering six physical sites in the region. Dave noted that four of the six properties in consideration are in private hands, with the others potentially being either Forest Service or State Park land. John said each would need to be not less than 200 acres to ensure a sense of separation and isolation. Proximity to Slade was a central concern, as Stantec felt it was the heart of the Red. In fact, sites as far out as the I-75/Mountain Parkway exchange had been considered but eliminated, as they were not close enough to Slade.

Entering the second phase of the resort study, Stantec would be examining physical and infrastructure options for each site, as well as barriers, such as endangered species and geological concerns. These include issues such as drinking water and sewer systems, existing roadway access, floodplain locations, and slope buildability. Concerns over broadband access and alcohol laws were also considered. Stantec has used several rural destination resorts for comparison purposes thus far, which include Big Cedar Lodge (Ridgedale, Missouri), Suncadia (Cle Elum, Washington), Nemacolin Woodlands (Farmington, Pennsylvania), Primland (Dan, Virginia), Old Edwards Inn (Highlands, North Carolina), Wilderness at The Smokies (Sevierville, Tennessee), and Blackberry Farm (Walland, Tennessee).

John shared some of their preliminary survey data on what potential visitors had rated as the top resort amenities they would like to see in a future Red River Gorge resort. These included (in order) gatherings and celebration spaces, food and drink, health and wellness, outdoor spaces, education, golf, outdoor adventure, and family opportunities. John noted that golf was not something being considered in terms of building an actual golf course, but the resort could include virtual golf activities. He felt that outdoor recreation was ranked seventh largely because so many opportunities were already available.

The presentation also addressed existing concerns. For example, both John and David said the proposed 10-mile zone limiting business development was not in their planning at this time. Instead, they collectively hoped the resort would open entrepreneurial opportunities for local residents. John felt that many residents in areas like Powell County drove outside the county (e.g., to Lexington) for work and said that the resort might help create job opportunities for them to remain closer to home. David stressed several times that there is no developer waiting in the wings. Rather, once the project proposal is completed, the resultant report would be opened to both public and private developers for discussion. Likewise, according to David, the resort certainly was not a done deal by any means; he placed 50-50 odds on the resort ever happening.

While it is too early to make a decision on this proposal, and a resort may never be in the works for the Red, this conversation does raise a valid question: What will the political economy of eastern Kentucky—and, more specifically, the Red River Gorge—look like in the coming decades? And thinking more broadly, what about the future of Appalachia as a whole? Could climbing have a place at the table as rural communities increasingly seek economic growth amid the decline of coal extraction and dwindling manufacturing jobs?

Quite relevant to the history of the Red, what role could climbers play in that conversation?

In recent years, the economic value of outdoor recreation has taken on new importance. The Outdoor Industry Association (OIA) offered an early glimpse of the national scale of outdoor recreation. Examining categories including camping, fishing, hunting, snow sports, trail sports (which includes climbing), and wheel sports, OIA set the economic contributions of outdoor recreation users at an astonishing $646 billion in 2012. By 2017, the Outdoor Industry Association estimated that the figure increased to $887 billion in annual expenditures.[15] Their research estimated that outdoor recreation also supported 7.6 million jobs, which include retail clerks, guides, gear manufacturing workers, park rangers, scientists, and more. This estimate placed outdoor recreation job numbers ahead of fields like construction (6.4 million workers) and computer technology (6.7 million workers).

One finding of the OIA 2017 report stands out: outdoor recreation created some highly skilled jobs, including technology, research and design, and manufacturing jobs. One drawback to tourism economic development is that it often creates far more unskilled than skilled jobs. While technology and R&D jobs are likely to require higher-education degrees, manufacturing is particularly valuable in areas where educated workers are at a premium. Tax benefits were another important piece of OIA's 2017 economic impact analysis. Nationally, outdoor recreation expenditures created $124.5 billion in federal, state, and local tax revenues. Overall, the findings indicate that outdoor recreation can be a big plus for local economies.

While notable both in their findings and scale, this historic report lacks texture at the local level, which could only be filled in by smaller, more specific reports. The OIA report utilized categories of outdoor recreation that created some unexpected bedfellows of backpackers and rock climbers, just as one example. Moreover, the report does not break down states by smaller regions, such as looking at a particular national forest or even a portion of the state.

Several studies have looked at the economic impact of climbing prior to the OIA report. For example, Ekstrand's work on Eldorado Canyon in Colorado estimated that climbers contributed $850,000 annually in 1994.[16] In 2002, Will Hobbs's economic study of climbing in the Red estimated expenditures of $2–3 million.[17] A 2004 study of Crowder's Mountain in North Carolina estimated climbers spend $125 per trip while there.[18] A 2004 study of Tennessee's Obed climbing area by Charles Sims and Donald Hodges placed expenditures by climbers at $146,000 per year.[19] W. Mark Anderson's 2006 study of Montana's Hyalite Canyon placed per-trip expenditures at $76–135 per visit.[20]

Starting in 2016, researchers released a series of new climbing economic impact studies that examined four of Appalachia's climbing areas. First up was the Red River Gorge, where climbers annually spent an estimated $3.8 million amid some of the poorest counties in the nation.[21] Those expenditures supported an estimated 34 jobs in the study area and $213,877 in state and local taxes. More studies followed, echoing similar findings. In Chattanooga, Tennessee, climbers were spending $6.9 million annually in Hamilton County.[22] When adding in two regional climbing destinations, *Foster Falls* and *Rocktown*, the expenditures increased to over $10 million annually. Next was North Carolina's thriving Nantahala-Pisgah climbing community, where climbers spent $13.9 million annually amid legendary tourism cities that everyone knows, like Asheville, and less-known rural towns like Cashiers.[23] In 2018, a study in West Virginia's New River Gorge continued to match the pattern from other economic impact studies—climbers there spent an estimated $12.1 million annually, supporting 168 jobs and $6.3 million in labor income for workers in the region.[24]

These studies consistently replicated some interesting demographic patterns among climbers. In the Red, education really stood out, with one in five respondents to the field survey holding graduate degrees and another 43 percent holding a bachelor degree. About a third of those without a college degree were currently in college. Climbers also had solid jobs. The common professions included engineers, teachers (including professors), nurses and physicians, accountants, entrepreneurs, and STEM scientists. Climbers' incomes also were quite surprising, with a third of the sample making $50,000 or more per year and around 7 percent making greater than $99,999 per year in personal income. In Nantahala-Pisgah, 85 percent of the sample had a college degree, with nearly half of the sample having a graduate degree. Income-wise, about half the sample made $50,000 per year or more. And adding a new question, the researchers found one in five climbers owned a business. In the New River Gorge, 45 percent made more than $50,000 per year, while 70 percent had a bachelor degree or higher, with one in five holding a graduate degree.

Taken as a whole, these recent climbing economic studies showed climbing had economic value, and yet that number was not something sufficient for being the singular driver of a regional economy. In short, regardless of location, several million in economic activity was not enough to keep an entire economy running. Even with the growing public awareness of climbing amid its increasing popularity, the findings did not support building an entire economy around climbing. Of course, this is not all bad: evidence long supports that monoeconomies (economies built around one employer) are not necessarily a good idea.[25] Eastern Kentucky's long dependence on coal-related jobs is good evidence of this.[26] Instead, climbing or outdoor recreation in general would be best seen as one part of an economy that could help provide sources for other economic activity without requiring investments and tax write-offs. Rather, it would simply require keeping climbing areas accessible and keeping them protected for future generations.

Collectively, the studies on Appalachian climbing do bring up some of the strengths of having climbing as one area of economic activity. First, climbers are interested in supporting local businesses. In the Red River Gorge and North Carolina studies, climbers reported being strong advocates for locally owned business and being fervently against national chain businesses being developed in the area. Second, climbers are well-educated professionals and sometimes entrepreneurs motivated to be part of the community where they climb. Climbers develop strong emotional connections to climbing areas. In fact, evidence from the North Carolina economic impact study shows that climbers will willingly relocate to live near climbing areas. Examples of professions in these areas include accounting, nursing, engineering, and teaching, which means that some of these talents could be relocated to areas like the Red. Third, climbers are frequent visitors. In the case of the Red's 2016 economic impact study, climbers were frequently returning from their home counties to the Red multiple weekends per year. As has been discussed already in this book, a percentage of climbers have set up semipermanent second homes in the Red in the form of RVs and even tents, returning here most weekends of the climbing season. This has led many to simply buy homes in the region or build new ones, which adds to the local tax base. Fourth, climbing's steadily increasing popularity (over multiple decades, in fact) shows that this is not merely a blip on the outdoor recreation radar—it is a serious, life-devoted form of outdoor recreation. As Shannon Stuart-Smith noted nearly two decades ago, "Well, I think this is a tsunami, and you're just looking at the wave rising up."

A yet-unexplored element of climbing is how it might provide an alternative economic use for natural areas. To date, uses of undeveloped natural areas throughout Appalachia have included timbering, oil and gas extraction, landfill construction, mountaintop removal mining, and strip-mining/open-pit mining, to name a few. These all create economic activity, without a doubt, and serve (or have served) some vital importance in the human story. However, each also leaves its mark on the area. For example, mountaintop removal areas are often difficult to reclaim and reuse. Coal washing storage ponds remain behind long after the mine has closed, as will the radioactive waste in the Estill County landfill. Moreover, in each case the intrinsic value of the land as a natural area is lost in favor of the instrumental value. As we see the documented decline of coal extraction, many rural areas that have previously pursued this approach to economic development are now looking for new opportunities. Climbing may offer another option.

Every state in Appalachia has, on some level, an established climbing area. Some are massive, such as West Virginia's New River Gorge, North Carolina's Linville Gorge, and certainly the Red. Some of them are quite small, like Tennessee's Obed or Kentucky/Virginia's Breaks Interstate Park. And then there are the countless new and still growing climbing areas all throughout the region, including Ijams Quarry and Devil's Racetrack in Tennessee, Alabama's Palisades Park and Yellow Bluff, and a long list of climbing and bouldering spots in western North Carolina. Still more fall just outside Appalachia's borders, such as New York State's Shawangunks. The commonality here is that each of these areas represents place-based resources that cannot be separated from where they exist. Developers cannot fully replicate (much to climbers' dismay) the Red in a gym environment or even find its resources in another place in such concentration. That unique Red sandstone is only found here. These resources are attached to a single location without exception, and climbers must (whether they like it or not) keep coming to the Red to experience that style of climbing. Compare this to timbering or extraction, which remove an asset, and once that asset is removed, the operator will move on.[27]

When rethinking natural areas in this way, it reframes how the community might approach extracting an instrumental value from natural areas. Communities can certainly use them as a resource, allowing businesses to remove whatever is of value before leaving the area. Respectfully, this hasn't boded well for Appalachia to date, which now holds a number of mountaintop removal areas that are devastated, with the land rendered largely unusable. Once coal extraction is complete, the coal and money leave Appalachia's borders, never to return. Another option, however, would be to keep these areas largely as they are and allow climbers, mountain bikers, hunters, fishers, and the many others seeking outdoor recreation to access these areas. This creates economic activity through visitation while maintaining the natural features. Of course, a key component here will be making sure that visitation does not itself damage the area. This is where policies of Leave No Trace and minimal-impact behaviors as well as sustainable trail designs and protective surfaces over archaeological areas are needed to keep the area sustainable, or even minimizing access to sensitive areas to protect cultural resources that cannot otherwise be protected.

If access is maintained and environmental impact from visitation can be minimized, these craggy place-attached resources, when handled correctly, can be *sustainable resources* for economic growth. Public lands are an ideal scenario, followed by something along the lines of climbing preserves, all of which should be made available to use by climbers and other outdoor recreation users. By assembling the two ideas together (a place-based resource and a sustainable resource), one can begin to rethink climbing—and outdoor recreation in general—as a useful tool for economic activity and begin to think about how this could create economic activity in places like the Red and beyond.

The current timing for rethinking these areas as potential sources of economic development is outstanding. Regionally, one finds rural areas facing declines in extraction and manufacturing, often alongside aging communities with few long-term opportunities for younger residents. It will not make an entirely sustainable rural economy run, but climbing and its related economic benefits can be a great starting point. Getting to that stage, however, is not easy.

One important first step, then, is exploring how climbers, including their organizations, can help make such an economic approach plausible and sustainable. If Appalachian areas with climbing were to pursue climbing as a means of preserving natural areas while also creating economic development, it falls squarely on climbers to do the very best they can with this gift of new climbing opportunities. The Red's climbing history has provided a valued list of experiences of how—and occasionally how not—to manage a climbing community's impact on the region. What follows, then, are policy recommendations for climbers and climbing organizations going into the coming decades. At first, these focus on local climbing organizations (LCOs) before turning to national climbing organizations (NCOs).

Climbing organization begins with the LCO. Without a doubt, LCOs are a critical part of climbing communities and a systematic necessity for addressing issues related to climbing. LCOs are the face of climbers to local politicians, community members, and businesses. They are necessary entities if climbers want to work to protect their resources while also maintaining the needs of local residents. In the Red, two LCOs have been important leaders and organizers for the climbing community: Red River Gorge Climbers' Coalition (RRGCC) and Muir Valley. And unofficially, the Cumberland Climbers functioned (if only briefly) as an LCO long before the term had a name or meaning. These organizations have been central to understanding how climbers cohesively function within the region with all facets of the local community. They are, in effect, the central voice representing climbers.

LCOs can accomplish a great deal among climbers. They can formalize problems, such as the example of the RRGCC announcing closures at Torrent Falls or *Roadside*, and give credence to solutions. The closures in and of themselves are brutal, but for an LCO to make clear the cause of the closure also gives a pathway for rectifying the issue in the future. LCOs can organize work parties, such as the multiple trail days happening in the Red, to make the most of limited resources and volunteer labor. LCOs also offer a functional pathway (when established as nonprofits) to grant funding, as has been the case in the Red. Importantly, LCOs operate as a face for the local community. In the Red's history, recall that Miller Fork Recreational Preserve was partly the result of a local resident being able to contact climbers via an LCO. Likewise, Rick Weber worked with Land of the Arches to link climbers with locals while RRGCC worked with Lee County Tourism. Throughout, one can see that LCOs are a functional piece of an engaged climbing community.

Perhaps one of the most important functions of any LCO would be working with public landholders like the Forest Service to ensure ongoing access to climbing. LCOs should certainly be in touch with local, state, and federal land organizations, such as the Forest Service or state parks offices, particularly if climbing areas share borders with these organizations. This is part of ensuring that there are no issues or miscommunications and that climbers are remaining compliant with any particular land use requirements. In the case of the Red, there has been an ongoing relationship with the DBNF through LCOs. For the most part, that relationship has been very productive, whether through negotiating climbing access, addressing climbing closures, or finding ways to work together in sharing access to public lands. It will never be a perfect story, and there undoubtedly will be miscommunications or cases of individuals breaching the trust between the two groups. MOUs (and the process for crafting MOUs) provide a useful way of minimizing many of these miscommunications, while also identifying and negotiating points of disagreement.

As a subset of LCOs working with public land managers, trail work is an ideal spot for building rapport. It makes sense that climbers should help maintain and even build trails that are used heavily by climbers on public lands. A good example of this is the current Forest Service trail to *Military Wall*. This trail is almost entirely now used by climbers, as it leads only to *Military Wall*. Trail work shows that climbers care about these areas and can be good land stewards. By participating in trail crews and limiting impacts on their heavy-use trails, climbers can engage in the work that inherently must be done to maintain access. Trail work also offers a chance to engage other related communities such as mountain biking and public land managers such as the Forest Service. The idea of LCOs building and maintaining trails to crags on public lands—with approval, of course—is especially valuable. Likewise, the lessons learned there can immediately be turned around to trail development on climbing preserves like the Pendergrass-Murray Recreational Preserve (PMRP).

Partnerships with public land managers can also open up new outlets for funding of climbing-related projects. For example, occasionally large employers offer grant programs that could support their employees' projects. Toyota's Environmental Activities Grant Program is one such grant program. In the last 20 years, Toyota has supported 413 different environmental projects to the tune of $100 million per year. While the Forest Service may not qualify for such programs, an LCO could, and this creates a new source of funding that could help fund trail development, support archaeological digs, or even support creating new climbing routes.

Even while managing relationships with public land partners, a central purpose of LCOs should be to gain access to new areas, whether public or private. In the Red, the creation of climbing preserves has worked very well in preserving climbing opportunities. Purchasing land can be an expensive endeavor, but fundraisers (which would certainly need to be part of any LCO presence), Access Fund loan programs, and private donors can make this process much easier. Moreover, climbers who work in law, surveying, and the like should consider serving at no cost in supporting LCOs and climbing access.

LCOs should also continue to address closures in their local area, whether that means ensuring that an area remains closed or finding solutions and resources to reopen closed areas. One possibility may include land swapping. For example, the PMRP has some land that is not currently of interest to climbers because it really doesn't contain any climbing areas. However, there are neighboring parts of the DBNF that *are* of interest to climbers (and have now been closed). Although far fetched, LCOs might be able to help broker a swap. Similarly, land swapping may work well with private organizations, such as nearby landholders who own property with climbing crags and who might be interested in trading it for climber-owned land that doesn't include crags.

While preparing for land purchases, LCOs must get a clear understanding of boundaries, mineral rights, and access to climbing areas and learn from the issues found in the PMRP. Ideally, it's best to buy land and any separated rights (such as timber or minerals) together, but this is often not an option in areas with lots of natural resources. Instead, it is the responsibility of the LCO to make sure climbing can happen in harmony with extraction. If access to a climbing area crosses actively extracted areas, the LCO must work out agreements and protocol with the extraction company so that climbers are not impinging on anyone's rights. In the Red, cars were towed and fights ensued over poor communication, misunications, and climbers breaking the rules. These things can generally be avoided with advance planning, and that responsibility falls to the LCO.

Following land purchases, LCOs (and nonprofit entities) should quantify their negative fiscal impact on the tax base and find ways to legitimately return this to the community. A frequent complaint against nonprofit climbing preserves in the Red is that the land, as a nonprofit, removes property taxes from the tax base. This is an example where climbers are, regrettably, impacting the sustainable resource by conflicting with local interests. Tax bases are particularly critical to schools in rural areas, so LCOs should consider giving the money directly to the school system as a donation, just as one example. If that is not possible, there may be resources that could be purchased, such as technology, for the school and its students, and the funds could be used to make that happen. Services, such as training programs created by climbers, could also be helpful here. This nullifies a legitimate resident complaint while also reiterating that climbers are interested in working together with and investing in local towns and cities.

Can there be more than one LCO in one region? Certainly. The Red is a classic example of this working in practice. There has definitely been a bit of chafing from time to time over the years between the RRGCC and FOMV, but this is to be expected. Much of this chafing was over miscommunication and different approaches to climbing management. These are issues that can be addressed. And even with the relatively minor problems, their messages are consistent in maintaining access and reducing climbing impact.

When there *is* more than one LCO, communication is key. Ideally, LCOs that overlap could have board members shared by both organizations to create a liaison linking the LCOs. This lessens opposition and leads to better communication among all sides. Likewise, LCOs can support each other in their work and missions. Communication prevents reinventing the wheel, shares new technologies and approaches (such as preventing environmental impact), and creates some level of consistency for all climbers to abide by. Looking through the Red's history, the activities of both LCOs often trickled through the forum from individuals rather than the LCOs. It would be far more ideal to have a central source, a clear, unfiltered message being communicated between LCOs.

LCOs gain strength and support from their national-level liaisons, the NCOs. NCOs can provide policy suggestions, guidance, and expertise that may not be available locally. NCOs should support data collection and studies examining climbers. Studies, such as economic impact, can be invaluable at the local level but are often just beyond the reach of LCOs. This is where grant activity can be immeasurably helpful to climbers. And once that data is collected, NCOs can help share that information in the community through outreach, research presentations, and conversations with local governments. NCOs should create and promote climbing policies, reduced impact programs, public perceptions of climbers, and the like through data-supported arguments. NCOs should also work with climbing scholars to have a cadre of researchers available to LCOs to help with studies like environmental impact. LCOs, although local, may not have the knowledge or tools to put policies into place, and this is where NCO leadership can help make that happen through media contacts and recommended best practices for sharing research.

NCOs should continue to support LCO land purchases. Presently, Access Fund offers support and guidance, as well as grants to help pay off properties. As we have seen in the Red, this has been a useful approach to preserving climbing and preserving the resource. As land purchases continue, NCOs should work with LCOs to provide surveying expertise at reduced or no cost. Again, this is something that may be available locally, but if not, NCOs should head off bad land buying practices early by making sure LCOs are fully clear on what is being purchased. This is also a valuable tool to help keep incidents like *Hominy Hole*—recall this climbing area on Forest Service land that nearly shut down all climbing in the Red—from happening. Borders need to be known and established, and NCOs can help make that happen.

Following land purchases, LCOs should also look at working with NCOs to have conservation easements placed to ensure that the land remains open to climbers regardless of the LCO's status. These easements create a lasting protection to the land, preventing it from being subdivided by the LCO or suddenly made into a profit-oriented business. These effectively ensure that public access will forever be free at this location. Currently, the Red's LCOs both have conservation easements in place to protect existing preserves.

NCOs need to lead the charge on protecting the climbing environment, but LCOs need to cover those unique differences at the ground level. NCOs such as Access Fund and American Alpine Club are already making great strides to support national (if not global) programs like the Climber's Pact and education for gym-to-crag transitions. Although the efficacy of these programs is not yet demonstrated, there is anecdotal evidence that they are working. Such programs must continue, but they should also be studied by scientists to examine what kind of effect NCO programs may have and where resources can be best spent to reduce impacts. This is especially true of understanding the gym-to-crag transition.

As climbers plot what the coming decades might entail for the climbing community, more research is sorely needed in multiple areas. Environmental research on climbing should now encompass how climbers' behaviors can be altered to reduce impact. A wealth of research examines climbers' impacts on cliff-line vegetation, and this is valuable. However, this research can be enhanced by further research examining what climbers can do in these areas to minimize impact beyond closing down climbing. Two recent studies out of Eastern Kentucky University have examined climbers' knowledge of minimum-impact practices and how these might correlate with their self-reported actions.[28] Both studies show that climbers who know more about minimizing their impact report putting those ideas into practice. This is welcome news, given that NCOs and LCOs are both working to educate climbers. The real question, however, is whether those programs are effective in raising climbers' knowledge of minimal impact. This issue is not examined in either study.

One major shortcoming of NCO programs such as the Climber's Pact, then, is that there are no public-facing studies examining whether this program truly has an impact on climbers' knowledge of how they might minimize their impact. Moreover, no public-facing research has examined if these programs are effectively teaching all elements of minimum-impact training or just focusing on some. A quantitative study of these programs is paramount to understanding how impacts can best be reduced. This could utilize measures of Leave No Trace that are applicable to climbing (e.g., chalk use, removing vegetation) and examine whether being engaged in environmental impact reduction programs impacts those measures.

Rural gentrification provides another area of concern for NCOs, LCOs, and climbing communities alike.[29] Gentrification is often more associated with changed cityscapes: communities being purchased house by house and then developed for new in-migrant use, leading to increased rents, increased tax bills, and the gradual evacuation and out-migration of the previous resident community.[30] The end result is the reinvestment of capital into creating a new space for the affluent in place of the previous, less affluent residents.[31] Kathleen Wong makes a profound point here regarding gentrification and climbing: climbing gyms in urban areas are sometimes following in the wake of gentrification, offering a new service (indoor climbing) to a changing demographic in gentrified communities such as Brooklyn.[32] However, rural areas like the Red are no longer immune to gentrification, though the causes may be different. Rural gentrification occurs when affluent persons from urban and suburban areas purchase land and homes in rural areas, which causes the same cycle of changes that push local residents out over time. The Red is certainly at risk for this in the coming decades, not only because of climbers arriving in the area but also owing to the countless tourists who come to the Red each year to hike and commune with nature.[33]

There is no single explanation for rural gentrification. Rather, there are several sometimes interrelated and overlapping reasons explaining the change. An important component would be in-migrants who are looking for a lifestyle change.[34] Rural areas can offer a clean break from urban or suburban life and provide opportunities to be close to outdoor recreation, bucolic experiences, and a pastoral life, which is perceived as more relaxing and healthier than urban life. Telecommuting (particularly post–COVID) may increase the movement of recreating users into new locations as their ability to telecommute becomes normalized. Consequently, the new generation of homesteaders and people looking to have a greater connection with the land have taken their role in rural gentrification while often bringing their jobs with them.[35] Still other causes are at hand. Relocating to a rural area provides a situation where their salary can buy more compared to their previous urban location. A good example would be paying rent in a city versus spending far less on a mortgage for a tract of rural land. Others are thinking in economic terms.[36] They may want resources available in rural areas (such as lots of land or water access) that match their economic plans, or they may aim to create businesses that link to the places where they are planning to move. In these cases, the land offers a form of capital that can be utilized to support economic activity.[37]

All of these triggers for rural gentrification seem quite relevant to rock climbing, although it is not quite clear this is happening in the Red *because* of rock climbing. Recall that climbers have been here now over 50 years without making marked changes in the local resident population. However, the recent uptick of homes being purchased in the area by climbers still gives cause to say this issue should be further researched. One profound finding among climbers living in the Nantahala-Pisgah and New River Gorge regions was that their attachment and interest in climbing in those areas was a major reason for their decision to relocate. This may mean climbers are quite resistant to wanting to change these areas in a dramatic fashion. Recall also that the Red's economic impact study on climbing indicated climbers strongly supported the idea of seeing more locally owned businesses, while showing strong resistance to the addition of national chains in the area. Still, climbers, as nonlocals, may have no say in this. The recent developments with the destination resort in the Red River Gorge show that others may be quite apt to pursue rural gentrification in this area whether climbers like it or not. Likewise, proliferating rental cabins or rental houses throughout the region through nationally owned organizations or even nonlocal owners may also exacerbate the issue. Again, more work is needed here to examine how outdoor recreation fits into rural gentrification patterns and what can be done to address this.

Further climbing economic impact studies across the nation would also prove beneficial. As of writing this book, three more economic impact studies are already under way in California's Bishop Region, Wyoming's Lander Region, and again in Kentucky's Red River Gorge. An important part of future economic impact research should include a focus on climbers' economic interests and the personal motivations for climbers who choose to relocate to be nearer to climbing. Additional information about how climbers feel about long-term development (e.g., rural gentrification) would also be enlightening. Overall, having more information about climbers and their behaviors, interests, motivations, and patterns will help NCOs and LCOs (as well as public land managers and local residents) better understand who these climbers really are.

Beyond LCO and NCOs working to serve the climbing community's interests, there is also lots of room for climbers to work in support of local residents' interests. Unpublished data from all the recent economic impact studies of climbing indicate that climbers are, by and far, professionals in their fields. These include physicians and nurses, lawyers, engineers, computer scientists, professors and teachers, craftspeople, and more. In their long quest to become part of the Red River Gorge's local community, climbers should consider what they are doing to support that community beyond their purchases. Ideas include supporting free mobile clinics and health counseling, pro bono legal service visits, collaborating with local towns in constructing new buildings, or teaching the next generation of Red River locals coding. The options are truly limitless, but it falls on climbers to put their best foot forward.

Hindsight can be one of the great gifts found in blending sociology and history because it gives us the rare chance to do things better in the future. Having the opportunity to reflect on the past, considering where things went particularly well or even where things went horribly wrong, provides a learning opportunity to shape a community's behaviors in the future. Climbers have now spent 50 years in Kentucky's Red River Gorge, working their way up its rock features, dwelling in its hollers, and embracing it as part of their lives.

Climbers' time in the Red has often been told by the history of their relationships. From the start, climbing organizations have considered the importance of mentorship among climbers, whether this was Ron Stokley testing climbers' belay skills or John Bronaugh sharing his self-reliant ideas on safety. They have long worked with the Daniel Boone National Forest from the days of the Cumberland Climbers right up to (and beyond) the 2019 MOU. This relationship has not always gone perfectly, with the misunderstandings about Forest Service policies regarding marking important crags and the *Military Wall* dig being temporary stumbling stones now overcome. In the last 15 years or so, climbers have also built increasingly strong relationships with local residents like David Terrill, the Pendergrass and Murray families, and the people of Beattyville. They have also built lifelong relationships with newer residents of the Red like Linda Black and the extraordinary Ventura family at Miguel's. These relationships have changed climbers for the better, and through these relationships climbers have constructed their long-standing ties to the region.

Maintaining these relationships will be a bellwether for climbers' collective future in the Red.

Reflecting on the last 50 years, the salient issues that climbing faces in the future are no mystery. Climbers must, within their own communities and without dependence on others, mitigate their environmental impacts without fail. Through mentorship, climbers must educate within their community on how they can be good partners with public land managers and local residents alike. Climbers must be ideal partners, whether supporting the Red's local residents or being an ally to the Daniel Boone National Forest. Climbers also face an uneasy compromise: they must find a way to manage their presence without irrevocably changing the Red they love so dearly. Much as the proposed Red River Dam could have flooded the Red some half a century ago, a crush of climbers (or even a destination resort) reinventing the very essence of the Red could render the region alien and distant. Where this book ends, the next 50 years of climbing in the Red begins. How these coming decades will transpire sits squarely in the calloused hands of the Red River Gorge's remarkable climbers.

Notes

INTRODUCTION

1. There are numerous videos and pictures online that can provide a visual sense of the Red. I suggest watching "Red River Gorge Petzl RocTrip" on YouTube to get a clear sense of the Red's unique erosion patterns. This event and its historical significance are discussed later in the book.
2. This book uses italics to identify climbing areas (or crags) and quotes to indicate climbing routes. Routes are generally named by the first people to climb the route (called a first ascent or FA), and the names range from the descriptive ("Table of Colors") to symbolic ("Amelia's Birthday") to humorous ("Kick Me in the Jimmie").

CHAPTER 1

1. For a detailed but accessible discussion of the geology of the Red, see Greb and Mason, "Geology of the Red River Gorge."
2. National natural landmarks are managed by the National Park Service in conjunction with land managers such as the US Forest Service. The Red River Gorge Natural Landmark area includes 41 natural bridges in Menifee, Powell, and Wolfe Counties.
3. The Daniel Boone National Forest officially spells this as Grays Arch, although it is sometimes misspelled as Gray's Arch in popular media.
4. There are numerous videos of Red River Gorge arches on YouTube. I suggest looking at videos of Grays Arch and Skybridge Arch, both of which are easily accessed by day hikers. Natural Bridge (which is in a state park) is probably the most famous arch in the area. There are also books and online media dedicated to so-called unofficial arches that are not noted on official DBNF maps. While enticing, visiting these often means stepping off the established user trails, risking damage to plants such as the white-haired goldenrod.
5. Royle, *Culloden*.
6. Collins's history of the DBNF notes that the formal dedication site for the DBNF was held in London at the Levi Jackson Wilderness Road State Park. The rationale given to the federal government was that this state park was located on the Old Wilderness Road (hacked out in part by Boone) and had been the site of two settler massacres by Native Americans. This inexplicably resolved the matter, and the ceremony went forward as planned. Collins, *History of the Daniel Boone National Forest*.
7. DBNF, "Forest Ownership Pattern."
8. The full list of crags on the Clifty Wilderness is *Mariba Fork*; *Tower Rock*; *Lower,*

Middle, & Upper Small Wall; *Moonshiner's Wall*; *Doorish Wall*; *Eagle Point Buttress*; *Wall of Denial*; *Woody's Wall*; *Funk Rock City*; and *Wildcat Wall*.

9. Stackelbeck and Mink, "Overview of Archaeological Research."
10. There is extensive research on this particular shelter and its importance in the region. See Southeastern Archaeological Conference, "Red River Gorge"; Jones, "Vegetal Remains"; Gremillion, "New Perspectives"; and Carmean and Sharp, "Not Quite Newt Kash."
11. Cherry, *Kentucky*.
12. Kentucky State Parks, "Fort Boonesborough State Park."
13. For an extraordinary history of the fort, see O'Malley, *Boonesborough*.
14. Collins, *History of the Daniel Boone National Forest*. Gist also has an interesting place in history in that he saved a certain important young future leader's life on two separate occasions: first from a Native American skirmish and second when that leader fell into the freezing Allegheny River. That leader's name? Future president George Washington.
15. For a full history of Pilot Knob, see Campbell, "Pilot Knob."
16. There is some debate in Daniel Boone biographies about his 1769 ascent of Pilot Knob and if there were two separate ascents. Enoch explores this issue and the relevant literature in "250th Anniversary." The *Red River Historical Society & Museum* journal also dedicated their Spring 2016 volume 24, issue 1 entirely to the history of Pilot Knob.

    In a strange twist of history, Daniel Boone and Christopher Gist actually knew each other, having been neighbors in North Carolina before Gist traveled into Kentucky. Younger generations may also be familiar with both Boone and Gist as they appear in the "Assassin's Creed" video game series.
17. Lowrey, "What's the Matter with Eastern Kentucky?"
18. Appalachian Regional Commission, "County Economic Status in Appalachia."
19. For an overview of addiction in the United States, see Caldwell, "American Carnage."
20. For an exploration of addiction as a national crisis, see Sullivan, "The Opioid Epidemic."
21. For a local perspective on the history of addiction in Kentucky, see Estep, "Toll of Eastern Kentucky's Drug Epidemic" and "Drug Overdose Deaths." For state statistics on addiction, see Kentucky Office of Drug Control Policy, "2016 Overdose Fatality Report."
22. For a discussion of how local communities are experiencing addiction, see Maser, "Perry County," and Galewitz, "Pharmacies Thriving."
23. Estep, "Toll of Eastern Kentucky's Drug Epidemic."
24. Sonka and Yetter, "Bevin Administration."
25. Desrochers and Brammer, "Bevin Proposes Ending."
26. "Kentucky Lost 11.1 Percent."
27. "Kentucky Quarterly Coal Report."
28. Outdoor Industry Association, "The Outdoor Recreation Economy."

CHAPTER 2

1. For those interested in seeing this gravel hill, search YouTube for "Climbing Vlog: Stuck at the Motherlode!"
2. See Nuttall, "Historic Oil Fields."

3. Jillian Rickly has extensively written about the climbing lifestyle in the Red. See Rickly, "Lifestyle Mobilities," "(Re)production of Climbing Space," and " 'I'm a Red River Local.' "

4. Here are some quick climbing terms found throughout the book. *Carabiners* are oval-shaped metal rings with a hinge on one side. The hinge is spring-loaded so that it stays closed but can easily have a rope pushed through the hinged side. Some carabiners also have a locking function that ensures they stay closed. Carabiners are used in myriad ways, most notably to attach the climbing rope to bolt anchors. *Quickdraws* are pieces of climbing webbing (a stiff material used in climbing harnesses) with carabiners on both ends. In sport climbing, quickdraws are attached to bolt anchors for protection. *Bolt anchors* are permanent anchors inserted into the rock via drilling and have a metal loop extending from the bolt to which a carabiner can be attached. Once the quickdraw is attached to the bolt anchor via one carabiner, the rope is then threaded through the other carabiner. Now, if the climber falls, their *belayer* (the person safeguarding the climber on the ground by controlling how much rope can freely move) can stop the climber's fall at the last bolt anchor into which the last quickdraw was attached. See Samet, *Climbing Dictionary*, for a detailed conversation about climbing language.

5. For an in-depth exploration of temperature and adhesion, see "Friction and Rock Climbing."

6. *Sending* a route (or indicating one has *sent* a route) means that the climber has completed the route. There are various more descriptive uses of the term. For example, *redpointing* is sending a route (typically a sport route) without falling after practicing it at least once. Redpointing does not allow for *hangdogging* (having the belay support one's weight via the rope so the climber can rest) or *toproping* (allowing someone else to climb the route and install the rope). Likewise, a route can be *onsighted* (sometimes listed as *onsited*) by sending the route the first time one sees the route without any advance preparation or information about the route. *Flashing* a route involves onsiting the route but allows for a bit of information from climbers about the route.

7. For a detailed conversation about projects, see Mann, "Dain Koyamada on Projects."

8. YouTube includes videos of climbing at *The Motherlode* that can help give perspective to the reader. Also, I suggest watching "Michaela Kiersch and The Golden Ticket" to get a sense of the terrain and its history in the surrounding area. "The Golden Ticket" is located at *Chocolate Factory*, which is in the holler next to *The Motherlode*.

9. The official full name of this crag is *The Motherlode* per the current Ellington guide, and that is what is used in this book. That said, other guides and websites have also listed it simply as *Motherlode*. In conversation, I have heard climbers also simply refer to it as *The Lode*, and I have also seen this in online discussion forums. Occasionally, it incorrectly appears as *The Motherload*.

10. See Boland, "How Miguel's Pizza Made."

11. Ellington, *Red River Gorge Rock Climbs*, 2nd ed., 351. It is useful to know that this route (a 5.13b) is notoriously difficult for people who are not particularly tall, largely because it requires a few big moves between holds. At the time, Katie was already climbing much harder routes, hence the route being in humor rather than being malicious. Bill Ramsey later echoed this being the case in the comments of Whitney Boland's article on sending the route "True Love" (see Boland, "The Day I

Sent True Love"). For more information about inclusivity in climbing, see Jun, "Accept and Adapt."

12. Chris Snyder was not alone in 1994 at this crag. Other important route developers included Brian McCray, Jeff Moll, Keith Moll, Tim Cornette, Roxana Brock, and Chris Martin. Each of these names appear elsewhere in the Red's climbing history in the 1990s.

13. To date, no private crags charge admission to climb. Instead, two (Muir Valley and Rock Domain) presently utilize a parking fee, but climbers are free to hike into the area and climb at no cost. Another area, Torrent Falls, rents cabins to climbers who are then given free access to routes on the property.

14. Ellington, *Red River Gorge Rock Climbs*, expanded 3rd ed. on *The Motherlode*.

15. Bald Rock Recreational Preserve, nearby Pendergrass-Murray Recreational Preserve, and Miller Fork Recreational Preserve, all RRGCC properties, include conservation easements. See Access Fund, "Land Holdings," for further discussion. This is also discussed further later in the book.

CHAPTER 3

1. Smith, "A Complete Guide."
2. Young, "Red River Rampage."
3. Lane Report, "Kentucky Counties Affected."
4. Puente, "Heavy Rain Causing Flooding."
5. "Kentucky Union Railroad."
6. Kentucky Union would later link Clay City to Winchester and Slade in June 1889 and Lexington directly in 1890. It would later default on their construction bonds and be placed into receivership. Lexington & Eastern Railway Company was organized in 1894 and would assume operations of Kentucky Union.
7. For a discussion of rural extraction towns, see Shifflett, *Coal Towns*.
8. For an overview of West Virginia's coal history in the New River Gorge, see Good and Stasick, "New River Gorge." Chris DellaMea's coalcampusa.com website also has extensive pictures of the New River Coalfield. For a detailed review of labor conflict in coal camps in the New River Gorge, see also Leebrick and Maples, "Landscape as Arena."
9. Gaventa, *Power and Powerlessness*, offers extraordinary insight on the role of power and labor in coal camps. It also serves as a useful history of the region's coal economy.
10. For a nuanced discussion of uneven development, see Eller, *Uneven Ground*. On a personal note, I am deeply appreciative of Dr. Eller's work in Appalachia.
11. Lerner, *Sacrifice Zones*.
12. For a detailed examination of life in sacrifice zones, see Cottle, "Land, Life and Labour."
13. For a review of coal mining and sacrifice zones, see Fox, "Mountaintop Removal in West Virginia."
14. See McSpirit et al., "EPA Actions."
15. For information on the Estill County landfill, see Van Velzer, "Radioactive Waste."
16. Reiser, *Cadillac Desert*, includes a full description of this extraordinary historical period of dam construction.
17. Bowen, "Bert T. Combs."

18. Eller, *Uneven Ground.*
19. Eller, *Uneven Ground.*
20. Enoch, "Bert T. Combs."
21. Bowen, "Bert T. Combs," 23.
22. Bowen, "Bert T. Combs."
23. Bowen, "Bert T. Combs."
24. Enoch, "Bert T. Combs."
25. Eller, *Uneven Ground.*
26. Enoch, "Bert T. Combs."
27. Eller, *Uneven Ground.*
28. Eller, *Uneven Ground.*
29. Lilley and Todd, "Controversy and Mystery."
30. Collins, *History of the Daniel Boone National Forest.* See also Shrake, "Operation Build and Destroy."
31. Kentucky Afield Radio, "Kentucky's Red November." Note that this audio includes an extraordinary online oral history of the dam.
32. Kentucky Afield Radio, "Kentucky's Red November."
33. Collins, *History of the Daniel Boone National Forest.* See also Shrake, "Operation Build and Destroy," 48.
    In the 1993 John Bronaugh climbing guide, there is a picture of a barn painted with the message ELECT COOK STOP THE DAM. It's not entirely clear who Cook would have been, but it does show at least one other politician (or perhaps candidate, as they may not have been elected) willing to openly resist the proposed dam. See Bronaugh, *Red River Gorge Climbs* (1st ed.), 6.
34. Shrake, "Operation Build and Destroy."
35. Even today, it is common to find local residents who lived through the dam and its subsequent protests who are unwilling to discuss the dam.
36. Kentucky Afield Radio, "Kentucky's Red November."
37. Kentucky Afield Radio, "Kentucky's Red November."
38. Kentucky Afield Radio, "Kentucky's Red November."
39. Combs returned again to run for governor in 1971 but lost in the primary to Wendell Ford, who would go on to win. Combs subsequently retired from political life but would continue to work for coal companies in the court system. See Eller, *Uneven Ground.*
40. Robert F. Collins notes an odd bit of history regarding the state governor's lack of support for the dam. Governor Nunn announced his support after meeting with Elvis Stahar, then president of the National Audubon Society. However, it was Stahar himself who, as secretary of the army in 1962, had signed off on the recommendation of authorizing the dam. See Collins, *History of the Daniel Boone National Forest.*
41. There is a bit of irony here, as NEPA would later be used against climbers in the Red in the 1990s.
42. Collins, *History of the Daniel Boone National Forest,* 275.
43. Shrake, "Operation Build and Destroy."
44. Becker, *Outsiders.*
45. Rutherford, "Saga of the Red River Gorge," 23.
46. Rutherford, "Saga of the Red River Gorge," 23.
47. Chaney, *In the Red.*

CHAPTER 4

1.   Regarding "Delta Blow": local legend (and Ellington's 3rd edition guide) has it that the route nearly killed its first ascensionist, Martin Hackworth, in the 1980s when a 20-pound flake broke off. Flakes are thin sections of rock that are separate from the rest of the wall, much like a flake on a croissant. They can come in all sizes. Sometimes flakes can hold a climber, and other times they may disconnect. More recently, technology now allows climbers to learn exactly how well a flake is attached to the wall. For a detailed conversation about this technology, see Kornie, "Peering beneath a Source," which also discusses some of the recent flake falls in Yosemite.

2.   The history of Yosemite climbing is an enthralling read that is beyond the scope of this book. For a complete history, I suggest Roper, *Camp 4*, followed by Taylor, *Pilgrims of the Vertical*. Both are captivating writers and storytellers.

3.   Note that "The Nose" was long considered unclimbable. It took Warren Harding and his evolving team (which included at different times Mark Powell, Bill Feurer, Rich Calderwood, Wayne Merry, and George Whitemore and summited using the latter three) 45 days to siege climb "The Nose." Siege climbing involves using pulleys and multiple trips to bring gear up and down the mountain. The current speed record on "The Nose" (as of June 2018) was set by newer climbing legends Alex Honnold and Tommy Caldwell. It took them less than two hours.

4.   For a detailed discussion of climbing ethics, see Taylor, *Pilgrims of the Vertical*.

5.   Like all good climbing stories, the story of how I came to find Ron deserves to be shared. Ron's last name was misspelled as "Stokely" in nearly all the guidebooks. I had nearly given up on finding him during this project, but in a weird twist of fate I accidentally Googled his name with the correct spelling (Stokley), leading to an article about him backpacking as a youth in Kentucky, which led to an email address. That random coincidence (and Ron's willingness to speak with me) unlocked much of the information in this chapter, including identifying "D. Britz" as Dieter Britz, which led me to find him, as well. Evidence suggests the typo may originate in the mailing list for the Cumberland Climbers, which lists "Ronald Stokely" as its first name on September 8, 1969. This mailing list is discussed later in the chapter.

6.   For the early history of this club, see Bluegrass Cycling Club, "Bluegrass Wheelmen Organize."

7.   Ron would later serve as a leader of Explorer Post 360. Explorer posts pop up a few times in the Red's climbing and caving history, and this would be a great area for future researchers to explore.

8.   Regarding jumars: *jumaring* is one great example of the links between climbing and caving as it involves one approach to ascending a rope while minimizing arm exertion. The basic jumaring technique can be done using ropes or a device called a *jumar* (sometimes more recently referred to as an ascender). The basic technique generally works in two steps using two connection points with the rope. First, one uses the jumar attached to the feet (with two loops, much like a stirrup on a saddle) to stand up on the rope, allowing the climber to raise the second jumar higher on the rope. Next, one can now put weight on that jumar while freeing the weight on the feet and raising the jumar attached to the feet. The cycle is repeated as needed.

9. See Ron's posts on redriverclimbing.com, "History of the Cumberland Climbers, Part 1."
10. Dieter's name was inexplicably listed only as D. Britz in the guidebooks, which created a long-standing mystery about his identity.
11. Taylor, *Pilgrims of the Vertical,* echoes several similarly unsafe (by today's standards) approaches that were commonplace at the time.
12. John Hubart (incorrectly spelled Hubbard in the guides per Dieter) was one of those mystery climbers who were present in the Red in 1969. Little is known about him today, aside from the fact that he may have just gotten out of the military when he showed up in the Red.
13. Chimney Top Rock was among the first lands acquired by the Daniel Boone National Forest in the 1930s. Chimney Rock was included in Tract 1. Nearby Chimney Top Creek was among later purchases and some may still have had private residences in the 1960s, including the Ledford property discussed later in this paragraph.
14. This report lists Dieter as D. Britz, which may explain the mystery as to why his name was listed as such in the early guides.
15. By coincidence, Floyd Ledford also appears in Edwin Shrake's 1968 article on the Red River Dam. There, Floyd explains that he felt many locals expected to get rich by selling their land after the dam was built. He also notes that land prices had increased in recent years as a result of the dam: "Land prices are booming. Over at Pine Ridge a fellow is asking $20,000 for less than 100 acres, and not one acre of it is level ground. There's going to be some very sad people when they understand this lake ain't going to make them wealthy." Shrake, "Operation Build and Destroy," 50.
16. Cumberland Climbers is not directly linked to today's Cumberland Climbers Coalition in Tennessee.
17. Taylor, *Pilgrims of the Vertical.*
18. Tom Seibert noted that Dave Kelly's name may actually have been Kelley. This same revision may also apply to Jim and Duane.
19. Regarding Cumberland Climbers founding date, a membership advertisement in the Cumberland Climber files lists September 8, 1969, as their official start date and that "Soon after, the purposes and aims of the club were determined."
20. Frank Becker dedicated his 1974 guide "To Cliff . . . and cliffs." In our conversations, he shared that Cliff was in fact Clifford Bond. On a related note, Tom Seibert shared a funny anecdote about Cliff's sense of humor. Cliff would tell Tom, "Never turn your back on a Cliff." Of course, as climbers, this has a double meaning, and Tom laughed that it was difficult not to do that when you were between a cliff and Cliff.
21. Sadly, Bill Andrews passed in 2012, so anecdotal evidence may be as close as we get to unraveling who started "Caver's Route."
22. Cohen, *History of the Sierra Club*, gives a great perspective on the function of the club.
23. Reportedly, the Cumberland Climbers also created a climbing guide that included at least some route descriptions. However, despite stories of copies existing, I have not personally seen a copy. Should someone reading this book have a copy, please contact me so we can discuss it.
24. Notably, these were directly in line with the kind of ideas Dick Leonard had

promoted in his time on the board of directors in the 1930s and as president, 1953–1955. See Taylor, *Pilgrims of the Vertical*.

25. Regarding arches and cathedrals quote, see Mead, "Gorge Protector." Regarding safety, see "No Title 950" (untitled article on Don Fig). Anecdotally, climbers also respected Don in that he was famously fit and had massive biceps. This may have made him feel more like part of the climbing community, too. In a Red River Climbers forum discussion about Fig's retirement in 2008, various climbers shared the following: "Don carries the torch for the Red and what is best for it, and he probably has the biggest biceps of any person I have ever seen." "Thanks Mr. Fig for being so cool and pro climber over the years. Now drop and give me 20. Seriously, that guy can kick all of our asses!" "Thanks Don, for your many years of devotion and hard work for the Red and the community. Even the ticket/fine you awarded me back in 90/91 for being in the wrong area at the wrong time never lessened my respect for you and your work." See "USFS Ranger Don Fig Retires." Additionally, 361 Adventures named one of their endurance racing events in the Red "The Fig." Sadly, Don passed away April 1, 2020, at the age of 83.

26. Personal correspondence between Frank Becker and Ranger John Moore, unpublished.

CHAPTER 5

1. There is some debate about the use of a backup knot on the figure eight. See "Do You Need to Back-up Your Tie-in Knot?" for a discussion of the arguments on both sides.

2. Although the website is now defunct, redriversaga.com (viewable via the Wayback Machine) centralized a folk history of the Red River Dam, including a detailed timeline and collection of photographs from the era.

3. Frank Becker's guide has extraordinary drawings in it by Diane Edith Blazy. The drawings include Courthouse Rock (as seen from CR 1067), the south side of Lookout Point at Natural Bridge, Chimney Top Rock from both the north and south sides, Half Moon Rock, Jewell Pinnacle (as seen from KY 715), and Tower Rock (as seen from KY 715, although the guide inaccurately says KY 175). Becker stated that Diane was not a climber. Diane graduated from the University of Kentucky in 1976 and worked in Lexington as a teacher and photographer in the 1970s and at the University of Kentucky from 1981 to 1982. She later received a MFA from Rochester Institute of Technology in 1991 and continued working in photography until her death in 2007. Diane created a drawing of the third Fayette County Courthouse (1806–1883) for Wright, *Lexington: Heart of the Bluegrass*. Diane's photography also appears in Bleicher, *Contemporary Color Theory and Use*.

4. See Becker, *Red River Gorge Climber's Guide*, preface.

5. Regarding "Tunnel Overhang," the notes on this route indicate that this guide was published, at earliest, in Fall 1974.

6. Regarding "Zig-Zag Bond," this route was later shortened to "Zig-Zag" and climbed by Ed Pearsall in 1977. It gets its name from having a few traverses similar to a zig-zag motion.

7. Regarding "Mighty Eidson," this route was FA'd by Bill and Nancy Eidson. Bill represents another tie back to the caving community and is referenced in Borden and Bruckner, *Beyond Mammoth Cave*.

8. Even today, the ties between the two communities exist, as BlueGrass Grotto holds their monthly meetings at LEF, the Lexington indoor climbing gym.
9. Becker, *Red River Gorge Climber's Guide*, 11.
10. Erick Bostrum's name was spelled "Erick" in the guide addendum, but Tom Seibert said it was actually "Eric."
11. Becker, *Red River Gorge Climber's Guide*, 13.
12. Dick Schori is included in Kor, *Beyond the Vertical*. Kor notes that Dick was "an American from Baton Rouge spending the summer in Europe as an exchange student" (145). He and Layton Kor soon committed to doing the *Direct Cima Grande* in the Dolomites. Bob Molzon's name appears in both regional caving and mathematics conferences. Although not confirmed, Bob also may have been a mathematics professor at the University of Kentucky.
13. Benjamin and Pearsall, *Rawk!*, 36. The Benjamin and Pearsall guide offers a unique example of how things change over time in climbing routes and crag names. In this guide, *Small Wall* added "Vine Climb," "Spiderweb Teahouse," and "85' Layback," although the guide had no information beyond the route names. In later years, *Small Wall* would be divided into *Lower Small Wall* and *Middle Small Wall*. The three routes listed at *Small Wall* were all first ascended by Tom Seibert and Larry Day in 1976. Some of the names were off or have changed with time, specifically "Devine Climb" and "Layback Crack." Even *Fortress Wall* had a second name listed: *Frenchburg Cliff*.
14. Benjamin and Pearsall, *Rawk!*, 14.
15. See Molloy, "Beauty and Death," for a conversation about tourist (not climber) deaths at *Chimney Top* and also nearby *Princess Arch*.
16. *Military Wall* was originally listed as *Military Walls* in Pearsall, *Climber's Guide to the Red River Gorge*, and subsequently in Hackworth, *Stones of Years*, in 1984.
17. *German-Irish* probably went up in the late fall to winter of 1974, while the Becker guide was in publication in Fall 1974. The 1978 Benjamin and Pearsall guide ideally would have included *Military Wall*, but it was either overlooked or simply not known by the authors at the time.
18. While discussing caving, Frank Becker noted in our oral history interview that BlueGrass Grotto was an affiliate of the National Speleological Society. The BlueGrass Grotto's newsletter was called *The Kentucky Caver*. Notably, Martin drew at least one newsletter cover for the organization, hinting at his many talents.
19. Ed Pearsall is included on the FA of "Jungle Beat" in this edition but not later editions.
20. Among those 20 routes was a route called "Dog Days Afternoon," which included Rich Gottlieb and Gene Hancock on the FA in June 1976. The route today is called simply "Dog Days." Rich was a climber from New York's Shawangunks (aka the Gunks) and would be an early example that the Red was already attracting climbers from other areas. The Pearsall guide listed "African Dogs" as an area for potential future development. The area was located on the same face as "Africa" and "Dog Days." Although the area was never specifically mentioned in future guides, Tom Souders added the route "Bleak Future," a 5.10d trad route there in 1989.
21. This picture can be seen at https://www.redriverclimbing.com/RRCGuide/?type=route&id=400.
22. Fantz, "Lloyd Fantz's Story," iii.
23. Becker, "Red River Gorge," 20.

24. For a history of nut development and this quote, see Achey, "The Nut Chronicles."
25. For a full perspective on Yosemite's technology use, see Roper, *Camp 4*. To place Yosemite into climbing's historical perspective, see Taylor, *Pilgrims of the Vertical*.
26. Achey, "The Nut Chronicles."
27. For a detailed history of climbing gear development, see Bright, "History of Rock Climbing Gear." For the evolution of nuts, see Achey, "The Nut Chronicles."
28. Van Leuven, "The History of Friends."
29. Hackworth, *Stones of Years*, i.
30. Hackworth, *Stones of Years*, i.
31. Regarding "Psycho Killer," later guides would list the first ascent of this route as Roger Pearson, John Bronaugh, Tina Feezel, and George Robinson in 1987. Hackworth, *Stones of Years*, specifically states that Greg produced the route alongside two other Greg Smith routes on the right side of "Roadside Attraction," so this may have been a route in development when the guide was going to the publisher.
32. Regarding "Harder Than Your Husband," the names of a fair number of routes in the Red have sexual connotations or innuendos. "Harder Than Your Husband" was one of the first of many to be named using puns and innuendos in later years. "Ball Scratcher," "Rug Muncher," and "The Reacharound" are a few other (of many) examples.
33. Regarding Tod Anderson, Tod's name is attached to only three routes in the Red: "Five Finger Discount," "Autumn" at *Long Wall* in 1984, and "Private Duty Nurses" at *The Dome*. All were first ascended in 1984, and all three included Martin Hackworth.
34. Regarding Snider and Hackworth's trip to *Muscle Beach*, as a historical note, this trip probably began on March 22 (a Monday), with the two climbing greats completing a first ascent of "Jaws."
35. Hackworth, *Stones of Years*, ii–iii.
36. Ellington, *Red River Gorge Climbs*, 3rd ed., 111.

CHAPTER 6

1. Today, there is a Jot'Em Down store in Lexington. L. C. and Ed Terrell opened the store in 1933, and it is still run by their family today. For the history of this store, see Crawford, *Kentucky Stories*, a fascinating book. There is further history on the store available at https://www.horseyhundred.com/Sites-Along-Route/Sites/Jot-em-Down.aspx. Another store now exists in Pine Ridge, Arkansas. Pine Ridge was originally called Waters but changed its name in 1936 as a reference to the radio show. The McKinzie general store renamed itself the Jot'Em Down Store. A snippet of the radio show, including the pronunciation of the store's name, is available on the museum's website at http://lum-abner.com. There is also a Jot-Em-Down shelter in the region. See White, "Lithic Analysis."
2. Note that the 1998 Bronaugh guide has an earlier picture of Miguel's from approximately the era described in this chapter. The words "The Rainbow Door" are visible at the top of the restaurant sign, along with mention of ice cream and sub sandwiches. See Bronaugh, *Red River Gorge Climbs*, 2nd ed., 9.
3. Boland, "How Miguel's Pizza Made."
4. Rickly, " 'They All Have a Different Vibe,' " provides an in-depth discussion of daily life at Miguel's.

5. Roper, *Camp 4*.
6. The correct spelling of Camp 4 uses the number, not the word "Four." The name itself comes directly from the Yosemite National Park sign marking the camp as "Camp 4." In 1971, it was renamed "Sunnyside Walk-in Campground" in an attempt to deter climbers' attraction to the site, but it was eventually (in 1999) renamed back to Camp 4. In 2003, it was added to the National Register of Historic Places. See Roper, *Camp 4*, for an authoritative and compelling history of the Yosemite climbing community.
7. See McDowell, *Porter Jarrard Climbs Moore's Wall*.
8. "Porter Jarrard: Climbing 5.14 at 44."
9. See Jarrard and Snyder, *Selected Climbs*, introduction. In this guide, Porter notes that his first route in the Red was "Crazy Fingers."
10. Doug Reed is a very respected climber in the Red River Gorge and is described in one source as the New River Gorge's strongest climber (Mellor, *American Rock*, 112). Doug and Porter worked on bolting many routes in West Virginia's New River Gorge.
11. There are occasional inconsistencies on YDS rankings for climbing routes over time. For example, "Another Doug Reed Route" is listed as a 5.11c in the print guidebook but as a 5.10c in the online guide. To add yet another level to this, "Another Doug Reed Route" has a 5.11a unofficial consensus ranking in the online guide, meaning that climbers who have completed the route have given their own ranking opinions on the route.
12. Ellison, "America's 100 Best."
13. Ellison, "America's 100 Best."
14. "Porter Jarrard: Climbing 5.14 at 44."
15. "Porter Jarrard: Climbing 5.14 at 44."
16. Rickly, "Lifestyle Mobilities"; Rickly, *On Lifestyle Climbers*.
17. Kentucky alcohol sales laws are quite complicated. The state currently has multiple alcohol designations: wet, dry, moist, limited, golf course, winery, and qualified historic site. "Wet" means alcohol may be sold in accordance with state regulations, while "dry" means no alcohol may be sold in the county. Cities may also vote to sell alcohol in a dry county, which results in "moist" designations. There are also limited designations for seating size (either 50 or 100 depending on the limited designation) of the location applying to sell alcohol. Golf courses and wineries in dry counties can also obtain limited status. Special considerations sometimes are made for historical districts and alcohol sales. For example, Boone Tavern (in a historically zoned area of Berea, Kentucky) had sufficient resident votes there to allow alcohol sales solely within that district (which only resulted in the tavern selling alcohol). Thus, one could have a glass of wine on Boone Tavern's porch in an otherwise dry city (and moist county). Berea itself subsequently allowed alcohol sales with food purchase in 2015, and local politicians indicate the city will likely have the chance to vote to go entirely wet in the coming years.

CHAPTER 7

1. *Bushwacking*, as it is often called in the climbing community, is an important part of finding new climbing destinations. It is often done either out of season (such as winter, when the leaves are off and cliffs are more easily seen from afar) or on off days when climbing muscles are simply too sore to climb.

2. "MV Anchor Cleaning Accident." Parentheses in original quote.
3. "Re: Johnny's Wall."
4. The guide also listed "Project" (a Jarrard project route later renamed "The Wheel of Time" and FA'd by David Hume in 1996) as a 5.13. "The Wheel of Time" is a good example of Porter's use of so-called Porter Hangers. A conversation about rebolting this route in the online guidebook notes that the route still contained some of these devices as of 2009.
5. Bronaugh, *Red River Gorge Climbs*, 12.
6. Stahl, "Rock Climbing in Gorge to Be Regulated."
7. Stahl, "Rock Climbing in Gorge to Be Regulated."
8. Achey, "Fixed Anchors in the Wilderness."
9. Stahl, "Rock Climbing in Gorge to Be Regulated."
10. For discussions of bans in these locations, see Procknow, "Cave Rock Permanently Closed"; Achey, "Fixed Anchors in the Wilderness"; and Mackley and Mackley, "Cave Rock." Note that Devils Tower is the correct spelling and does not include an apostrophe.
11. Grijalva et al., "Valuing the Loss," 103.
12. For further conversation about the Aladağ mountains incident, see Griffin, "Foreign Climbers Cause Controversy."
13. Regarding "Pulling Pockets," in talking with Tom Souders, he noted that the person who bolted the route (whose name is presently lost to history) did contact him and ask permission to retro-bolt the route, which Tom agreed to allow, noting that he didn't own the route regardless.
14. US Forest Service, "Rock Climbing Management Guide," i.
15. US Forest Service, "Rock Climbing Management Guide."
16. US Forest Service, "Rock Climbing Management Guide," i.
17. US Forest Service, "Rock Climbing Management Guide."
18. US Forest Service, "Rock Climbing Management Guide," 3.
19. There is a slight inconsistency in the CMG in that page 3 states the DBNF would *not* consider routes in Clifty Wilderness, while page 4 says the DBNF is *unlikely* to consider routes in the Clifty Wilderness. For the Tight Hollow Research Natural Area, the same applies on page 6.
20. US Forest Service, "Rock Climbing Management Guide."
21. Clark and Hessl, "The Effects of Rock Climbing."
22. Juan Lorite, et al., "Rock climbing alters plant species"; Bruno Baur, Lars Fröberg, and Stefan W. Müller, "Effect of Rock Climbing."
23. Walendziak, "Longitudinal variation."
24. Kuntz and Larson, "Influences of Microhabitat Constraints."
25. Kris again reflected some of the early ties to caving in the Red. For example, she was invited by the BlueGrass Grotto to go on a spelunking trip to Pine Mountain Caves. Also, note that Chris Snyder and Kris Snyder are different persons.
    John was the first president of the RRGCC, serving from 1996 to 1998. Later presidents included Hugh Loeffler (1998–2003), Gretchen Finniff (May 2003–May 2004), Bill Strachan (May 2004–December 2005), Bob Matheny (December 2005–February 2009), Charlie Rittenberry (February 2009–June 2010), Rick Bost (July 2010–December 2011), Paul Vidal (January 2012–April 2013), Bentley Brackett (May 2013–June 2015), Josephine Sterr (July 2015–December 2016), Yasmeen Fowler (January 2017–December 2017), Adam Gregory (January 2018–December 2020), and current president Jereme Ransick.

26. Donnie Richardson with the DBNF also helped the RRGCC in their early search for members. Donnie placed a flier at the Slade exit asking for members. Jeff Neal was reportedly the first member, per Shannon Stuart-Smith.
27. "The Madness" was originally listed as "Madness."
28. Bronaugh, *Red River Gorge Climbs*, 2nd ed., 299.
29. Jarrard and Snyder, *Selected Climbs*, iv.
30. Jarrard and Snyder, *Selected Climbs*, iv.
31. Chipping remains even today an issue in the climbing community. See Kardaleff, Huey, and Haab, "Open Letter."
32. Jarrard and Snyder, *Selected Climbs*, v.
33. Jarrard and Snyder, *Selected Climbs*, 80.
34. Jarrard and Snyder, *Selected Climbs*, viii.

CHAPTER 8

1. For a full discussion of plants in the Red, see McFadden, "Vascular Flora."
2. McFadden, "Vascular Flora."
3. US Fish and Wildlife Service, "White-haired Goldenrod."
4. Long before he served as RRGCC executive director, Bill established a 5.11c trad route called "Here Comes Batman" in 1978 at *Staircase Wall*. This route was the first 5.11 route in the Red, making it the most difficult skill route in the Red at the time.
5. For a detailed exploration of John and Gifford's relationship, see Clayton, *Natural Rivals*. See also Lorbiecki, *A Fierce Green Fire*, for a detailed exploration of Aldo's impact on the Forest Service and his ideas on conservation.
6. Collins, *History of the Daniel Boone National Forest*, 276.
7. Collins, *History of the Daniel Boone National Forest*, 279.
8. Veno, "Chris Schimmoeller."
9. Kalisz and Boettcher, "Active and Abandoned."
10. Brown, "Odd Little Red-Cockaded Woodpeckers."
11. Bronaugh, *Red River Gorge Climbs*, 8.
12. See Balf, "Climbing," for a conversation about aging and competition within the community.
13. Bronaugh, *Red River Gorge Climbs*, 329.
14. Boland, "(There's No Place Like) The Lode."
15. Boland, "(There's No Place Like) The Lode," includes a similar summary of the conversation between Murray and Loeffler while also noting Loeffler's interest in being honest with Murray about the land use.
16. There are important differences between grindstones and millstones. Grindstones are used to sharpen tools, while millstones are used for grinding food. There are also subtle differences in millstones, such as using flint to shear wheat versus using conglomerate sandstone for grains. Charles D. Hockensmith wrote two excellent books examining millstones in Powell County and beyond. See Hockensmith, *Millstone Quarries of Powell County*, and Hockensmith, *Millstone Industry*, for a detailed historical exploration of millstone production and use.
17. Fig and Knudsen, "Niter Mining." See also O'Dell, "Saltpeter Manufacturing and Marketing."
18. De Paepe, *Gunpowder from Mammoth Cave*.
19. O'Dell, "Saltpeter Manufacturing and Marketing."
20. Cornette, *High Rock Petroglyph*.

21. DBNF, "Site Protection Laws."
22. *Hominy Hole* was also the location of a niter mine. Archaeologists found a leather shoe left by a niter miner. They also made another rare find: an intact niter mining trough. Niter troughs were once a fairly common find, but Johnny Faulkner explained why they are now rare: "They were easy to find years ago, but the long history of recreational camping in the Gorge, back when I was doing the monitoring work . . . I would see wooden remains all the time." The number one killer of those niter mine troughs? Campfires. Folks mistook those pieces of rugged Kentucky history as ideal firewood dried in the rain shadow of the shelter.
23. RRGCC and DBNF, Memorandum of Understanding.
24. For a comprehensive and occasionally updated list of the world's most difficult bouldering problems, see "Hardest Boulder Problems."
25. For more information on the "Lappnor Project," see "Nalle Hukkataival." The picture alone is worth the visit.
26. For more information on "Fontainebleu," see Corrigan, "Charles Albert."
27. Bronaugh, "To Include or Not" (redriverclimbing.com).
28. Redmond, *Red River Gorge Bouldering*, 3.
29. Redmond, *Red River Gorge Bouldering*, 3.

CHAPTER 9

1. Schlarb and Pollack, "An Archaeological Evaluation."
2. Jillian Rickly has examined the social nature of climbing in several articles and a dissertation. See Rickly, *On Lifestyle Climbers*"; (Re)Production of Climbing Space"; "Lifestyle Mobilities"; and " 'I'm a Red River Local.' " The social nature of climbing has now grown to include climbers bringing nonclimbers with them to campgrounds and crags. One issue today is the social use of crags, which increases impacts. This is reexamined in subsequent chapters.
3. Schlarb and Pollack, "An Archaeological Evaluation."
4. See Schlarb and Pollack, "An Archaeological Evaluation."
5. See Schlarb and Pollack, "An Archaeological Evaluation."
6. More modern humans had also made their contribution. The report included 69 modern debris samples from the late twentieth century and early twenty-first century. These included a AAA battery, cigarette filters, bits of plastic and wood, US pennies (1994 and 1996), US nickels (1991 and 1994), a bandage, a match, green bottle glass, aluminum pull tab, melted aluminum, a wooden button, an ox shoe, wire nails, burlap fragments, a US dime from 1987, and a 1979 Canadian penny. Perhaps the most damning modern evidence? A rubber tent-pole tip. See Schlarb and Pollack, "An Archaeological Evaluation."
7. Although the exact date of the closure is not known, the date listed here is generally accepted as the date *Military Wall* was closed per the climbing community.

CHAPTER 10

1. *Hueco* is Spanish for hole or hollows. It traditionally refers to indentions in the rock that hold water. In climbing, this term specifically describes circular spots in the rock where climbers can put a finger, hand, or in extreme cases such as those at *Pocket Wall*, their entire bodies. The term was probably borrowed from Hueco Tanks, a climbing area in El Paso, Texas, where this kind of hold is commonly found.

2. Lago Linda Hideaway was listed in Ellington, *The Red River Gorge*. She recalled that listing in our interview: "Money was tight," Linda said, "so it was Ray Ellington and (Michelle Ellington) [who] said, 'So we could trade for an advertisement in this guidebook.' I forgot how much it was but I said, 'Well, that's quite a lot of money really even if I'm trading.' . . . I was thinking it was going to be something that would last a year, and they said, 'It will be out there forever.' . . . That was when we started to take off with the rock climbers."

3. Doug dubbed this room the "shake out" room. When asked what you call a room where you're supposed to relax, Doug told Linda that he'd call it "shaking out." This is also the term climbers use when actively resting (i.e., resting without using the rope to take their weight.) They shake out the pump (fatigue) so they can keep climbing. Either way, the name stuck. Sadly, Doug Black died February 16, 2012, aged 82.

4. For conversations about this closure, see "Roadside Camping" and "Roadside Dumping."

5. See "Roadside Beware" and "Thiefs at Roadside."

6. "Murray Property Update." Parentheses included in original text.

7. There is no formal listing of climbers in Team Suck, and any effort to list them will inevitably leave someone out. That said, members include Terry Kindred, Blake Bowling, Bob Matheny, Brian Maslyar, Stephanie Meadows, Gerald Goodpasture, Wes Allen, Ryan Adams, Bill Strachan, and certainly others.

8. Interesting historical note: An early fundraising discussion included a charity auction in which climbers could sponsor a route at the new crag. See "Murray Property Update."

9. "Murray Property Update."

10. Boland, "(There's No Place Like) The Lode."

11. "Johnny." Parentheses in original text.

12. All quotes in this paragraph are from "Johnny."

13. Ellington, *Red River Gorge Rock Climbs*, 2nd ed.

CHAPTER 11

1. Ellington, *Red River Gorge Rock Climbs*, 3rd ed., 141.

2. Ellington, *Red River Gorge Rock Climbs*, 3rd ed., 13.

3. As a historical note, the climbing community held a trail day the weekend of the posting, so impact was certainly on many Red climbers' minds.

4. "Potential Closure of Torrent Falls Crag."

5. "Potential Closure of Torrent Falls Crag."

6. "Potential Closure of Torrent Falls Crag." Parentheses in original text.

7. See "Torrent Falls Closed." Forum user Sarah Bellam later set the urination incident to memory in a poem entitled, "The Urinator of Torrent Falls," available on the Red River Climbing forum at https://www.redriverclimbing.com/viewtopic.php ?f=11&t=8151&start=60.

8. "Potential Closure of Torrent Falls Crag."

9. Chris discusses his experiences when his family owned the store in Chaney, *In the Red*.

10. See "Terry Kindred Day."

11. See "Terry" for all quotes in this paragraph.

12. As a historical note, Muir Valley also used the 2007 guide to make the

announcement that, as of January 1, 2008, dogs would no longer be allowed in the preserve.

13. *The Boneyard* was named by Craig Luebben in remembrance of Todd Skinner, per the Ellington guide. Todd Skinner was a well-known climber who held several notable first ascents. Todd died in a climbing accident on October 23, 2006, in Yosemite. For more about his life, see Piana, "The Renegade."

14. "Red River Outdoors Fire." Typos in original text corrected.

15. Roth, "Red River Outdoors Burns Down."

16. Rocktoberfest would continue to be held at Natural Bridge Cabin Company Campground from 2007 to 2015. It was moved to Land of the Arches in 2016 and has remained there since.

17. See "Rock Star Watch."

18. Petzl also supported the event by sending along countless carabiners and quick draws to replace existing gear at *The Motherlode*. It was twofold: it would provide a major technology investment in the Red, but also (since Petzl is a for-profit organization) the shiny new gear looked really good in the pictures. But to keep them looking good (and from possibly being pilfered), climbers had to wait until RocTrip to hang them. Bentley was doubled over with work prepping for this event. Climber Mike Doyle saved the day and told Brackett, "Dude, I got this." He reportedly hung the entirety of those draws at *The Motherlode* the day before the event started.

19. Migeon, "Ensure Access to Red River Gorge."

20. Migeon, "Ensure Access to Red River Gorge."

21. Migeon, "Ensure Access to Red River Gorge."

22. It is conjecture, but Rocktoberfest 2007 may also have driven a wedge between RRGCC and Muir Valley. It is important to reiterate that Muir Valley is not represented by the RRGCC. To my knowledge, Muir Valley saw no funds from this event or subsequent Rocktoberfest events. Still, the RRGCC's name, which includes the phrase Red River Gorge, implies at face value that it represents the entire area. While the name predates Muir Valley, it seems logical to think that the RRGCC probably intended to represent the entire region at the time. Despite subtle differences and approaches today, the two climbing organizations continue to work together in keeping climbing open in the region.

23. "Rock Star Watch."

24. Ellington, *Red River Gorge Rock Climbs*, 2nd ed., recollects some of the controversy that ensued on sending "Fifty Words for Pump." The crux of this particular route (as noted in Ellington, *The Red River Gorge*, 243) included "a very hard clip at the 4th bolt. 5.14?" Fuselier completed the route using the original bolted path by Hugh Loeffler (including the scary fourth clip), but shortly after the FA Mike Doyle added bolts slightly right of the original fourth clip (arguably following the path of least resistance) to remove this crux. The prevailing argument behind the additional bolts was that a clip shouldn't be the crux of the climb. However, the two new bolts reportedly made the route easier (by a letter grade). At least one climber (Adam Taylor) remained interested in climbing the more difficult original route and had installed his own permadraws on the original route. However, as the result of an unspecified climber's photo shoot, one or more permadraws were removed and never replaced. In reaction, Taylor smashed the two hangers to minor internet outcry. The hangers were replaced, but the moment would be forever remembered through Kris Hampton's song, "Fifty Words for Chump." The article

"Fifty Words for Chump" on the event also includes a picture of the smashed hanger and links to the song.

25. "Rock Star Watch."

26. These areas are still worth visiting, however; Ellington, *Red River Gorge Rock Climbs*, 3rd ed., notes that *Friction Slab* holds one of the best boulder problems in the Red ("Bulldog"), while *Auxier Ridge* holds "Excalibur." He also notes that these include a couple of historic sites, such as *Courthouse Rock*. In other cases (like *Wildcat Wall*), Ellington notes the hike to the crag is probably the best part.

27. This crag receives global attention even today. News of the ascent of "The Golden Ticket" broke on the forum (see "Nice Job!!!" and later "Adam Taylor Punches Golden Ticket"). Adam Ondra (globally recognized as a top climber) would later take a trip to the Red and complete "The Golden Ticket" as well as "Pure Imagination" in 2012. See "Adam Ondra."

28. There are historical clues that hint *Crossroads* was probably McCray's work. In discussing the crag in the online guide, climbers noted the use of open cold shuts, which were found on other routes McCray was known to have equipped. Cold shuts are cheap and easily obtained, often used to join two chains, but they are perhaps less likely to be used safely in climbing. Sandor Nagay describes a basic test of the strength of cold shuts for climbing purposes, and the results were not exactly confidence inspiring. See Nagay, "Blind Faith." For a discussion of cold shuts and accidents, see "A Tragic Lesson" about Brian's affiliation with this crag.

29. Although the historical record is not clear, Brian most likely also found *Area 6*. There he equipped and completed a route called "Diablo," a 5.11d, and "Red Bull," a 5.11c. However, this crag (which was off RRGCC property) would be closed in the coming years at the landowner's request and remains closed today.

CHAPTER 12

1. Regarding the "complex land ownership," Grant is an attorney and there are similarities here in how John Bronaugh (also an attorney) worked with Lee County records to identify the ownership of the PMRP. Shannon Stuart-Smith has similarly worked with the RRGCC and climbing community on legal issues. This illustrates the value of climbers who are also attorneys working closely with climbing organizations for this reason.

2. Permadraws (or fixed draws) are another point of conflict in the Red. These devices hang from fixed gear (such as a bolt in the rock wall) and are left in place as a convenience. Not all climbers feel they should be left hanging, and common arguments are that they visually distract from the experience and may cause some climbers to push themselves beyond their own limits. The Red recently underwent a fixed gear initiative to replace worn bolts and increase safety. See Boland, "Point Break."

3. For clarity, I have used *Roadside* to describe the crag, which is located on the Graining Fork Nature Preserve, as opposed to describing the entire nature preserve as being the same as *Roadside*.

4. See "More Thoughts on RRG."

5. "Roadside Impact."

6. "Roadside Impact."

7. For discussion of the closure, see Access Fund, "Roadside in the Red River Gorge Closed," and "Re: ROADSIDE IS NOT OPEN."

8.   John Haight sadly passed in December 2017. Since his passing, his wife April has run Graining Fork and kept it open to climbing. As of December 2019, Graining Fork was temporarily closed as they worked on trail and erosion projects on the property, ensuring the stability of climbing there for future generations.
9.   "Torrent Opening." Parentheses in original text.
10. "Who Does It Belong To?" Parentheses in original text.
11. "Who Does It Belong To?" Emphasis in original quote.
12. Davis, "Gym to Crag Handbook." The idea that gym climbers have a different outdoor ethic compared to any other type of climber is something that should be examined at the national level.
13. Access Fund, "Access Fund Launches."
14. Access Fund, "Making the Transition from Gym to Crag."
15. Access Fund, "Red River Gorge Climbers' Coalition."
16. Access Fund, "Red River Gorge Climbers' Coalition."
17. Ellington, *Miller Fork Climbing*, 218. Regarding illustrations, in some ways, this guide's illustrations are somewhat reminiscent of those done by Diane Blazy for Becker, *Red River Gorge Climber's Guide*.
18. Sawhill, *The Forgotten Americans*.
19. Beattyville is often pronounced by locals as "Bay-ta-vull," removing the long *y* ("Bay-tee") sound that many nonlocals add to the name. This creates a bit of an accidental pun in that beta ("Bay-ta") is a climbing term used to describe information given about a particular route.
20. Truman, "Cathedral Domain Celebrates."
21. RRGCC, "Red River Gorge Climbers' Coalition."
22. "The Climbing Advocate."

CHAPTER 13

1.   The full Ale-8-One name goes back to marketing describing the drink as *the latest thing* (or per the label, *a late one*) in the soft drink world. Arguably it is now climbers who are *the latest thing* in the Red—and perhaps also in the outdoor recreation world.
2.   Authur, "Mission Impossible II."
3.   "Meet the Rock-Climbing Legend."
4.   Synott, "Exclusive."
5.   Bradley, "Rise of the Climbing Ninja Warriors."
6.   Corrigan, "Climbing Officially Approved."
7.   For information on Bears Ears, see Merica, "Utah Senator," and Access Fund, "Access Fund Will Sue."
8.   For info on climber lobbying, see American Alpine Club, "Climbers Lobby for Public Lands," and Access Fund, "Climbers Move the Needle."
9.   For info on the Red in the national conversation, see Honnold, "Alex Honnold to Politicos."
10. For the full concept description, see "Concept Paper" and American Planning Association, "Masterplan for Destination Resort."
11. KCC notes from the first public discussion of the proposal are available; see Explore Kentucky Initiative, "KCC Notes from Public Meeting."
12. AECOM, "Potential for Tourism Development," 2–3.
13. For the report, see HVS, "Eastern Kentucky Tourism Study."

14. Oliver, "Possible Resort."
15. Outdoor Industry Association, "The Outdoor Recreation Economy."
16. Ekstrand, "Economic Benefits of Resources."
17. Hobbs, "Economic Impact of Rock Climbing."
18. Siderelis and Attarian, "Trip Response Modeling."
19. Sims and Hodges, "Obed Wild and Scenic River."
20. Anderson, "Estimating the Economic Value."
21. Maples, et al., "Climbing Out of Poverty."
22. Bailey and Hungenberg, "Managing the Rock Climbing Economy."
23. Maples and Bradley, "Economic Impact of Rock Climbing."
24. Maples, et al., "Climbing Out of Poverty."
25. Gaventa, *Power and Powerlessness.*
26. Eller, *Uneven Ground.*
27. See Woods and Gordon, "Mountaintop Removal and Job Creation."
28. Clark, Maples, and Sharp, "Awareness and Application of Minimum Impact Practices," and Sharp, Maples, and Gerlaugh, "Factors Influencing Knowledge."
29. DeSena, *Gentrification and Inequality in Brooklyn.*
30. Fullilove, *Root Shock.*
31. Smith, *Uneven Development.*
32. Wong, "Rock Climbing Studios."
33. Nelson and Nelson, "Rural Gentrification."
34. Phillips, "Rural Gentrification."
35. Leebrick, "Environmental Gentrification and Development."
36. Ghose, "Big Sky or Big Sprawl?"
37. Flora and Flora, "Creating Social Capital."

Bibliography

Access Fund. 2014. "Access Fund Launches Climber Education Program with Black
    Diamond." https://www.accessfund.org/news-and-events/news/access
    -fund-launches-climber-education-program-with-black-diamond.
———. 2017. "Access Fund Will Sue to Protect Bears Ears National Monument."
    https://www.accessfund.org/news-and-events/news/access-fund-will-sue-to
    -protect-bears-ears-national-monument.
———. 2018. "Climbers Move the Needle on Capitol Hill." https://www.accessfund
    .org/news-and-events/news/climbers-move-the-needle-on-capitol-hill.
———. 2019. "Land Holdings." https://www.accessfund.org/meet-the-access-fund
    /our-approach/land-acquisition-protection/land-holdings.
———. "Making the Transition from Gym to Crag." Accessed October 15, 2020.
    https://www.accessfund.org/uploads/pdf/Gym-to-Crag_PDF-2-copy.pdf
———. 2013. "Red River Gorge Climbers' Coalition Teams up with Access Fund to
    Purchase New Climbing Area in Kentucky." https://www.accessfund.org
    /news-and-events/news/red-river-gorge-climbers-coalition-teams-up-with
    -access-fund-to-purchase-new-climbing-area-in-kentucky.
———. 2011. "Roadside in the Red River Gorge Closed to Public Access." https://
    www.accessfund.org/news-and-events/news/roadside-in-the-red-river
    -gorge-closed-to-public-access.
Achey, Jeff. 2013. "Fixed Anchors in the Wilderness." *Climbing Magazine* (April 8).
    https://www.climbing.com/people/fixed-anchors-in-the-wilderness/.
———. 2013. "The Nut Chronicles." *Climbing Magazine* (June 5). https://www
    .climbing.com/people/the-nut-chronicles/.
"Adam Ondra, Two 8c+ On-Sights at the Red River Gorge." 2012. https://www.planet
    mountain.com/en/news/climbing/adam-ondra-two-8c-on-sights-at-the-red
    -river-gorge.html.
"Adam Taylor Punches Golden Ticket in the Red River Gorge." 2009. https://
    climbingnarc.com/2009/10/adam-taylor-punches-golden-ticket-at-the-red
    -river-gorge/.
AECOM. 2013. "Potential for Tourism Development in eastern Kentucky." http://
    www.redriverky.com/wp-content/uploads/2019/03/EKY-Tourism-AECOM
    -Report-FINAL-1.pdf.
American Alpine Club. 2017. "Climbers Lobby for Public Lands." https://
    americanalpineclub.org/updates-from-your-policy-team/2017/5/15
    /climbers-lobby-for-public-lands.
American Planning Association. 2019. "Masterplan for Destination Resort." https://
    www.planning.org/consultants/rfp/9180663/.

Anderson, W. Mark. 2010. "Estimating the Economic Value of Ice Climbing in Hyalite Canyon: An Application of Travel Cost Count Data Models That Account for Excess Zeros." *Journal of Environmental Management* 91(4) (March–April).

Appalachian Regional Commission. 2017. "County Economic Status in Appalachia, FY 2017." https://www.arc.gov/research/MapsofAppalachia.asp?MAP_ID=116.

Authur, Charles. 2000. "Mission Impossible II Climbing Scenes Special." *UK Climbing*, July 9. https://www.ukclimbing.com/articles/features/mission_impossible _ii_climbing_scenes_special-18.

Bailey, Andrew W., and Eric Hungenberg. 2018. "Managing the Rock-Climbing Economy: A Case from Chattanooga." *Annals of Leisure Research*, June 26. https://www.tandfonline.com/doi/full/10.1080/11745398.2018.1488146.

Balf, Todd. 1995. "Climbing: Dad, Am I Over the Hill?" https://www.outsideonline .com/1830091/climbing-dad-am-i-over-hill.

Baur, Bruno, Lars Fröberg, and Stefan W. Müller. 2007. "Effect of Rock Climbing on the Calcicolous Lichen Community of Limestone Cliffs in the Northern Swiss Jura Mountains." *Nova Hedwigia* 85(3-4): 429–444.

Becker, Frank. 1974. "Personal correspondence between Frank Becker and Ranger John Moore." Letter in Frank Becker's possession.

———. 1981. "Red River Gorge." *Climbing* 68 (September-October): 18–19.

———. 1974. *Red River Gorge Climber's Guide*. Self-published by Frank Becker.

Becker, Howard. 2008. *Outsiders: Studies in the Sociology of Deviance*. New York: Free Press.

Benjamin, Ed, and Ed Pearsall. 1978. *Rawk!: A Climbers Guide to the Red River Gorge*. Self-published.

Bluegrass Cycling Club. "The Bluegrass Wheelmen Organize." Accessed October 15, 2020. https://www.bgcycling.net/content.aspx?page_id=22&club_id= 740127&module_id=151227.

Boland, Whitney. 2014. "The Day I Sent True Love." https://eveningsends.com /day-sent-true-love/.

———. 2017. "How Miguel's Pizza Made the Red River Gorge What It Is Today." *Climbing Magazine* (June 9). https://www.climbing.com/places/how-miguels -pizza-made-the-red-river-gorge-what-it-is-today/.

———. 2013. "Point Break: Fight Over Fixed Draws." *Rock and Ice* (January 9). https:// rockandice.com/opinion/point-break-fight-over-fixed-draws/.

———. 2008. "(There's No Place Like) The Lode." *Rock and Ice* 165 (January). Online version at https://rockandice.com/snowball/americas-best-climbing-area -red-river-gorge/.

Borden, James, and Roger W. Bruckner. 2000. *Beyond Mammoth Cave: A Tale of Obsession in the World's Longest Cave*. Carbondale, IL: Southern Illinois Press.

Bowen, Joe. 2004. "Bert T. Combs Had Progressive Administration as Governor." *Kentucky Explorer* 19(4): 22–25.

Bradley, Ryan. 2015. "Rise of the Climbing Ninja Warriors." https://www.outside online.com/1972896/rise-climbing-ninja-warriors.

Bright, Casandra Marie. 2014. "A History of Rock Climbing Gear Technology and Standards." Mechanical engineering honors thesis, University of Arkansas, Fayetteville.

Bronaugh, John. 1993. *Red River Gorge Climbs*. Lexington, KY: Geezer Press.

———. 1998. *Red River Gorge Climbs*. 2nd edition. Lexington, KY: Geezer Press.

Brown, Horace. 2011. "Odd Little Red-Cockaded Woodpeckers Now Carve Their Lives Outside Kentucky." https://www.sentinelnews.com/content/odd-little-red -cockaded-woodpeckers-now-carve-their-lives-outside-kentucky.

Caldwell, Christopher. 2017. "American Carnage: The New Landscape of Opioid Addiction." *First Things* (April). https://www.firstthings.com/article/2017 /04/american-carnage.

Campbell, Julian. 2016. "Pilot Knob: New View of an Old Scene." *Red River Historical Society & Museum* 24(1): 5–13

Carmean, Kelli, and William E. Sharp. 1998. "Not Quite Newt Kash: Three Small Rockshelters in Laurel County." In *Current Archaeological Research in Kentucky*, volume 5. Edited by Charles D. Hockensmith, Kenneth C. Carstens, Charles Stout, and Sara J. Rivers. Frankfort, KY: Kentucky Heritage Council.

Chaney, Chris. 2019. *In the Red: Adventures in Kentucky's Red River Gorge.* Stanton, KY: Ascensionist Press.

Cherry, Thomas Crittenden.1935. *Kentucky: The Pioneer State of the West.* Boston: D.C. Heath.

Clark, Brian G., James N. Maples, and Ryan L. Sharp. 2020. "Awareness and Application of Minimum Impact Practices among Rock Climbers in the Red River Gorge, Kentucky." *Journal of Outdoor and Environmental Education* (January). https://doi.org/10.1007/s42322-019-00048-0.

Clark, Peter, and Amy Hessl. 2015. "The Effects of Rock Climbing on Cliff-Face Vegetation." *Applied Vegetation Science* 18 (May 19): 705–715.

Clayton, John. 2019. *Natural Rivals: John Muir, Gifford Pinchot, and the Creation of America's Public Lands.* New York: Pegasus Books.

"The Climbing Advocate Episode #9—Ashlee Milanich." 2019. *Climbing Advocate.* https://soundcloud.com/climbing_advocate_podcast/episode-9-ashlee -milanich.

Cohen, Michael P. 1988. *The History of the Sierra Club: 1892–1970.* New York: Random House.

Collins, Robert F. 1975. *A History of the Daniel Boone National Forest, 1770–1970.* Lexington, KY: Daniel Boone National Forest Service.

"Concept Paper: Eastern Kentucky Destination Resort." 2019. http://www.redriverky .com/wp-content/uploads/2019/07/E.-Ky.-Destinaton-Resort-Concept-Paper -10-30-18-FINAL.pdf.

Cornette, Alan. 2015. *The High Rock Petroglyph: Red River Gorge Rock Art.* Slade, KY: Earth Macro Vision.

Corrigan, Kevin. 2019. "Charles Albert Proposes World's Second V17 in Fontainebleau (Barefoot)." https://www.climbing.com/news/charles-albert-proposes -worlds-second-v17-in-fontainebleau-barefoot/.

———. 2016. "Climbing Officially Approved for 2020 Olympics." *Climbing Magazine* (August 3). https://www.climbing.com/news/climbing-officially-approved -for-2020-olympics/.

Cottle, Drew. 2013. "Land, Life and Labour in the Sacrifice Zone: The Socio-Economic Dynamics of Open-Cut Coal Mining in the Upper Hunter Valley, New South Wales." *Rural Society* 22(3) (June): 208–216.

Davis, Shannon. 2016. "Gym to Crag Handbook: 36 Tips from the Pros." https://www .climbing.com/skills/gym-to-crag-handbook-36-tips-from-the-pros/.

DBNF. "Forest Ownership Pattern." Accessed on October 15, 2020. https://www
    .fs.usda.gov/detail/dbnf/about-forest/?cid=stelprdb5277049.
DBNF. "Site Protection Laws." Accessed on October 15, 2020. https://www.fs.usda
    .gov/detail/dbnf/learning/history-culture/?cid=stelprdb5278969.
DellaMea, Chris. 2014. "New River Coalfield." https://coalcampusa.com/sowv/river
    /newriver.htm.
De Paepe, Duane. 1985. *Gunpowder from Mammoth Cave: The Saga of Saltpeter Mining
    before and during the War of 1812*. Hays, KS: Cave Pearl Press.
DeSena, Judith N. *Gentrification and Inequality in Brooklyn: The New Kids on the Block*.
    New York: Lexington Books.
Desrochers, Daniel, and Jack Brammer. 2018. "Bevin Proposes Ending 70 Government
    Programs and Deep Cuts for Many State Agencies." *Lexington Herald Leader*,
    January 16. https://www.kentucky.com/news/politics-government/article
    195017314.html.
"Do You Need to Back-up Your Tie-in Knot?" 2018. *Northeast Alpine Start*, August 9.
    https://northeastalpinestart.com/2018/08/09/do-you-need-to-back-up-your
    -tie-in-knot/.
Ekstrand, Earl R. 1995. "Economic Benefits of Resources Used for Rock Climbing at
    Eldorado Canyon State Park, Colorado." PhD dissertation, Colorado State
    University.
Eller, Ronald D. 2008. *Uneven Ground: Appalachia since 1945*. Lexington, KY: University
    of Kentucky Press.
———. 2013. *Uneven Ground: Appalachia since 1945*. Illustrated edition. Lexington,
    KY: University of Kentucky Press.
Ellington, Ray. 2015. *Miller Fork Climbing: A Guidebook for Rock Climbing at the Miller
    Fork Recreational Preserve in Kentucky's Red River Gorge*. Lexington, KY: Red
    River Publishing.
———. 2005. *The Red River Gorge: A Rock Climbing Guide*. New Castle, CO: Wolverine.
———. 2007. *Red River Gorge Rock Climbs*. 2nd edition. Ft. Collins, CO: Wolverine.
———. 2010. *Red River Gorge Rock Climbs*. Expanded 3rd edition. Ft. Collins, CO:
    Wolverine.
Ellison, Julie. 2016. "America's 100 Best Sport Climbing Routes." *Climbing Magazine*
    (May 31). https://www.climbing.com/places/americas-100-best-sport
    -climbing-routes/.
Enoch, Harry. 2014. "Bert T. Combs: Kentucky's Education Governor." *Red River
    Historical Society & Museum* 22(2): 8–16.
———. 2019. "250th Anniversary of Daniel Boone at Pilot Knob." *Red River Historical
    Society & Museum* 27(2): 3–10.
Estep, Bill. 2016. "Drug Overdose Deaths Climb to Record Level in Kentucky in 2015."
    Lexington Herald Leader, June 14. http://www.kentucky.com/news/state
    /article83770067.html.
———. 2013. "Toll of Eastern Kentucky's Drug Epidemic: Violence and Heartache."
    Lexington Herald Leader, December 1. http://www.kentucky.com/news
    /special-reports/fifty-years-of-night/article44456310.html.
Explore Kentucky Initiative. 2019. "KCC Notes from Public Meeting on the Proposed
    Red River Gorge Development." https://www.explorekentucky.us/field
    journal/redrivergorgedestinationresortnotes.
Fantz, Lloyd. 2014. "Lloyd Fantz's Story." *Red River Historical Society & Museum* 22(1): 15.

"Fifty Words for Chump." 2008. https://climbingnarc.com/2008/11/fifty-words-for
-chump/.
Fig, Donald, and Gary Knudsen. 1984. "Niter Mining: An Incipient Industry of the
Red River Gorge, Kentucky." *Proceedings of the Symposium on Ohio Valley
Urban and Historic Archaeology* 2: 67–73.
Flora, Cornelia B., and Jan L. Flora. "Creating Social Capital." In *The Earthscan Reader
in Sustainable Agriculture*, 39–63. Edited by Jules Pretty. London and
Sterling, VA: Earthscan.
Fox, Julia. 1999. "Mountaintop Removal in West Virginia: An Environmental Sacrifice
Zone." *Organization & Environment* 12(2) (June): 163–183.
"Friction and Rock Climbing." Accessed October 19, 2020. http://threerockbooks.com
/friction-and-rock-climbing/.
Fullilove, Mindy T. 2016. *Root Shock: How Tearing Up City Neighborhoods Hurts America
and What We Can Do About It.* New York: New Village Press.
Galewitz, Phil. 2017. "The Pharmacies Thriving in Kentucky's Opioid-Stricken Towns."
The Atlantic (February 7). https://www.theatlantic.com/health/archive/2017
/02/kentucky-opioids/515775/.
Gaventa, John. 1982. *Power and Powerlessness: Quiescence and Rebellion in an
Appalachian Valley.* Urbana, IL: University of Illinois Press.
Ghose, Rina. 2013. "Big Sky or Big Sprawl? Rural Gentrification and the Changing
Cultural Landscape of Missoula, Montana." *Urban Geography* 25(6) (May 16):
528–549.
Good, Gregory A., and Lynn Stasick. 2008. "New River Gorge National River
Administrative History." https://www.nps.gov/parkhistory/online_books
/neri/neri_admin_history.pdf.
Greb, Stephen F., and Charles E. Mason. 2005. "Geology of the Red River Gorge
Geological Area and Natural Bridge State Resort Park." In *42nd Annual
Meeting of the American Institute of Professional Geologists Field Trip Guidebook.*
Lexington, KY: AIPG.
Gremillion, Kristin. 1997. "New Perspectives on the Paleoethnobotany of the Newt
Kash Shelter." In *People, Plants, and Landscapes: Studies in Paleoethnobotany*,
23–41. Edited by Kristen J. Gremillion. Tuscaloosa: University of Alabama
Press.
Griffin, Lindsay. 2012. "Foreign Climbers Cause Controversy with Unwelcome
Retro-Bolting." https://www.thebmc.co.uk/foreign-climbers-again-cause
-controversy-with-unethical-bolting-practices.
Grijalva, Therese C., Robert P. Berrens, Alok K. Bohara, Paul M. Jakus, and W.
Douglass Shaw. 2002. "Valuing the Loss of Rock Climbing Access in
Wilderness Areas: A National-Level, Random-Utility Model." *Land Economics*
78(1) (February): 103–120.
Hackworth, Martin. 1984. *Stones of Years: A Climber's Guide to Red River Gorge.*
Lexington, KY: Pro Printers.
"The Hardest Boulder Problems in the World." Last modified March 5, 2019. https://
www.99boulders.com/hardest-boulder-problems.
Herzog, Maurice. 1952. *Annapurna: The First Conquest of an 8,000-Meter Peak.* New
York: E. P. Dutton.
Hill, Lynn. "Lynn Hill Attends the Petzl Roctrip." https://www.patagonia.com/stories
/petzl-roctrip/story-20683.html.

"History of the Cumberland Climbers, Part 1." 2007. https://www.redriverclimbing
.com/viewtopic.php?f=12&t=8022.

Hobbs, Will. 2002. "Economic Impact of Rock Climbing on the Communities
Surrounding the Red River Gorge, Kentucky." Master's thesis, Department
of Kinesiology, Recreation and Sport, Western Kentucky University.

Hockensmith, Charles D. 2009. *The Millstone Industry: A Summary of Research on
Quarries and Producers in the United States, Europe and Elsewhere*. Jefferson,
NC: McFarland.

———. 2009. *The Millstone Quarries of Powell County, Kentucky*. Jefferson, NC:
McFarland.

Honnold, Alex. 2018. "Alex Honnold to Politicos: Leave Our Public Lands Alone."
Outside (May 25). https://www.outsideonline.com/2313076/alex-honnold
-politicos-leave-our-public-lands-alone.

HVS. 2017. "Eastern Kentucky Tourism Study Destination Resort and Tourism
Assessment:" Report available in two downloads at http://www.redriverky
.com/studies/#page-content.

Jarrard, Porter, and Chris Snyder. 1997. *Selected Climbs at Red River Gorge Kentucky*.
Lexington, KY: El Rancho Relaxo Press.

"Johnny." 2004. https://www.redriverclimbing.com/viewtopic.php?f=11&t=3265.

Jones, Volney H. 1936. "The Vegetal Remains of Newt Kash Hollow Shelter." In *Rock
Shelters in Menifee County, Kentucky*, 147–165. By William S. Webb and
William D. Funkhouser. Lexington, KY: University of Kentucky.

Jun, Shelma. 2016. "Accept and Adapt: Women in Climbing." *Climbing Magazine*
(September 13). https://www.climbing.com/people/women-in-climbing
-accept-and-adapt/.

Kalisz, Paul J., and Susan E. Boettcher. 1991. "Active and Abandoned Red-Cockaded
Woodpecker Habitat in Kentucky." *Journal of Wildlife Management* 55(1)
(January): 146–154.

Kardaleff, Charlie, Aaron Huey, and J. B. Haab. 2019. "Open Letter: Chipping and
Manufacturing Climbs in Ten Sleep Canyon Needs to Stop." *Rock and Ice*
(February 18). https://rockandice.com/climbing-news/open-letter-chipping
-and-manufacturing-climbs-in-ten-sleep-canyon-needs-to-stop/.

Kentucky Afield Radio. 2016. "Kentucky's Red November." https://www.youtube.com
/watch?v=zM30OdwUckA.

"Kentucky Lost 11.1 Percent of Its Manufacturing Jobs over the Past 24 Months."
2011. https://www.reliableplant.com/Read/27254/Kentucky-lost-manu
facturing-jobs.

Kentucky Office of Drug Control Policy. 2017. "2016 Overdose Fatality Report."
https://odcp.ky.gov/Documents/2016%20ODCP%20Overdose%20
Fatality%20Report%20Final.pdf.

"Kentucky Quarterly Coal Report." 2018. https://eec.ky.gov/Energy/News
-Publications/Quarterly percent20Coal percent20Reports/2018-Q1.pdf.

Kentucky State Parks. "Fort Boonesborough State Park—Historic Pocket Brochure
Text." Accessed October 16, 2020. https://parks.ky.gov/sites/default/files
/listing_documents/29f62b4b45eb647e941a630345c5b709_
Ftboonepktbrohtext.pdf.

"Kentucky Union Railroad." 2009. http://lexhistory.org/wikilex/kentucky-union
-railroad.

Kor, Layton. 2013. *Beyond the Vertical*. Helena, MT: Falcon Guides.

Kornie, Katherine. 2019. "Peering beneath a Source of El Capitan's Deadly Rockfalls." *New York Times*, May 20. https://www.nytimes.com/2019/05/20/science/el -capitan-yosemite.html.

Kuntz, Kathryn Lynn, and Douglass W. Larson. 2006. "Influences of Microhabitat Constraints and Rock-Climbing Disturbance on Cliff-Face Vegetation Communities." *Conservation Biology* 20(3) (June): 821–832.

Lane Report. 2020. "Kentucky Counties Affected by Historic Flooding Receive Disaster Declaration." https://www.lanereport.com/124922/2020/04 /ky-counties-affected-by-historical-flooding-receive-disaster-declaration/.

Leebrick, Rhiannon A. 2015. "Environmental Gentrification and Development in a Rural Appalachian Community: Blending Critical Theory and Ethnography." PhD dissertation, University of Tennessee–Knoxville.

Leebrick, Rhiannon A., and James N. Maples. 2015. "Landscape as Arena and Spatial Narrative in the New River Gorge National River's Coal Camps: A Case Study of the Elverton, West Virginia 1914 Strike." *Southeastern Geographer* 55(4) (Winter): 474–494.

Leopold, Aldo. 1947. "The Ecological Conscious." In *The River of the Mother of God and Other Essays by Aldo Leopold*, 338–348. Edited by Susan L. Flader and J. Baird Callicott. Madison, WI: University of Wisconsin Press.

Lerner, Steve. 2012. *Sacrifice Zones: The Front Lines of Toxic Chemical Exposure in the United States*. Cambridge, MA: MIT Press.

Lilley, Jessica, and Roxy Todd. 2018. "Controversy and Mystery Still Surround Lakes Built by the Army Corps of Engineers." *Inside Appalachia*. http://wvpublic .org/post/controversy-and-mystery-still-surround-lakes-built-army-corps -engineers#stream/0.

Lorbiecki, Marybeth. 2016. *A Fierce Green Fire: Aldo Leopold's Life and Legacy*. New York: Oxford University Press.

Lorite, Juan, Fabio Serrano, Adrián Lorenzo, Eva M. Cañadas, Miguel Ballesteros, and Julio Peñas. 2017. "Rock Climbing Alters Plant Species Composition, Cover, and Richness in Mediterranean Limestone Cliffs." *PLoS One* 12(8) (August 2).

Lowrey, Annie. 2014. "What's the Matter with Eastern Kentucky?" *New York Times Magazine*, June 26. https://www.nytimes.com/2014/06/29/magazine/whats -the-matter-with-eastern-kentucky.html.

Mackley, Matthew S., and Michael J. Mackley. 2010. *Cave Rock: Climbers, Courts, and a Washoe Indian Sacred Place*. Reno: University of Nevada Press.

Mann, Neal. 2017. "Dai Koyamada on Projects, Grades, and the Impact of the Olympics." *Project Magazine* (December 18). https://www.theprojectmagazine.com /features/2017/9/1/dai-koyamada-interview.

Maples, James N., and Michael J. Bradley. 2017. "Economic Impact of Rock Climbing in the Nantahala and Pisgah National Forests." https://static1.squarespace .com/static/54aabb14e4b01142027654ee/t/59d5452c12abd93de5f7b021 /1507149106153/ OA_NPNF_ClimbingStudy.pdf.

Maples, James N., Michael J. Bradley, Sadie Giles, Rhiannon Leebrick, and Brian Clark. 2019. "Climbing Out of Coal Country: The Economic Impact of Climbing in West Virginia's New River Gorge." *Journal of Appalachian Studies* 25(2) (Fall): 184–201.

Maples, James N., Ryan L. Sharp, Brian Clark, Katherine Gerlaugh, and Braylon Gillespie. 2017. "Climbing Out of Poverty: The Economic Impact of Rock

Climbing in and around Eastern Kentucky's Red River Gorge." *Journal of Appalachian Studies* 23(1) (Spring): 53–71.

Maser, Jeffrey. 2017. "Perry County Has Highest Opioid Abuse Hospitalization Rate in Nation at Nearly 6 Percent." https://dexur.com/a/perry-county-has-highest -opioid-abuse-hospitalization-rate-nation-nearly-6/57/.

McDowell, Bodie. 1990. "Porter Jarrard Climbs Moore's Wall at Hanging Rock." News and Record (July 7). https://greensboro.com/porter-jarrard-climbs-moores -wall-at-hanging-rock-jarrard-climbs-with-zeal/article_3657c384-1e0f -5aa3-82c9-da143225c7b5.html.

McFadden, Thomas Steele. 2018. "The Vascular Flora of the Red River Gorge in Powell, Menifee, and Wolfe Counties Kentucky." Master's thesis, Eastern Kentucky University.

McSpirit, Stephanie, Shaunna L. Scott, Sharon Hardesty, and Robert Welch. 2005. "EPA Actions in Post Disaster Martin County, Kentucky: An Analysis of Bureaucratic Slippage and Agency Recreancy." *Journal of Appalachian Studies* 11(1/2) (Spring/Fall): 30–59.

Mead, Andy. 2008. "Gorge Protector." https://www.kentucky.com/latest-news/article 43973400.html.

"Meet the Rock-Climbing Legend Who Conquered El Capitan in Yosemite." 2017. https://www.today.com/video/meet-the-rock-climbing-legend-who -conquered-el-capitan-in-yosemite-1009928259591.

Mellor, Don. 2001. *American Rock: Region, Rock, and Culture in American Climbing.* Woodstock, VT: Countryman Press.

Merica, Dan. 2017. "Utah Senator: Trump Plans to Shrink Size of Utah National Monuments." https://www.cnn.com/2017/10/27/politics/trump-bears-ears -hatch-utah/index.html.

Migeon, Christophe. 2014. "Ensure Access to Red River Gorge Climbing Site, Kentucky." https://www.redriverclimbing.com/viewtopic.php?f=5&t=8971& hilit=roctrip&start=30.

Molloy, Johnny. 2018. "Beauty and Death Are Both Found in the Red River Gorge." *Johnson City Press*, July 7. https://www.johnsoncitypress.com/Hobbies -Interests/2018/07/08/Beauty-and-Death-Are-Both-Found-in-the-Red -River-Gorge.

"More Thoughts on RRG and Access Situations in General." 2011. https://climbing narc.com/2011/05/more-thoughts-on-rrg-and-access-situations-in-general /comment-page-1/.

Muir, John. 1916. *A Thousand-Mile Walk to the Gulf.* New York: Houghton Mifflin.

"Murray Property Update." 2003. https://www.redriverclimbing.com/viewtopic .php?f=11&t=1032.

"MV Anchor Cleaning Accident." 2011. https://www.redriverclimbing.com/viewtopic .php?f=11&t=14165.

Nagay, Sandor. 2003. "Blind Faith: Can We Really Trust Cold Shuts." http://www .safeclimbing.org/education/blindfaith.htm.

"Nalle Hukkataival Sends World's First V17." 2016. *Rock and Ice* (October 24). https:// rockandice.com/climbing-news/nalle-hukkataival-sends-worlds-first-v17/.

Nelson, Lise, and Peter B. Nelson. 2010. "Rural Gentrification and Linked Migration in the US." *Journal of Rural Studies* 26(4) (October): 343–352.

"Nice Job!!!" 2009. https://www.redriverclimbing.com/viewtopic.php?f=5&t=12163& start=15&sid=e4f7ecebf77c623eeadac0deeb6ed309.

"No Title 950." 2004. Untitled article on Don Fig. *Kentucky Living* (October 1). https://www.kentuckyliving.com/archives/no-title-950.

Nuttall, Brandon C. 2001. "Historic Oil Fields of Eastern Kentucky and Big Andy Ridge." https://kgs.uky.edu/kgsweb/olops/pub/kgs/GB%202001%20KSPG.pdf.

O'Dell, Gary A. 1996. "Saltpeter Manufacturing and Marketing and Its Relation to the Gunpowder Industry in Kentucky during the Nineteenth Century." In *Historical Archaeology in Kentucky*, 67–105. Edited by Kim A. McBride, W. Stephen McBride, and David Pollack. Frankfort, KY: Kentucky Heritage Council.

Oliver, Nick. 2020. "Possible Resort Near Red River Gorge Moves Forward with Latest Approval." wkyt.com/content/news/Community-discusses-possible-resort-at-Red-River-Gorge-567079741.html.

O'Malley, Nancy. 2019. *Boonesborough: Frontier Archaeology at a Revolutionary Fort*. Lexington, KY: University Press of Kentucky.

Outdoor Industry Association. 2017. "The Outdoor Recreation Economy." https://outdoorindustry.org/wp-content/uploads/2017/04/OIA_RecEconomy_FINAL_Single.pdf.

———. 2018. "The Outdoor Recreation Economy." http://oia.outdoorindustry.org/OIA-receconomy.

Pearsall, Ed. 1980. *Climber's Guide to the Red River Gorge*. Lexington, KY: Sky Bridge Guides.

Phillips, Martin. 1993. "Rural Gentrification and the Processes of Class Colonisation." *Journal of Rural* Studies 9(2) (April): 123–140.

Piana, Paul. 2007. "The Renegade: The Dreams and Lifetimes of Todd Skinner." https://rockandice.com/snowball/the-renegade-todd-skinner/.

"Porter Jarrard: Climbing 5.14 at 44." 2010. *Dead Point Magazine*. https://web.archive.org/web/20111017004725/http://www.dpmclimbing.com/articles/view/porter-jarrard-climbing-514-44.

"Potential Closure of Torrent Falls Crag." 2006. https://www.redriverclimbing.com/viewtopic.php?f=11&t=6589.

Procknow, Hillary. 2008. "Cave Rock Closed Permanently." *Alpinist* (March 6). http://www.alpinist.com/doc/web08s/newswire-cave-rock-closed-permanently.

Puente, Victor. 2020. "Heavy Rain Causing Flooding in the 'Usual Places' of Powell County." https://www.wymt.com/content/news/Heavy-rain-causing-flooding-in-the-usual-places-of-Powell-County-570602851.html.

Redmond, Christopher. 2000. *Red River Gorge Bouldering*. A Production of Endless Works. Self-published.

"Red River Outdoors Fire." 2007. https://www.redriverclimbing.com/viewtopic.php?f=11&t=8295.

Red River Saga. 2012. "The Red River Valley Dam Timeline." Archived website. https://web.archive.org/web/20120125072333/http://www.redriversaga.com/rrvd_02.html.

Reisner, Marc. 1993. *Cadillac Desert: The American West and Its Disappearing Water*. New York: Penguin Books.

"Re: Johnny's Wall." 2005. https://www.redriverclimbing.com/viewtopic.php?f=5&t=4026.

"Re: Roadside Is Not Open—It Is Closed." 2014. https://redriverclimbing.com/viewtopic.php?f=28&t=16256&start=15.

Rickly, Jillian M. 2017. " 'I'm a Red River Local': Rock Climbing Mobilities and Community Hospitalities." *Tourist Studies* 17(1) (March 1): 54–74.

———. 2016. "Lifestyle Mobilities: A Politics of Lifestyle Rock Climbing." *Mobilities* 11(2) (April): 243–263.

———. 2012. *On Lifestyle Climbers: An Examination of Rock Climbing Dedication, Community, and Travel*. PhD dissertation, Indiana University, Bloomington.

———. 2017. "The (Re)production of Climbing Space: Bodies, Gestures, Texts." *Cultural Geographies* 24(1) (May 25): 69–88.

———. 2016. " 'They All Have a Different Vibe': A Rhythmanalysis of Climbing Mobilities and the Red River Gorge as Place." *Tourist Studies* 17(3) (July 11): 223–244.

"Roadside Beware." 2003. https://www.redriverclimbing.com/viewtopic.php?f=11&t =1279&p=16573&hilit=roadside#p16573.

"Roadside Camping. . . . CLOSED." 2003. https://www.redriverclimbing.com/view topic.php?f=11&t=857&p=10729&hilit=roadside#p10729.

"Roadside Dumping." 2003. *Red River Climbing*, May 27. https://www.redriverclimbing .com/viewtopic.php?f=11&t=1103&p=14026&hilit=roadside#p14026.

"Roadside Impact." 2005. https://www.redriverclimbing.com/viewtopic.php?f=11&t =5320.

"Rock Star Watch." 2007. https://www.redriverclimbing.com/viewtopic.php?f=5&t =8971&start=30.

Roper, Steve. 1998. *Camp 4: Reflections of a Yosemite Rockclimber*. Seattle: Mountaineers Books.

Roth, Justin. 2007. "Red River Outdoors Burns Down." https://www.climbing.com /news/red-river-outdoors-burns-down/.

Royle, Trevor. 2016. *Culloden: Scotland's Last Battle and the Forging of the British Empire*. New York: Pegasus Books.

RRGCC. 2017. "Red River Gorge Climbers' Coalition and Access Fund Record Easements to Strengthen Permanent Protection." http://www.rrgcc.org /announcements/2017/09/07/rrgcc-and-access-fund-strengthen-permanent -protections.html.

RRGCC and DBNF. 2000. Memorandum of Understanding. US Forest Service, February 7.

Rutherford, Glen O. 1972. "The Saga of the Red River Gorge." *American Forests Magazine* 78 (February): 20–23.

Samet, Matt. 2011. *Climbing Dictionary: Mountaineering Slang, Terms, Neologisms, & Lingo*. Seattle: Mountaineers Books.

Sawhill, Isabel. 2018. *The Forgotten Americans: The Economic Agenda for a Divided Nation*. New Haven, CT: Yale University Press.

Schlarb, Eric J., and David Pollack. 2002. "An Archaeological Evaluation of the *Military Wall* Rockshelter (15Po282), Daniel Boone National Forest, Powell County, Kentucky." DBNF Report No. 44.

Sharp, Ryan, James N. Maples, and Katherine Gerlaugh. 2018. "Factors Influencing Knowledge and Self-Reported Application of Leave No Trace Principles amongst Rock Climbers in Kentucky's Red River Gorge." *Journal of Adventure Education and Outdoor Learning* (December 7): 1–14.

Shifflett, Crandall A. 1991. *Coal Towns: Life, Work, and Culture in Company Towns of Southern Appalachia 1880–1960*. Knoxville: University of Tennessee Press.

Shrake, Edwin. 1968. "Operation Build and Destroy." *Sports Illustrated* (April 1). https://www.si.com/vault/issue/42933/47.

Siderelis, Christos, and Aram Attarian.2004. "Trip Response Modeling of Rock Climbers' Reactions to Proposed Regulations." *Journal of Leisure Research* 36(1) (December 13): 73–88.

Sims, Charles B., and Donald G. Hodges. 2004. "Obed Wild and Scenic River Rock Climbing Survey Results." https://www.researchgate.net/publication /228434040_Obed_Wild_and_Scenic_River _Rock_Climbing_Survey _Results.

Smith, Neil. 2008. *Uneven Development: Nature, Capital, and the Production of Space.* Athens: University of Georgia Press.

Smith, Shaine. "A Complete Guide to Kentucky's Wild and Scenic Red River." Accessed October 19, 2020. https://www.kentuckytourism.com/a-complete-guide-to -kentuckys-wild-and-scenic-red-river.

Sonka, Joe, and Deborah Yetter. 2019. "Bevin Administration Says Kentucky Faces $1.1 Billion Budget Shortfall over Next Two Years." *Louisville Courier-Journal*, December 4. https://www.courier-journal.com/story/news/politics /ky-legislature/2019/12/04/bevin-administration-releases-stark-budget -forecast-kentucky/2608880001/.

Southeastern Archaeological Conference. 2008. "Red River Gorge: A World Hearth of Plant Domestication." http://www.southeasternarchaeology.org/wp -content/uploads/LAW_Plant_Domestication_Handout.pdf.

Stackelbeck, Kary, and Philip Mink. 2008. "Overview of Archaeological Research in Kentucky." In David Pollack, *The Archaeology of Kentucky: An Update*, volume 2, 27–108. https://heritage.ky.gov/Documents/TheArchaeologyofKYAn UpdateVol2.pdf.

Stahl, Linda. 1994. "Rock Climbing in Gorge to Be Regulated." *Courier-Journal*, September 6.

Stoll, Steven. 2018. *Ramp Hollow: The Ordeal of Appalachia.* New York: Hill and Wang.

Sullivan, Andrew. 2017. "The Opioid Epidemic is This Generation's AIDS Crisis." *New York* Magazine, March 16. http://nymag.com/daily/intelligencer/2017/03 /the-opioid-epidemic-is-this-generations-aids-crisis.html?mid=fb-share-di.

Synott. Mark. 2017. "Exclusive: Climber Completes the Most Dangerous Rope-Free Ascent Ever." *National Geographic* (November 8). https://www.nationalgeo graphic.co.uk/video/tv/exclusive-climber-completes-most-dangerous-rope -free-ascent-ever.

Taylor, Joseph. 2010. *Pilgrims of the Vertical: Yosemite Rock Climbers & Nature at Risk.* Cambridge, MA: Harvard University Press.

"Terry." 2006. https://www.redriverclimbing.com/viewtopic.php?f=11&t=6922& start=30.

"Terry Kindred Day." 2008. https://www.redriverclimbing.com/viewtopic.php?f=11 &t=10139.

"Thiefs at Roadside—Description and License Plate Number." 2004. https://www .redriverclimbing.com/viewtopic.php?f=11&t=2984&p=53076&hilit=road side#p53076.

"Torrent Falls Closed to Public Climbing." 2006. https://www.redriverclimbing.com /viewtopic.php?f=11&t=7711.

"Torrent Opening." 2008. https://www.redriverclimbing.com/viewtopic.php?f=11&t =10424&start=15.

"A Tragic Lesson: Anchor Shuts from Above." 2012. https://www.mountainproject
.com/forum /topic/107614432/a-tragic-lesson-anchor-shuts-from-above.

Truman, Cheryl. 2013. "Cathedral Domain Celebrates 100 Years of Welcoming
Visitors." *Lexington Herald*, July 6. https://www.kentucky.com/living
/religion/article44432817.html.

US Fish & Wildlife Service. 2015. "White-Haired Goldenrod Proposed for Removal
from the Federal List of Endangered and Threatened Plants." https://www
.fws.gov/frankfort/pdf/White-hairedGoldenrod_final.pdf.

US Forest Service. "Rock Climbing Management Guide." 1996. Forest Service report.

"USFS Ranger Don Fig Retires." 2008. https://www.redriverclimbing.com/viewtopic
.php?f=11&t=9530.

Van Leuven, Chris. 2017. "The History of Friends." *Climbing Magazine* (July 17).
https://www.climbing.com/gear/the-history-of-friends/.

Van Velzer, Ryan. 2018. "Radioactive Waste Will Stay in Estill County." *WEKU News*,
May16. https://www.weku.fm/post/radioactive-waste-will-stay-estill
-county.

Veno, Chanda. 2017. "Chris Schimmoeller Awarded for Land Protection Efforts." *State
Journal* (September 1). http://www.state-journal.com/2017/09/01/chris
-schimmoeller-awarded-for-land-protection-efforts/.

Walendziak, Nicholas. 2015. "Longitudinal Variation in Environmental Impact at
Rock Climbing Areas in the Red River Gorge Limits of Acceptable Change
Study Area, Daniel Boone National Forest, Kentucky." Master's thesis,
Eastern Kentucky University.

White, Mary M. 2014. "Lithic Analysis of the Jot-Em-Down Shelter (15mcY348)
Collection: Utilization, and Shelter Activities Along the Cumberland
Plateau." Master's thesis, University of Kentucky.

"Who Does It Belong To?" 2011. https://www.redriverclimbing.com/viewtopic.php
?f=28&t=13926.

Wong, Kathleen. 2016. "Rock Climbing Studios Follow the Tide of Gentrification to
Bushwick." https://brooklynbased.com/2016/03/29/rock-climbing-brooklyn
-follow-gentrification-bushwick/.

Woods, Brad R., and Jason S. Gordon. "Mountaintop Removal and Job Creation:
Exploring the Relationship Using Spatial Regression." *Annals of the
Association of American Geographers* 101(4) (July): 806–815.

Young, Cheyenne. 2010. "Red River Rampage." *Clay City Times*, May 6. http://www
.claycity-times.com/news/?p=1456.

Index

www.ingramcontent.com/pod-product-compliance
Lightning Source LLC
Chambersburg PA
CBHW071738270326
41928CB00013B/2723